THE BATTLE OF THE BEANFIELD

Edited by Andy Worthington

With photos and contributions by
Alan Lodge, Tim Malyon, Neil Goodwin,
Gareth Morris, Alan Dearling and others

AN ENABLER PUBLICATION

THE BATTLE OF THE BEANFIELD

Edited by Andy Worthington

With photos and contributions by
Alan Lodge, Tim Malyon, Neil Goodwin,
Gareth Morris, Alan Dearling and others

First published June 2005 by:

Enabler Publications

16 Bitton Avenue
Teignmouth
Devon
TQ14 8HD

Front cover photograph copyright Tim Malyon.
Back cover photographs copyright Alan Lodge.

Designed and typeset by Jez Tucker.

Printed by Latimer Trend & Company Ltd, Plymouth.

ISBN 0-9523316-6-7

'Do not judge us by the media reportage, or a panicking government – but talk to us and help us build a unity amongst people of all cultures.'
Fiona Earle, new traveller, from A Time to Travel? (1994)

THE BATTLE OF THE BEANFIELD

Edited by Andy Worthington

Contents

Introduction   1

_____ **The background**

Chapter One   5
Stonehenge and the road to the Beanfield
By Andy Worthington with Alan Dearling

_____ **The travellers**

Chapter Two   26
Interview with Phil Shakesby
Conducted by Gareth Morris and Caroline Thomas

Chapter Three   41
Interview with Maureen Stone
Conducted by Neil Goodwin and Gareth Morris

Chapter Four   54
'Stonehenge '85: Souvenir Issue'
Written and compiled by Sheila Craig

_____ **The media**

Chapter Five   79
Interview with Nick Davies
Conducted by Neil Goodwin and Gareth Morris

Chapter Six   88
Interview with Kim Sabido
Conducted by Neil Goodwin and Gareth Morris

The landowner

Chapter Seven   **94**
Interview with the Earl of Cardigan
Conducted by Neil Goodwin and Gareth Morris

The police

Chapter Eight   **109**
Excerpts from the police radio log, June 1st 1985

Chapter Nine   **139**
Interview with Deputy Chief Constable Ian Readhead
Conducted by Richard Hester

The trial

Chapter Ten   **146**
'Beanfield Battle Trial'
By Don Aitken and Alex Rosenberger

Chapter Eleven   **151**
Interview with Lord Gifford QC
Conducted by Neil Goodwin and Gareth Morris

The film

Chapter Twelve   **166**
The Making of the 'Operation Solstice' film
By Neil Goodwin

The aftermath

Chapter Thirteen   **181**
A conclusion of sorts
By Andy Worthington

Chapter Fourteen   **202**
The legacy of the Beanfield
By Andy Worthington

About the contributors   **233**

Further reading (and viewing, and listening...)   **236**

Lest we forget

There's no point in remembering an anniversary
without a reason to remember.

What happened on that dread June day in 1985
was fired by prejudice against traveller culture.

This prejudice is still rife.

And it will not go away until
an adequate network of legal sites
is established around the country,
and reasonable planning guidelines drawn up
for travellers who have bought
their own piece of land on which to live.

Lest we forget.

Tim Malyon, June 2005

Introduction

This collection of eye-witness statements, archive material and new essays has been published to mark the 20th anniversary of an event that has become known as the Battle of the Beanfield. This took place on June 1st 1985, after a convoy of 140 vehicles, containing around 450 men, women and children – including new travellers, peace protestors, green activists and festival-goers – had set off from an overnight camp in Savernake Forest near Marlborough to establish the 12th Stonehenge Free Festival.

They never reached their destination. Eight miles from Stonehenge the convoy was ambushed, assaulted and arrested with unprecedented brutality by a quasi-military police force of over 1,300 officers drawn from six counties – Wiltshire, Hampshire, Thames Valley, Avon and Somerset, Gloucestershire and Dorset – as well as from the Ministry of Defence.

History – as many commentators have noted – tends to be written by the victors, and in the case of the Beanfield the establishment view is perhaps best represented by the prevailing tone in the majority of the print media, who regularly vilified the travellers as 'Giro gypsies' and 'Sponging scum', and who, after the Beanfield, gleefully misinterpreted the event as the 'Stonehenge riot' (*The Western Daily Press*), and published misleading articles, disguised as news stories, which included headlines like 'Stonehenge hippies attack police at festival' (*The Mail on Sunday*).

To redress this imbalance, I hope that this book will be a useful reference tool for all those interested in the history of counter-cultural movements in Britain over the last 40 years, particularly in relation to the new travellers' movement, the free festival scene, and creative forms of protest and dissent. This first full-length analysis of 'The Battle of the Beanfield' draws upon the detailed recollections of a number of people who were actually there on the day, and includes a number of full-length interviews that have never been reproduced before. These interviews – with travellers Phil Shakesby and Maureen Stone, journalists Nick Davies (of *The Observer*) and Kim Sabido (of ITN), and the Earl of the Cardigan, part of the family that owns Savernake Forest – were conducted by film-makers Neil Goodwin and Gareth Morris during the making of 'Operation Solstice', their acclaimed 1991 documentary about the Beanfield.

This project was actually conceived during discussions between myself and Neil Goodwin, and it's fair to say that the role played by both Neil and Gareth has been so significant that, without the interviews that they made at the time, the book would never have come into being. Both have been extremely helpful in providing tapes and transcripts, and I'd like to express my particular thanks to Neil for also providing a chapter which details the detective work and paranoia involved in the making of 'Operation Solstice.'

Also included is the complete text of a contemporary report that has been published before, but that is currently out of print – the pamphlet 'Stonehenge '85: Souvenir Issue', written and compiled by Sheila Craig and originally published by Bruce Garrard's Unique Publications in Glastonbury in 1986. I'd like to express my heartfelt appreciation to Sheila – with whom I spent an excellent evening in Kennington discussing the turbulent events of 1984-85 – for permission to reproduce this document, in which the recollections and observations of 20 people who experienced the brutality of the Beanfield are interspersed with a perceptive and heartfelt commentary by Sheila herself.

Of particular interest may be the two chapters which shed light on the activities of the police. The first of these contains lengthy extracts from the police radio log, covering the events of the day from the time that the convoy left Savernake Forest in the early afternoon to the winding-down of most parts of the operation at 9 pm. The second contains an interview, conducted by Richard Hester, as part of a PhD thesis, with Deputy Chief Constable Ian Readhead, who was an Inspector with Hampshire Constabulary on the day of the Beanfield. I'm grateful to Richard for granting permission to reproduce it. An analysis of what actually happened on the day, which is pieced together from all of the chapters described above – but with particular reference to the activities of the police – is contained in the book's penultimate chapter, which I have described, in the absence of a few absolute certainties, as 'A conclusion of sorts.'

Also included are two chapters dealing with the Beanfield trial, which took place at Winchester Crown Court from November 1990 to February 1991, in which 24 of those arrested at the Beanfield sued the Wiltshire Constabulary for false imprisonment, assault and damage to property. The first of these reproduces an article by Don Aitken and Alex Rosenberger – luminaries of the travellers' scene – which was originally published in *Festival Eye*, and which contains a detailed breakdown of the trial's successes and failures. I'd like to thank both Don and Alex for permission to reproduce it. The second contains a previously unpublished interview with Lord Gifford QC, who headed the team of barristers representing the travellers. Like the majority of the previous interviews, this was conducted during the making of 'Operation Solstice', and in it Lord Gifford provides a wide-ranging and perceptive review of the case, as well as looking at its implications for civil liberties in the UK in general.

I owe an enormous debt of gratitude to Alan Dearling, who stepped in at the 11th hour to give shape and meaning to the rather unfocused collection of interviews and archive material that I had been attempting to marshal at short notice and under increasing duress over the previous few months. As well as providing essential support and acres of research material, Alan also provided an invaluable contribution to the opening chapter of the book, with insights into the early life of Phil Russell (aka Wally Hope), the founder of the Stonehenge Free Festival, and information about the early free festivals and the development of the travellers' movement which would otherwise have eluded me. He also pointed out – and helped fill – gaps in my analysis of the police's perspective on the Beanfield in Chapter Thirteen, and added pertinent comments and detailed information about the development of various Gypsy and travellers support groups to the last chapter, in which I attempt to summarise the effects of the Beanfield on counter-cultural movements and civil liberties over the last 20 years.

I'd also like to thank the photographers, in particular Alan Lodge, who has not only been extremely generous with his extraordinary archive of photos, but who also looked after me on a recent visit to Nottingham, and also Tim Malyon, Adrian Arbib, Roger Hutchinson, Celia Kibblewhite and Graeme Strike. I also strongly suspect that the majority of the unattributed photos of the Beanfield were taken by Ben Gibson for *The Observer*, but as these photos do not seem to officially exist, and I've had no success in locating Ben Gibson, this remains speculative. Thanks are due to Chris Riley for his Spirals-era stuff, but he seems to have disappeared. Particular thanks are due to Jez Tucker, who not only provided photos but also designed and typeset the book at exceedingly short notice with consummate style. Also the cartoonists: Pete Loveday, who seemed both touched and amused that I'd bothered to ask his permission to reproduce his hilarious cartoon of the Stonehenge Free Festival, the incomparable Kate Evans, and new traveller artist Gubby.

For contributions above and beyond what might reasonably be expected, I'd like to thank my mum, my wife Dot and my son Tyler, and I'd also like to extend my gratitude to the counter-cultural pioneer Greg Sams for his generosity. Thanks are also due to the following people, who have contributed to this project in all manner of ways, both seen and unseen: Wesley Burrage, Jim Carey, Fraser Clark, Shane Collins, Richie Cotterill, Bruce Garrard, Dice George, Mark Graham, Charlie Hart, Andy Hemingway, Andy and Sally of the Green Roadshow, Ronald Hutton, Rik Mayes, George McKay, John Michell, Mogg Morgan, Steve Muggeridge, Brig Oubridge, Arthur Pendragon, Mike Pitts, Alex Plows, Sid and Jules, Rowan (Pagan Warriors), Andy Smith, Chris Stone, David Taylor and Brian Viziondanz. Also Mark Saunders, Polly Nash and Joyce Amparbeng at Spectacle Productions in London, Warren, Paul and John Hodge at *SchNEWS* and the Cowley Club in Brighton, Max, John and Paul at Kebele in Bristol, Lokabandhu of Buddhafield, Tim and Jean at Libra Aries in Cambridge, Des Kay and John Johnson of the Kingston Green Fair, Scott Wood of the South East London Folklore Society (SELFS), Patrick and Eleanor at Sumac in Nottingham, Tim Neate at the Strawberry Fair, Neil and Jo of the Stroud Valleys Artspace, the late Jeremy Sandford, who was a lifetime friend of Gypsies, travellers and free spirits, and – last but not least – George Firsoff, festival-goer, pagan priest and founder of the Stonehenge Truth and Reconciliation Commission, who was a tireless campaigner for access to Stonehenge from the time of the Beanfield until his death last year.

The Battle of the Beanfield

George's comments on the Beanfield, made during an interview with Roisin McAuley for a programme on the Beanfield that was broadcast on Radio 4 in 2002, provide what I believe are the most fitting words to end this introduction, and I'd like to dedicate this book to his memory, as well as to the memory of Maureen Stone, who, sadly, is also no longer with us. The 20th anniversary of the Beanfield is not an occasion to raise the spirits, but it's a pity that George and Moz aren't around to see it:

'The story of the festival – and the suppression of the festival – has continued, so you get a younger generation of people, who were never there and who never even went to a free festival, but they are somehow still angry about it. It's like a myth, you know, it's very hard... these two myths [of the travellers and of the police] are obviously different, and to write a true history of what happened, in the end, is a means of how all civil disorders are reconciled eventually. There is a history – this is what happened, this is what really happened, and then people can be calm about it, talk to each other.'

Andy Worthington, London, June 2005

Chapter One

Stonehenge and the road to the Beanfield

By Andy Worthington with Alan Dearling

Before launching into the first-hand accounts of the so-called Battle of the Beanfield, which expose the events of that dreadful day with a chilling clarity, I'd like to present some background to the confrontation, looking at the significance of Stonehenge and the rise of the travelling free festival culture, which, by 1985, was considered such a threat to the state that it was deemed necessary to suppress it with extreme prejudice.

The catalyst for the violence of the Beanfield was, ostensibly, the Stonehenge Free Festival, the central focus of a cycle of free festivals established by what has become known as the new travellers' movement. The festival had been growing year on year from its humble roots on the summer solstice in 1974, so that a decade later, when the decision was taken at the highest levels that it would no longer be tolerated, it attracted up to 100,000 people over the course of the month that it squatted so resolutely on National Trust land to the north of Stonehenge. Behind this rationale, however, there was also a strong desire to 'decommission' the whole of the travellers' movement, which had become increasingly politicised throughout the early 1980s.

Stonehenge and its festival, summer solstice 1984.

The Battle of the Beanfield

To understand the significance of the festival and the culture of the travellers' scene, we need to look in particular at the development of both forms of counter-cultural dissent during the social and political uprisings of the 1960s and early 1970s. It's also worth pointing out, however, that long before the counter-cultural awakening of the 1960s began, Stonehenge had been a magnet for popular gatherings on the summer solstice for at least a hundred years. From the 1890s to the 1950s, crowds of up to 3,000 people turned up when the weather was fine, bringing their own entertainment with them — mandolin players and gramophones in the 1920s and 1930s, and skiffle groups and student jazz bands in the 1950s.

Despite these precedents, however, by the early 1960s the establishment had become so outraged by the rowdy behaviour of a minority of the solstice-goers that steps were taken to curb the gatherings — even though many observers noted that the most persistent trouble-makers were not members of the general public but off-duty military personnel from the nearby army bases. Temporary barbed-wire fences were installed in 1962, and by 1964 access was restricted to everyone except the elite membership of a group of white-robed Druid revivalists, who had also been gathering on the solstice since the early years of the century.

The mid- to late-1960s were the seed-bed of festival culture. A prime mover was Harold Pendleton, who had run the legendary Marquee Club in London and a series of increasingly rock- and blues-focused festivals at Richmond and Kempton Parks, starting with the Rolling Stones at Richmond in 1963. By 1965, Pendleton's programme notes were calling it 'the teenagers' Ascot.' In 1966 and 1967, the event moved to Windsor racecourse with many more rock acts including the Who, the Small Faces, and Arthur Brown, who was lowered from a crane with his hell-fire hair ablaze. Essentially, these festivals were amongst the earliest 'lifestyle experiments' for the new generation — they were not just music festivals anymore.

While the first of these 'lifestyle experiments' were taking place, the first 'hippies' were also being drawn to Stonehenge, ignoring the prohibition and turning up on the solstice anyway. A police report from the mid-1960s, reproduced on the *Festival Zone* website, described how 'people came and strummed guitars in the field next to the monument.' According to the police, 'It was generally a pretty happy event, with no policing problems', although it was also obvious that the policy of exclusion was only adding to the temple's growing role as a counter-cultural icon. As the movement's indignation grew stronger, the fences at Stonehenge duly gave way. At the solstice in 1969, 2,000 revellers crashed through the fence and drowned out the Druids with their own spontaneous ceremony, and in 1970 a crowd of 3,000 people held a gigantic party around the temple's perimeter.

1970 was also the year that the free festival movement really took off in Britain, at Phun City and the Isle of Wight. The Phun City festival, near Worthing, was coordinated by the *International Times* (IT), and was originally intended as a benefit for the magazine's editors in their obscenity trial. Their promotional leaflet claimed that the festival would be 'attempting to provide a three-day environment designed to the needs and desires of the freak', and this – along with the encouragement to 'Get your end away at Phun City' – scared local people so much that they took out an injunction to prevent it happening. Ironically, the would-be festival-goers were undeterred, and the event became not only an impromptu free festival but also the wildest expression of the counter-culture to date, with thousands of people camping in the woods. As one of its organisers, the musician and activist Mick Farren, described it, 'Free food operations sprung up, the [Hell's] Angels stole beer wholesale and distributed it to the kids, dealers stopped selling dope and gave it away, [and] collections were made to keep the generators going.' At the third Isle of Wight festival in 1970, anarchists and agitators demanded a free festival and established one on a hill outside the site. Together with other festival-goers, who found the huge, fenced auditorium intimidating, they began to pull down the perimeter fence, and on the final day the organisers gave up the struggle and the festival was declared free.

In the long run, however, the most significant developments took place in 1971 and 1972, with the establishment of two particular free festivals: the Glastonbury Fayre and the Windsor Free Festival. The 1971 Glastonbury Fayre took place over the solstice weekend at Worthy Farm in Pilton, which was owned by Michael Eavis, a dairy farmer with 'crowd-gathering tendencies.' In the 1987 book, *Glastonbury Festivals*, Eavis said he was bored by the prospect of 'years and years of just milking,' and was 'enthusiastic for the spirit of youthful revolution' he'd witnessed at the Bath Festival of Blues and Progressive Music in June 1970, when 150,000 people had turned up to watch Led Zeppelin, while underground heroes the Pink Fairies had played off the back of a lorry to a free festival that had sprung up outside the gates. As a result, Eavis and his wife Jean held a small festival at Worthy Farm in September 1970 – entry cost a pound and included free milk – and hoped to hold a similar event at Stonehenge in 1971 until they 'realised that the authorities would make every effort to block an event at the Stones.'

In the end, the 1971 festival was largely organised by Andrew Kerr and Arabella Churchill, well-connected friends of the Eavises, who formed a company called Solstice Capers Ltd, and who ran the festival as a privately funded free event with high ideals – no alcohol was for sale on the site, and all the food was vegetarian – and a pronounced spiritual angle. Kerr in particular was inspired by John Michell's *The View Over Atlantis*, published in 1969, which introduced ley-lines and sacred geometry to a public hungry for spiritual alternatives, and which revived, as centres of mystical power, Stonehenge, Avebury and Glastonbury. He hired Bill Harkin to design the festival's centrepiece, the celebrated pyramid stage, which was planned as a scaled-down model of the Great Pyramid, with its proportions based on the dimensions of Stonehenge. It was also situated in a supposedly sacred location – close to the Glastonbury Abbey/Stonehenge ley-line.

In the history of free festivals, the 1971 Glastonbury Fayre is widely remembered as 'the legendary one', even though it was 'free' only insofar as the punters didn't have to pay for entry, and was, in all other respects, a licensed, quite tightly organised legal event, very different from the far more anarchic festivals that were to follow at Windsor and Stonehenge. As the cultural commentator George McKay has questioned, 'how far does 'free' equate with 'non-commercial'?' For Alan Dearling, 'it doesn't really; the organisers sold the film rights to the Fayre and subsequently established Revelation Enterprises, which sold, between 1972 and 1973, 16,000 copies of the *Glastonbury Fayre Revelation* album, which even featured bands like the Grateful Dead who were meant to have played at the event, but somehow got lost en route.'

In contrast, the Windsor Free Festival, which began on the August Bank Holiday weekend in 1972, was a far more political affair – though one shot through with 'acid prankster' humour. As Alan Dearling described it, 'Even the title – 'Rent Strike: The People's Free Festival' – had a feel to it that was more about political and social change, rather than just another music bash for weekend hippies.' Its organiser, Bill 'Ubi' Dwyer, who worked in Her Majesty's Stationery Office by day, printed 100,000 leaflets to promote the event. Some of these proclaimed that 'Between one and five million people are expected including many thousands from overseas', and others, under the headline 'The Revival of Free Festivals' – which featured a nude statue of Aphrodite and the claim that they were circulated by the Church of Aphrodite Pandemos – advised potential festival-goers that, 'Everything we do is approved by a god or goddess since there is a deity for every aspect of human life. Hence drinking strong wine is pleasing to Dionysus, the playing of music is pleasing to Apollo, the making of sexual love pleases Aphrodite and Priapus and they would be offended were it not performed to the full.'

In reality, the first festival was a bit of a shambles. Bill Dwyer didn't get his millions of people, and the 700 or so attendees were nearly outnumbered by police, but the following year it hit its stride, attracting up to 8,000 people over a period of ten days. Unlike Glastonbury, Windsor was a genuinely 'free' event. As Alan Dearling put it, 'There were no fences, no gate charges, and the ethos was purposely one of self-help, anything-can-happen anarchy.'

Behind his prankster façade, Bill Dwyer had worked hard to ensure the success of the 1973 festival. His friend Bruce Bradley remembers, 'We worked many long hours putting the whole thing together, making flyers and distributing them, contacting artists and agents, dealing with police and press – it was a heady time. Bill was a gentle guy with a grizzled beard, but he could be fierce when he needed to be. The problems he encountered demanded that he be tenacious and I loved watching him with the media and the naysayers. His passion for the festival was something to behold. I also remember that he was impressed that I knew the derivation of his nickname – 'Ubi' is Latin for 'everywhere'.'

In addition to Bill Dwyer, the Windsor festivals also involved many of the cult figures of the time – colourful individuals like Nick Albery, Nick Saunders and Heathcote Williams, many of whom were heavily into the squatting movement (hence the frequent encouragement to 'pay no rent.') Alan Dearling suggests that, 'In their own ways those characters became

The People's Free Festival, Windsor Great Park, August 1973. Copyright Roger Hutchinson.

some of the legendary, charismatic, difficult, colourful oddballs of late 20th century Britain. This was serious alternative weirdness and somehow it was infectious. It certainly laid the foundations of what became the counter-culture and alternative economy of the festival circuit.'

To quote Sid Rawle, one of the most extrovert of this band, and the self-proclaimed King of the Hippies: 'We have to find out how all us individuals in the world can have enough space to live in love and harmony, enough to be self sufficient and be ourselves, and how to give everyone else this space. That is the Vision of Albion, that is the vision of the rainbow people... All over the world there are still other people who do remember what their roots are, people who are still in touch with their tribal history. What lies deep in their systems must also lie deep in our own system. We have to learn to find it again.'

That's the fluffy, hippy vision, and it was certainly there embedded in the whole paraphernalia of the underground; newspapers such as *IT, Oz, Friends, Ink* and *Strange Days* and most of the self-help aid groups/organisations of the period, such as BIT Information Services, Release and even the Dwarfs. A prankster group who described themselves as 'freak ambassadors', the Dwarfs first appeared at the Portobello Carnival in 1971, where Hawkwind and the Pink Fairies played beneath the flyover. A bemused *West London Observer* reported that, 'Working out what the Dwarfs stand for is like trying to grab a fist full of air and bottling it in a jam jar.'

Significantly, one of those involved with both the Dwarfs and the Windsor festivals was a charismatic young man called Phil Russell – better known as Wally Hope – the founder of the first Stonehenge Free Festival. As Alan Dearling has commented, 'No other hippy icon or folk legend has proved as long lasting as Phil Russell.'

Phil Russell, aka Wally Hope. Photo provided by Alan Dearling.

Phil had worked on one of the festival's free newsletters, in which he had advanced John Lennon and Yoko Ono's notion of 'nutopia', a 'state of the brotherhood of man, recognising no national boundaries or artificially imposed lines over our beautiful planet', but according to Tim Abbott, who met Phil at Windsor in 1973, 'He was disillusioned by what was already happening at the 'People's Free Festival', notably the sight of someone going haywire on the gate demanding money from traders for a 'free' festival. As well as being a psychedelic anarchist he had a strong traditionalist streak, and was upset that the Queen's back garden should be littered and fouled. He had a vision that it could be done in a purer way. Later in the autumn he arrived at my father's vicarage in Wiltshire with a vision of a massive tribal gathering at Stonehenge the following summer.' His friend Jeremy Ratter, who took the name Penny Rimbaud and who later co-founded the anarcho-punk collective Crass, recalls that it was at a well-known hippie café on Ibiza – one of Phil's regular haunts – that he first came up with the idea of a free festival at Stonehenge. He 'wanted to claim back Stonehenge (a place that he regarded as sacred to the people and stolen by the government) and make it a site for free festivals, free music, free space, free mind.'

Much has been written about Phil Russell over the years, but until now little has been known of his background. By chance, however, a few years ago in a bar in Lyme Regis, Alan Dearling met a man called Nick, who was Phil's closest friend in the Windsor area from 1965 to 1967. According to Nick, 'He was a loner, but needed people around him – he always wanted to be a leader of something.' Phil and Nick became good friends, often spending time together, talking and listening to music in Phil's house, the Lodge. Nick described how 'Phil's dad was dead and he got trust money – about £12 a week, a lot in

One of Phil Russell's flyers for the first Stonehenge Free Festival, 1974. Image provided by Alan Dearling.

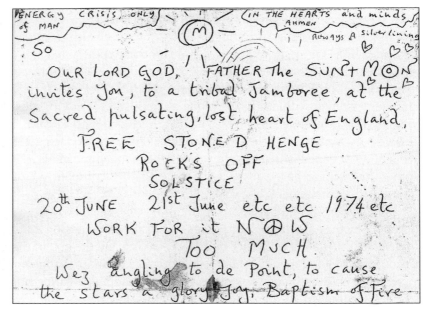

those days – and was due to inherit a bigger property when he reached 30. Sometimes his guardian, John Snagge, the broadcaster, would see him too.'

Nick also described how Phil's Danish mother 'would drop in on journeys from Germany and Denmark', and explained that 'They had a very strange relationship. She was strange anyway, quite strong, about 40, I think. She'd organise the house and have a lot of influence over him, but no clout over the property... Anyway, one night in 1967 there were seven or eight of us at the Lodge. The police came in and knew exactly what they were looking for – they pulled some cannabis out of an umbrella in the hall. We were all charged, but they wanted to make an example of Phil since it was his house. Phil was sure that his mother had set him and us up. Maybe she thought if he was locked up, she'd get the house, I don't know. Phil got 18 months starting in the Scrubs and then moved to Ashford in Kent. My charges were dropped and all my parents did was to arrange that I had to go and see a psychiatrist. But I wrote to Phil while he was inside and he wrote back. You can see from his letters what sort of a guy he was at that time. I visited him inside.'

Nick kept three of Phil's letters, the first from Wormwood Scrubs, the other two from Ashford HM Remand Centre. The letters reveal a young man – Phil was about 21 at the time – struggling to cope with his incarceration. In his first letter he wrote (his spelling): 'I feel so hopeless and lost and I don't really know what to do... I'm here in sort of solitry confinement', and explained how he 'would rather go to a hospital and be treated as a human instead of a criminal.' In another he described how 'It's damaging me here, because I'm someone else and a slave to society, and it's breeding a lot of hate and grief inside of me.'

Even so, the letters contain hints of Phil's submerged personality – and also, perhaps, of the metamorphosis that was to come. In Ashford, where he made a few friends, he described how 'We sit down at meals and pump our politics and ideas into the people to make them understand this weird society', and in his final letter he explained that being inside had given him 'time to think about the future of this society and how we can change it', adding, 'I think they've made a big mistake.' Perhaps most revealing are the ways in which Phil ended his letters. The first concluded with 'Regards from your local God behind bars, Mutant Phil' (the two friends frequently referred to each other as 'Mutants'), while the last ended with 'Dear me, haven't they robbed me of life. Mind you our day will come where we can have our say. It will come. Maybe very soon. As truth always conquers ignorance... Commander Energy or Phil to You.'

Certainly, by the early 1970s, Phil Russell wasn't the same person that Nick from Windsor had been best friends with. Nick told Alan Dearling, 'By the end of the 1960s I moved to Devon, and Phil and myself kind of lost contact... I was into woodland crafts and I didn't want to be an urban hippy any more. Phil would appear wearing bright multi-coloured shirts made by Mon, his Danish girlfriend. By this time he was living with her in Surbiton, I think. He'd taken acid, seen God in Cyprus, and we weren't talking the same language anymore. I went and visited him in his flat with Mon, and he came down and stayed with us. His stories of organising events or whatever would come out in one long rush and go on for as long as you could stay awake. He couldn't come down and just enjoy a normal day out. We'd all take a lot of acid, we kind of humoured him. He wanted to lead and felt that he had a divine right to be listened to. We'd get pissed off with him after a couple of days. He brought a couple of Wallies with him one time, right plankheads. He needed people who weren't as bright as him that he could push around. There were a very limited number of people who would listen to him or could cope with him. I think he lost the plot when he became a 'visionary'. We tried to get him to come and live with us in the country – I was into farming at the time – but it wasn't for him.'

The leaflets for Phil's great dream – a free festival at Stonehenge – reveal where he'd reached in his head. Duplicated by hand, they nearly always included one of his child-like drawings of the Sun and/or the Stones, and he had become a fount of cosmic catch phrases, including, 'Every Day is a Sun Day. Every One is a Wally. Every Where has a Heart. Every Festival is a Cosmic Battle Honour. Every Body is a Department of the Environment.'

The first Stonehenge festival – planned at Penny Rimbaud's commune in Essex, just down the road from Phil's guardian – duly took place at the Stones on the summer solstice in 1974. Despite a leafleting campaign and promotion by Radio Caroline, it was a small gathering, numbering about 500 people at the most. The festival would have had little impact if it had stopped soon after the solstice was over, but by this time Phil had persuaded 30 people to stay on in the field beside the stone circle. Calling themselves 'The Wallies of Wessex', they lived a rudimentary communal lifestyle, inspired, as one visitor,

The envelope for the letter (reproduced on the following page) that Phil Russell sent to 'the Farmer, who owns Land Round Stone Henge', requesting permission to hold a festival on his land. Image provided by Alan Dearling.

Nigel Ayers, put it, by 'the common purpose of discovering the relevance of this ancient mysterious place by the physical experience of spending a lot of time there.'

The Wallies were taken to court in August, but when they were evicted they simply returned to Stonehenge, resurrecting their camp on a public by-way that ran beside the perimeter fence. In August, they took a fateful trip to the third Windsor festival. Attracting anything up to 60,000 people – depending on whose reports you read – the 1974 festival took place without Bill Dwyer, who had been imprisoned for two years while promoting it, charged with possession of acid and for 'incitement to cause a public nuisance, causing large crowds to gather unlawfully, and thereby causing a foul and loathsome amount of litter and waste, and causing excessively loud music to be played into the night.'

As Alan Dearling described it, 'The festival was far from being a laid-back event. The Queen's Crown Commissioners had made a point of banning the event, and had put in steel posts to stop vehicles for the bands getting onto site. The Thames Valley police were present in an enormous show of strength, but hadn't arrived early enough to stop thousands of people occupying the Great Park.' A week after the festival was set up, the police took their revenge. Phil Russell and his Wallies witnessed the unprecedented police violence that closed the festival down, when, in an early morning raid, hundreds of police officers gave the crowd little or no time to disperse before laying into them with truncheons. In Phil's words, 'I saw a pregnant woman being kicked in the belly, and a little boy being punched in the face. All around, the police were just laying into people. I went to one policeman who had just knocked out a woman's teeth and asked him why he'd

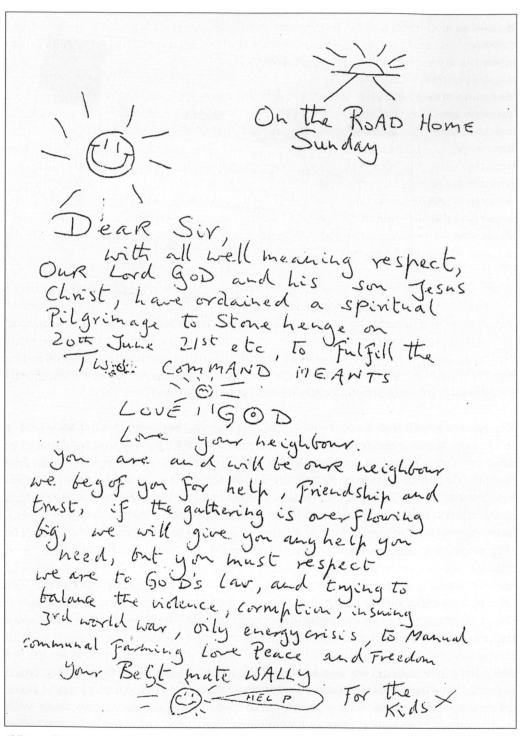

On the ROAD HOME
Sunday

Dear Sir,
        with all well meaning respect,
Our Lord GoD and his son Jesus
Christ, have ordained a spiritual
Pilgrimage to Stone henge on
20th June 21st etc, to fulfill the
Two COMMAND MEANTS
            LOVE 11GOD
        Love your neighbour.
You are and will be our neighbour
we beg of you for help, Friendship and
trust, if the gathering is overflowing
big, we will give you any help you
    need, but you must respect
we are to GoD's law, and trying to
balance the violence, corruption, insuing
3rd world war, oily energy crisis, to Manual
communal Farming love Peace and Freedom
    Your Best mate WALLy
        — ☺ — HELP — For the
                                Kids ✗

Phil Russell's bizarre yet endearing letter, with references to God, Jesus, the 'oily energy crisis' and
'Manual communal Farming.' Image provided by Alan Dearling.

done it. He told me to fuck off or I'd get the same. Later on, I did.' After Windsor, the Wallies attended a protest that was held in Hyde Park, and on both occasions Phil recruited more visitors to the experimental camp on Salisbury Plain.

The camp lasted until after the winter solstice, when some of the group moved into a squat in Amesbury, and Phil went off to Cyprus. In the meantime, Nick Albery, Heathcote Williams and Diana Senior sued David Holdsworth, the Thames Valley Chief Constable, for creating a riotous situation at Windsor. Along with their supporters, such as Don Aitken and Sid Rawle, they turned the court case into something more akin to a carnival than a trial, providing a focus for many of the future Stonehenge organisers. The high point of BIT's report of the proceedings was Diana Senior's exchange with a senior officer: 'Diana asked why they'd moved in, and he said, 'Because we apprehended a breach of the peace.' 'At eight in the morning, when almost everyone was asleep? What breach of the peace did you apprehend then? Snoring?"

While the Windsor activists secured an extraordinary victory, not only gaining damages but also receiving the assurance of Home Secretary Roy Jenkins that the government would provide an alternative site for the Windsor festival, Phil Russell spent the spring of 1975 preparing for the coming festival at Stonehenge. In May, however, after stopping at the squat during a journey from London to Cornwall, he was arrested for possession of a small amount of LSD during an unexpected raid by the police, when he apparently threatened to give the arresting officer 'a cosmic kick in the balls.'

The second Stonehenge festival – when the weather was hot and sunny, and a crowd of 3,000 turned up on the solstice – took place without him. He was released two days after the last vehicle left the festival that he'd inspired, but in the meantime he had been diagnosed as having schizophrenia, and was sectioned under the Mental Health Act and held in the Old Manor hospital in Salisbury. According to Penny Rimbaud, in the space of two short months, large doses of anti-psychotic drugs turned the 'sun-worshipping warrior' into a broken, bloated and fearful shadow, afraid of the sun. His old friend Nick described how, after Phil's release, he 'came and stayed with us in Branscombe in Devon. He was like an old man. He could barely speak or walk. He said the doctors had overdosed him on purpose, saying, 'Get off Cloud Nine, sonny.' We tried to walk him along by the beach, but he'd lost it by then. We put him on the train for Ongar in Essex where he was to stay with the Hatfields, who were doctors. We never saw him again. He was totally burnt out.'

Phil's last public appearance was at Watchfield, a disused airfield in Oxfordshire, which was the alternative venue provided for the People's Free Festival by the Labour government. He died soon after, although even after his death the full details of what had happened to him never emerged. Two coroners' inquests were adjourned, and by the time of the third his medical notes had conveniently disappeared. Penny Rimbaud began an investigation, but abandoned it when he became convinced that he was under permanent surveillance and that his life was in danger. Nevertheless, Phil's death provided the basis for a vibrant contemporary mythology. In the blazing hot summer of 1976, when over 5,000 people turned up for the Stonehenge festival, hundreds of the festival-goers staged an invasion of the temple on the day of solstice, honouring Phil's memory by scattering his ashes from a box, inscribed with the epitaph 'Wally Hope, died 1975 aged 29: a victim of ignorance', which Penny had brought along, and acquiring, in the process, a right of religious access to the stones that was begrudgingly respected for as long as the festival continued.

With Phil's death, the organisation of the festival devolved to a loose-knit network of other groups and individuals, including a group of young agitators known as the Polytantric Circle, Sid Rawle, John Pendragon, immortalised by C.J. Stone as *The Last of the Hippies*, the musician Nik Turner, who lent his pyramid stage to the festival each year, and Bev Richardson, who was central to the festival's connection with the Stones as a pagan free spirit and prominent traveller. It was also at this time that the free festival scene began to expand into a summer-long season, with events springing up from May to September in locations as diverse as Wales, the West Country, Lancashire, the Lake District and East Anglia – festivals whose names are synonymous with the subversive spirit of the times: Meigan Fayre, the Psilocybin Festival, the Trentishoe Whole Earth Fayre, Deeply Vale and the Albion Fairs. And whereas, in the early days, the majority of people had simply hitch-

The Stonehenge Free Festival, 1977: the giant 'Atomhenge' stage under construction.
Copyright Roger Hutchinson.

hiked to the festivals, many now began to buy their own vehicles – often old trucks and buses – and to investigate new ways of living on the land, in tepees and benders. In the process, of course, a new travellers' movement was born.

Alan Dearling describes how "travelling' took on a meaning borrowed and amended from the social and economic nomadism of the Gypsy peoples of the world. It gradually dawned on a growing number of festival goers that the glimpses of an 'alternative lifestyle', which the festivals of the late sixties and first half of the seventies had offered, could be turned into a full-time reality. A bus, bender, tipi or truck were cheaper to obtain than the sedentary life and so-called 'security' offered by a house or flat. And these new homes allowed their occupants to move relatively easily from venue to venue. The first wave of these 'new travellers' had grown up with a loosely defined hippy lifestyle of marijuana, Hawkwind and indigenous third world clothing. They were the traders, stage builders and sometime performers of the festivals. And, shock, horror – some may even have traded in drugs! Add to them a 'new wave' of anti-Thatcher town and city kids nurtured on 1976-78 anarcho-punk, and you have some idea of the melting pot that brewed up the traveller culture that was to become the most despised scapegoat of successive Conservative governments.'

As the free festival scene continued to grow, the solstice gathering at Stonehenge remained its central focus, and by the early 1980s it had become a truly massive event. The widespread eviction of squatters at the time spurred the growth of the travellers' movement, with thousands of people buying up old vehicles and taking to the road each year, and across the country people from all walks of life who were opposed to the new mood of intolerance in Margaret Thatcher's government discovered that at Stonehenge a social, political and spiritual alternative was already well established. In the pages of *Squall*, Jim Carey captured the essence of the Stonehenge festival's success: 'Entirely unlicensed, unpoliced and free from the profit motivation that drives modern day commercial festivals, it was one of the great people-led social experiments of modern times. The festival existed in sharp contrast to the vacuous modern political rhetoric about 'community', for despite its many foibles, it was a genuine example of people working through the realities of the word.'

Alan Dearling's memory of the Stonehenge festivals is that they 'provided a space and place in which you could experiment, become another person, and try on new identities. Many of my new traveller friends learned through this process to become the people they wanted to be, and the Stones, along with their nomadic homes, helped with that creation of a shared cultural identity.' One (un-named) traveller, quoted by the academic Kevin Hetherington in his book *New Age Travellers*, underlined Alan's analysis, commenting that Stonehenge 'was the space that allowed people to get a community going. It created a kind of space in which people could do things that they couldn't do anywhere else... You could do what you wanted at Stonehenge and no one would bat an eyelid.'

Another early traveller who re-invented himself on the road was Gary, who formed the business Rainbow Marquees. He remembers, 'I bought myself a tepee and a van and learned how to do leather craftwork. I started making moccasins, made to measure, street moccasins with hard soles. I was ready for my first Stonehenge proper. Stonehenge was about freedom. The freedom to actually blossom, to do what you wanted to do as long as it didn't harm anybody else. It was far out.' The opportunities provided by the festival scene were also remarked upon by a traveller called Scott, in Richard Lowe and William Shaw's *Travellers: Voices of the New Age Nomads*: 'When I first went on the road, going to Stonehenge and all the festivals, I didn't think to myself, 'This is great – I'm going to get a lorry and go into the iron business', but that's how it turned out, really. It's one of the only ways of earning money like this and it's traditional for travellers to do it – gypsies have been doing it for years.'

As well as offering the space to pursue alternative forms of employment, the festival circuit also combined the social and the spiritual in a way that was sorely lacking in the world of the commercial festivals, as is apparent in this description by Fiona Earle: 'I arrived on June 3rd on the back of a trials bike with one bag of possessions, and saw the 'Henge for the first time – a magnificent monument with a few hundred people on the grass across the road, setting up along the drags. It evolved really quickly, and the month is a haze of images: swimming in the river at Amesbury; Hawkwind and the Enid on stage; siphoning petrol to blag bike rides; nights by the fire, days lying in the sun; Pete's sagging bender leaking in the rain; a sense of total freedom, timeless energy... and solstice morning; the chill of pre-dawn darkness, walking to the stones, chanting, dancing – the sun rising majestically above the Heel Stone while the music echoed around.'

Early travellers: the Polytantric Circle truck, Camden Town, 1976. Copyright Roger Hutchinson.

Stonehenge and the road to the Beanfield

It was also at this time that travellers first began to form themselves into the 'convoys' that were to gain such notoriety by the time of the Beanfield. Brig Oubridge has suggested that the first convoys actually appeared as early as 1976, as 'an enjoyably sociable means of travel' between festivals, but it was not until 1981, and the establishment of a Peace Camp at Greenham Common, the first proposed airbase in the UK for American Cruise missiles, that the phenomenon became firmly established. In keeping with the counter-cultural significance of Stonehenge, it was at the great temple on Salisbury Plain – and its attendant festival – that this new movement had its roots. As Alan Dearling has observed, 'The Stones were their party, their shrine, their emblem (literally emblazoned on the side of many trucks and rainbow coloured buses) and – in a real way – 'home', the annual meeting place of the tribes and traveller 'families'.'

In *A Time to Travel: an introduction to Britain's newer Travellers* , compiled by Fiona Earle, Alan Dearling, Helen Whittle, Gubby and Roddy Glasse, a traveller called Andy described how 'The 'Peace Convoy' really began in '81 when we went from 'Henge to Greenham Common to support the women camping there.' In that first year, the camp at Greenham wasn't for women only. Indeed, Don Aitken of Festival Welfare Services later claimed that they had shown the women how to build benders. Andy described how 'A group went beforehand to check out the site, then everyone painted up their vehicles, and a core of 120 snaked away from Wiltshire. It was all peaceful. When we met a roadblock, we'd stop, get out, and just lift the cars out the way, with the police inside.'

Pete Loveday's frankly hilarious take on the popularity of the Stonehenge Free Festival, from 'Stones Again' in 'Festival Eye', Summer '89. Copyright Pete Loveday.

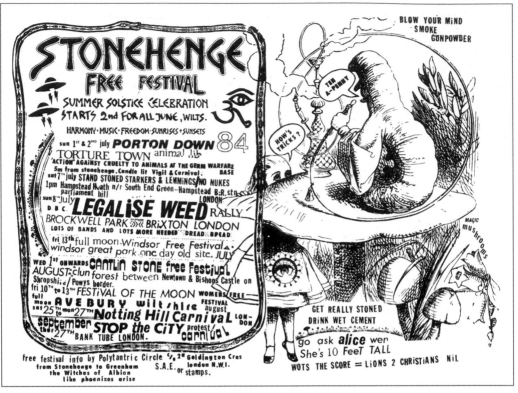

Poster for the 1984 Stonehenge Free Festival – and a host of other events throughout the summer.

In 1982, when Thatcher went to war in the Falklands, an even larger 'Peace Convoy', comprising 135 vehicles, again set off for Greenham at the end of the Stonehenge festival, where they established a number of stages, participated in direct action by pulling down sections of the fence, and endured random acts of police brutality. A statement at the time, reproduced on the *Festival Zone* website, declared, 'The unstoppable convoy has taken another site. But not just another site; the most important site we have ever taken... It's what we've been practising for all these long years... every Windsor free festival, every Stonehenge has in a way been a preparation for this – this is the one that really matters.'

Although the established free festival circuit was still in existence, by 1982 radical politics had permeated almost every event. That summer the first Green Gathering took place at Worthy Farm, after the main Glastonbury Festival had come to an end, attracting over 5,000 people and establishing a template for sustainable gatherings that were able to maintain the ethos of the free festivals – 'Bring what you expect to find. If you want to contribute in any way, don't wait to be asked: do it' – in the face of a growing influx of less focused 'consumers.' The only music was acoustic, everyone was encouraged to participate – financially, physically and spiritually – and it's significant that a number of small-scale gatherings are still run along the same lines today.

Stonehenge and the road to the Beanfield

By 1983, the increasingly intertwined expressions of celebration and dissent – the free festival scene and the political protest movement – expanded beyond anyone's wildest dreams. At Stonehenge, welfare volunteer Penny Mellor estimated that 'There were at least 30,000 people attending the festival over the solstice weekend, with as many as 70,000 people visiting the festival over the duration.' Inevitably, however, the festival began to show signs of cracking under the pressure. Penny Mellor noted ruefully that 'There seemed to be less caring amongst the festival people', hundreds of trees were cut down in the nearest plantation – until the National Trust provided alternative supplies – and the stage crews threatened to walk out unless something was done about the heroin dealers who had begun to make their way onto the site. To their credit, the representatives of the festival's tribes – who were as appalled as anyone else by these developments – took the problem seriously, and those that could be found were subsequently evicted.

Nevertheless, by the time of the festivals in 1983 and 1984, many of those who had been a part of its earlier history became aware that the gathering no longer resembled the never-ending months of Sun Days that Phil Russell had envisaged back in 1974. In these final years – and particularly in 1984, when the festival grew even larger – it began, at its fraying edges, to reflect the darkness that was permeating society as a whole, a deep undercurrent of anger and frustration that was to see riots breaking out across the inner cities, and the first 'Stop the City' demonstrations in London, at which Class War activists

Is this what all the fuss was about? The crowd – and a horse – at Stonehenge, summer solstice 1984. Copyright Alan Lodge.

Convoy en route to Porton Down, July 1984.
Copyright Celia Kibblewhite.

targeted the Bank of England, Barclays Bank, Soho's sex shops and the offices of Saatchi and Saatchi. Gary, the traveller who established Rainbow Marquees, suggested that 'New age travellers of the seventies and early eighties were driven by visions, ideals, inspiration', whereas 'The influx of what I would call economic refugees changed it completely... It's what went wrong with Stonehenge... The breadheads came in and it was all about how much they could make selling drugs.'

Looking back on the events of the time in the 1989 issue of *Festival Eye*, Krystof, another free festival regular, was also aware of the failings of the overloaded infrastructure of the 1983 and 1984 festivals. He suggested that 'whereas a few thousand people can communicate successfully enough to create and maintain a community, groups of fifty thousand and more require a proportionate amount of activists to keep them together.' Krystof continued with a pertinent analysis of the elements required not only for a successful free festival, but also for alternative visions of society as a whole: 'In a way, the festival can be thought of in two ways: as an actual physical event, the gathering of people in one place at one time, and also as a spiritual event, in other words as a state of mind... History shows the price of ignoring this other aspect. The spiritual side does not have to involve ritualistic mumbo-jumbo or far fetched cultism – care, respect for others and the environment, and sharing, would guarantee a real celebration of life and a happy time for everyone.'

Even so, although the festival was becoming 'soured' for the old hands, new generations of people continued to arrive each year, and for many of them it was still a life-changing and life-affirming experience. I was one of them. My first visit to the Stonehenge festival took place in 1983, and in my social history of Stonehenge – *Stonehenge: Celebration and*

Stonehenge and the road to the Beanfield

Subversion – I described how 'this seasonal settlement of impossibly weathered and wildly decorated tents, tipis, vans, buses and old army vehicles was little short of a revelation, an alternative state within Thatcher's Britain that seemed to have rooted itself to the ancient sacred landscape with nonchalant ease.'

I returned the following year, to discover, like so many others in their late teens and early twenties, that this edgy, exuberant, anarchic jamboree still provided a thrilling antidote to the grim reality of everyday life under the Tories. The unprecedented mingling of the tribes continued unabated, breaking down social barriers that were all too noticeable elsewhere, and, most spectacularly of all, on solstice morning the fences came down, the sun shone out in all its summer glory, and the festival-goers once more gathered at the stones to celebrate their anarchic, pagan-tinted visions of a new Albion.

Behind the scenes, however, the authorities responsible for the temple and its immediate environment – the government, the National Trust, local landowners, the police and English Heritage, a quango that had taken over management of the monument on April Fool's Day – were already working on plans that would prevent access to Stonehenge at the summer solstice for the overwhelming majority of people for the next 16 years.

In the summer of 1984, while the majority of the festival regulars pursued their annual cycle of events, the first signs of a new and disturbingly violent intolerance on the part of the authorities took place at Boscombe Down airfield near Stonehenge, and at Nostell Priory in Yorkshire. The first of these incidents came about after a group of militant travellers hijacked a peaceful animal rights protest at Porton Down in early July, pulling down fences before moving on to the US air force base at Boscombe Down, where a peace camp was already in existence and a free festival had been held just a few weeks before. At Boscombe Down, the fences came down once more, 'undoing weeks of careful

Police advance on protestors at Boscombe Down, July 1984. Copyright Celia Kibblewhite.

confidence-building between peace activists and the USAF base security', as one observer, Celia Kibblewhite, described it. The authorities took their revenge shortly after, when the protestors were, according to Celia, 'cut up by riot vans, boarded, attacked and trashed by a squad of Special Branch police.'

In some ways, this retaliation by the police could be regarded as the end result of a deliberately confrontational game of cat-and-mouse that had been bubbling away for years. At Nostell Priory, however, the police violence was unprovoked and far more severe. At the end of a licensed weekend festival, riot police, who had only recently been suppressing striking miners at the Orgreave coking plant, raided the site at dawn, ransacking vehicles and arresting the majority of the travellers – 360 people in total – with a savagery that had not been seen since the last Windsor Free Festival in 1974. The travellers were held without charge for up to a fortnight in police and army prisons, finally appearing before a magistrate who found them all guilty on allegedly trumped-up charges, and the events of that time are vividly described in a sometimes harrowing and sometimes hilarious account by Phil Shakesby in the following chapter.

Some of the battered survivors made it to Molesworth in Cambridgeshire, a disused World War II airbase that had been designated as the second Cruise missile base after Greenham Common, where they joined peace protestors, other travellers and members of various Green organisations to become the Rainbow Village Peace Camp. In many ways, Molesworth, which swiftly became a rooted settlement, was the epitome of the free festival-protest fusion, cutting across class and social divides and reflecting many of the developments – in feminism, activism and environmental awareness – that had been transforming alternative society since the largely middle class – and often patriarchal – revolutions of the late sixties and early seventies. One resident, Phil Hudson, recalled the extent of the experiment: 'There was a village shop on a double-decker bus, a postman, a chapel, a peace garden, a small plantation of wheat for Ethiopia (planted weeks before Michael Buerk 'broke' the famine story in the mainstream media), and the legendary Free Food Kitchen.' The Rainbow Village was finally evicted in February 1985 by the largest peacetime mobilisation of troops in the UK, and the unprecedented scale of the operation, and the effect it had in creating even stronger bonds between the various groups of travellers, are brought to life in the interview with Maureen Stone in Chapter Three, and in the recollections of Sheila Craig in Chapter Six.

The convoy shifted uneasily around the country for the next few months, persistently harassed by the police and regularly monitored by planes and helicopters. In April they were presented with an injunction, naming 83 individuals who supposedly made up the leadership of the convoy, which was designed to prevent them from going to Stonehenge. As Sheila Craig put it, however, 'it was difficult to take it seriously, it seemed meaningless, almost comical, just a bit of paper... So the festival was banned, but we were the festival. It didn't seem to make a lot of difference, especially as we seemed to be banned anyway, wherever we were.'

Stonehenge and the road to the Beanfield

Such was the awareness that a noose was tightening around the travellers – through the well-publicised banning of the festival, as well as the constant persecution and the injunction – that even those like the Green Collective, who continued to assert the right of people to attend the 1985 festival, knew that they were effectively drawing up 'battle plans.' In the face of the National Trust threatening further injunctions against organisations like Festival Welfare Services and the St John's Ambulance Brigade if they showed up at Stonehenge, Bruce Garrard wrote in a Green Collective mailing newsletter, 'After years of talking about it, this year it seems the authorities will be making a concerted effort to stop the next midsummer festival... but they won't succeed; what they'll probably do is to politicise the 50,000+ free festival goers who will arrive there anyway... Thousands of people will be on the move this summer. We'll all look back and remember the Spirit of '85.'

As it transpired, people would remember the Spirit of '85 for far different reasons. On June 1st, after groups of travellers from around the country had stopped overnight in Savernake Forest near Marlborough, 140 vehicles set off for Stonehenge in the hope of setting up the 12th free festival. The atmosphere, as described by many eye-witnesses in the accounts that follow, was buoyant and optimistic. It remains apparent, however – especially in light of the persecution of the previous nine months – that behind this façade lurked generally unvoiced fears. Mo Poole, for example, recalled, in a conversation with Roisin McAuley for an edition of 'In Living Memory' that was broadcast on Radio 4 in 2002, that 'When the convoy had left Savernake that day, there was a police helicopter that had followed us all the way. There was police everywhere, really. It was obvious to us that we were being followed by the police and that they were monitoring our journey, and therefore I knew that something was going to happen, because they'd never done that before.'

Sid Rawle was so convinced that the state was planning a disproportionate response to the threat posed by the convoy that he stayed behind in Savernake, arguing that if all the travellers stayed put and waited for thousands more people to join them, the authorities would be powerless to break up the ever-growing movement that he had worked for so long to encourage. While it's also apparent that some of those who set off for Stonehenge that day were prepared for some kind of confrontation, few could have suspected quite how well-armed and hostile their opponents would be. The violent ambush that followed has become known as the Battle of the Beanfield, but it might be better described as a one-sided rout of heart-breaking brutality, and a black day for British justice and civil liberties whose repercussions are still felt to this day.

This chapter is partly adapted from Andy's book 'Stonehenge: Celebration and Subversion' (Alternative Albion, 2004) and partly from Alan's unpublished manuscript 'Not only but also... reminiscences on the festies, the Stones and the new Travellers, 1969-2001.'

Chapter Two

Interview with Phil Shakesby

Conducted by Gareth Morris and Caroline Thomas

Nostell Priory, 1984

It was the back end of the summer time. We'd done the normal summer circuit – Stonehenge, Inglestone Common – and then people went on to Cumbria and then down to Nostell Priory. It was a paying do. They had all kinds of bands on, some big name bands. We were all parked up in this big horseshoe affair, and it was all going quite nicely. Then the trouble started.

It was the time of the miners' strike, and the police had been herding them off into a field and battling it out with them. When the police steamed into Nostell Priory, they were fresh from beating up this bloody mega-wodge of miners. The first we knew of it was about half past eleven, when Alex came steaming past my gaff shouting, 'The Old Bill's coming up!' As I leapt outside and looked up this huge field, there was these great big blocks of bobbies, just like the Roman epics, at least four or five hundred of them. And they came charging across the field towards us, with these batons banging on their riot shields, shouting a war cry. Oh, my goodness!

They surrounded us just right of the marquee. At that point we were well and truly sorted. As I say, they had these mega bloody riot sticks, and wagons chasing through the site running into benders. Now they didn't know whether there was anybody in these benders, and they'd run into them at high speed, just loving the way that they exploded. The tarp and all the poles would blow out, scattering the contents all over the place. And they did several of these. One of the lads managed to fire up his truck and chase after this thing, and, of course, a few more riot wagons came in then, and they eventually stopped him by ramming him from either side.

The main Super Duper comes over when they've actually surrounded us, and he's asking for Boris and Doris, who are the ring-leaders as far as he's concerned, because we'd billed ourselves as, 'The Peace Convoy, backed by Boris and Doris' – who were two geese that we had on site. So on all the fly-posters it was 'Boris and Doris proudly presents...' sort of thing. So they wanted to arrest Boris and Doris. And of course, your arse is tweeting like nobody's business because there's all this thing going on. Your gaffs are being wrecked right before you, and you're surrounded by all this police, and then the Chief Super Duper marches up and says, 'Right, I want Boris and Doris to step out here now!' as all 200 of us fell about guffawing. I mean, you couldn't do anything else. Your arse is tweeting away one moment, and then there's this loony toon asking for two geese to step forward. It was the funny moment of it all. Wicked!

The other thing that went down: these guys that looked just like us – there was about seven of them. They'd infiltrated us that summer and done a bloody good job. They'd been wheeling and dealing along with some of the other lads that did that kind of thing. As we're surrounded, people are getting these lumps out of their back pockets and shoving them to one side. They were arresting us – arm up the back – and filing us out through the crowd and pushing us into the main bulk of the bobbies with the tackle.

It came to my turn to hand myself in. As I did, these two bobbies took hold of me and cuffed me up with two lots of cuffs, and quite smartly marched me away down the field. As they marched me down I looked to the right at my home. I had a Pilot Showman's trailer, and the contents are literally flying out of the windows that they'd broken. They were supposedly looking for drugs but they were systematically smashing up every home in the place. In fact, the trailer next to me, the inside was a total and utter wreck. There was nothing left.

I've got down to where they're photographing us and I'm complaining to this sergeant that my home is being smashed up. They're not searching it at all –they're smashing it up. And he just scribbled this number on my forehead and the camera went flash and I was dragged away. I told them what I felt about them. I told them that they were a gorgeous bunch of bastards. And so I was immediately nicked for that, and then they flung me headfirst into the riot wagon.

Anyhow, I slid down across the steely floor of this wagon, and they've seen this screwdriver in my back pocket. They pulled me back out by my feet, whipped me round in front of this sergeant, and showed him this screwdriver that I was supposedly going to use on them. And in fact, what the crack was, when they steamed in at half past eleven I was just finishing me fittings. You know, as you do when you're working, you slip things in your back pocket so you know where it is. It was about five minutes later when the police came in.

We were taken off into the police cells, where we spent three days and nights. And that was pretty wicked. Those that were kicking up, if they didn't get hosed down, they got a good hiding. I wouldn't make a statement. When they asked your name it was 'Joe Clone.' I wouldn't let them take me prints, and so they were going to get me sorted. They wanted to sort me there and then, so I offered them, 'Come on then, let's have it out now. I'll have all five of you.' And they thought that was too cocky for them, so they got these guys in from this borstal training thing, you know, and these guys actually turned up that night.

And there were these guys a few cells down from me who were being, like myself, non-cooperative. You could hear flesh and bone smacking against the brick wall as these borstal types were pummelling them down the way. And the three guys that were in the cells with me, I told them about how they were getting these guys in to sort me later, and these three are literally crying and whimpering away, because you could hear what was happening to the others down there.

I managed to blag their mattresses and put them in front of me, which made it very spongy for these gorillas to stand on, and I was going to be on the bench doing the business, letting fly with everything. I felt that they were going to snuff me out. A bit extreme, I suppose, but you read about people being battered to death in the cells and nothing ever being done about it. And when you heard these bodies being slapped down the way there, my goodness!

They came up to the door, and I was sat meditating on the bed, sort of thing, trying to keep my composure. All I could hear was my cell-mates going wobbly-lip. And one of these borstal types ripped the latch down on the cell door. I opened my eyes and I looked at these two eyeballs peering through, and my heart was thumping away as these manic eyeballs roamed around the cell. But for some reason they never came in. They just carried on down.

We were regularly rioting throughout the day. Then they decided to give us all tea and coffee, and we thought, 'Oh brilliant!' We hadn't had a drink of tea and coffee in days. You only got water and jam sandwiches and that was it. And of course, an hour or so later, after we had these drinks, it went deadly silent for the first time in days. They'd put Largactil – wodges of it – in the tea. Loads of people actually passed out or fell asleep, or they were laying there with their eyes open but couldn't do anything. The same thing happened to me. There were just one or two people who hadn't had this chemical cosh, and they sussed out what was going on pretty quick and started creating even more.

On the third or fourth day we were moved to army jail. This was quite a miserable experience for all concerned. You were banged-up 23 out of 24 hours, with only two half-hour exercise times. It was a miserable place. But when we first got out in the exercise yard we were quite chirpy, and John and I tried to crack a few laughs and warm proceedings up a bit.

In dribs and drabs I served ten days. Most people got up to a fortnight before they were taken to court. If you didn't give your right name they were going to keep you in indefinitely, but after a fortnight they sussed most of our names out. Loads of us were filed into court in front of this magistrate, who systematically went through us all, finding us guilty and nicking us for whatever it was. Myself, I got two lots of suspended sentences, for six months each, for just being at a festival and complaining that these people were smashing my home up. I felt quite bitter about that, really.

When I came out and found my gaff in the state it were in – it were a total wreck. They'd actually ripped the hangings down that I'd just put up, and ripped out all the panels too, so-called looking for drugs. They were just being totally and utterly destructive. They just

King of the Road: a traveller's vehicle (with Stonehenge on the side). Copyright Alan Lodge.

wanted to smash our homes up, because they still had this strange thing that if they decommissioned the homes they're decommissioning us, sort of thing.

I hadn't been on site long when some of the solicitors and barristers turned up that had been dealing with our cases. And they informed us that the police intended to do the very same thing the next day – to come in and arrest everybody there for whatever fairy tale charge they could make up. Well, of course, that sent paranoia charging right through the whole site.

Operation Amethyst

The next morning everybody was up bright and early. We were running and set off down the motorway, and at every exit we came to there were police cars and riot wagons all the way up and across the bridge. A mega-turnout. You couldn't leave the motorway. And this carried on in every county and at every exit as we charged down the M1 all the way to London. It just didn't stop until we actually hit London.

We ended up at this lovely place in Kent, and at the end of a month staying there, there was just about ten or so left out of the original convoy, and we moved on from there and we went... well, we couldn't go any further south without becoming amphibious. We thought they were going to run us straight into the sea, as it were. So we started going up north and ended up on this disused airfield. That was where this particular 'Operation Amethyst' took place.

The Battle of the Beanfield

As I say, there was very few of us. We'd had the usual hassle with them. They'd dumped about five tons of this clay on our only route in and out. They'd blocked it good and proper. We spent a couple of days hacking a way through that and eventually shifted it all. And as soon as we'd shifted it, they came along with this reinforced concrete and dumped umpteen tons of that. So we started hacking away at that, but it was almost impossible to get through. Dan, who was with us – The Neck, as he's known by the London firm – hijacked this JCB that was working just down the way from us, and he set about hacking away at this stuff. There was all this metal intertwined. He had to drive back and charge at it full-pelt with the bucket wide open, sort of thing, and grab into this stuff.

Anyway, we're working on top of this mound of tackle at the same time with sledgehammers and picks, as this guy, our nearest neighbour, turns out with his shotgun and starts letting go. I was on top of the mound smashing away at this tackle, and all these leaves came floating down from this branch a few feet above my head. I was well impressed by that. People sort of stopped, and I said, 'No, come on, let's get on with it. It's getting to the point when they're going to have to kill us if they want to stop us. Let's just carry on.' And we did. And he fired another shot. The police turned out, and we explained what had happened, and of course they wanted the JCB back. Everything was sorted and sort of fell into place, and we thought things were ok. We finished the work for the night and went back to our homes.

At the crack of dawn the next morning, Special Branch came in with a warrant for guns and drugs. I'd just smoked me last bit of drug as they were banging on the door. I smiled and popped it in the range. It was burning away quite merrily as they steamed in. They had guns under their armpits and guns on their hips, and there was these riflemen set out round about. They were quite frightening, really. It did give you this impression that you were on a short bit of string, that, short of a bullet, some of us are not going to go away. And it seemed that that day was not far off, really, because all of a sudden they're turning out with guns.

They arrested everyone on site again for whatever it was. As they're going through my kit for the second time, because they haven't found anything to arrest me on, Paddy's being dragged past and he's saying, 'You'll never guess what they're arresting me for. They're arresting me for being in possession of my own milk churn.' These bobbies looked at my milk churn by the door and said, 'Right, you're under arrest for being in possession of that milk churn and that tarpaulin.'

When we got down to the local nick there were these blackboards, and all our names are on these blackboards and what cells we were going in. So they knew. They'd already pre-planned to have that particular set of people down the cells, regardless of whether they found anything or not. We were interviewed by Special Branch. As far as they were concerned, we were terrorists. We were to be dealt with as terrorists. They couldn't find anything to nick us on, and so at the end of the day they've said, 'Psst, if you leave the area we'll drop the charges – the theft of the milk churn and the tarp.' And the same with the others. But we dug our heels in and stayed in the area and they never nicked us.

Molesworth

When we got this site established, we pulled off and went up to Molesworth, where the Peace Convoy actually came about then. We'd been told that a few people were up there. We moved on to the Rainbow Village and joined in with the protest. And by just being there you were protesting against these Cruise missiles. I didn't like Britain being used as a front line defence by some other country. It's us that'll get it in the head come the time, so I thought. So I ought to throw my threepence ha'penny's worth in and see what can be done.

And that's where I met lots and lots of new faces, and it was all working out pretty well there, though they'd been nicking bods for theft of firewood. It was freezing cold, you know. Winter. So I felt that that was really out of order. I'd never heard of it before. All the years that I'd been on the road, I'd never been nicked for theft of firewood. Being nicked for trying to keep warm, sort of thing.

High-ranking bobbies and officials would regularly come on, and I took them to one side and had a word with them about it. But they weren't having none of it. I put it to them that we can have it tit-for-tat, if you like. 'If you're going to carry on nicking people for collecting firewood, I can always block off your main entrance', I told them. They sort of

Peace Convoy bus.
Copyright
Alan Lodge.

said, 'Go ahead', so we did. Ten of us moved onto their main road, which only left them the one way in. There was no exit. And it stayed like that all the time, because they carried on nicking people for collecting the firewood. And we told them, when they stopped nicking people or when they dropped the charges, we'd open the road up, but until then it would be tit-for-tat. Well, they never did relent, so we kept the road blocked for three weeks.

It was quite a good do. Loads of Joe Public turning out at weekends, and coming along with old Wellingtons and old sets of work boots, and all kinds of stuff. There was this free food area, where loads of potatoes were done in the ovens, and loads and loads of food was always on the go at weekends. It was quite a good do down there.

But on the night when they came in... It was about half past eleven. There's this huge trail of motors that you could see in the distance. I'd never seen so many headlights in all my life, sort of Old Bill-wise. You knew who it was straight away. It was the Old Bill and the army, and there were thousands of them coming in. As they came closer and closer, the panic set in. People were running around with lumps of stash and sort of bimbling off in different directions and doing like they do. They steamed in and surrounded us. They had it well-timed. We were promptly ringed by the Old Bill, as these army sappers were running around with coils of barbed wire.

Talk about overkill. There were 1,500 Royal Engineers, 100 military police, and about 500 riot cops. It were the biggest Royal Engineer operation since the war. And Michael Heseltine flew in like Action Man. You know he has this long hair – well, he had this bloody hair-net on as well – quite a cod! Yeah, that was the do – Michael Heseltine.

Long Marston

After Molesworth, this main lump was put up in Bedford, and then on to Long Marston. We had a wodge of jam sandwiches steam in. They were trying to cut us up and slow us down. All you could do was keep going at the same speed and go up their back end and push them along, you know. As we went through the different counties we had jam sandwiches, then we had these riot vans doing the same thing, and then all these motorcycle cops. It was quite a wacky race, if you like, from Bedfordshire to Long Marston. And then, in the last twenty miles, all the Old Bill that had been interfering with us disappeared. Instead of trying to stop us, the local Old Bill in Stratford are going, 'Yeah, yeah, it's alright. Just steam on up there.' They even gave us directions.

When we got to the site, of course, there was the landowner in this bloody great mechanical digger, not letting us in. And the entrance was quite a big entrance. Jed was over one side and I was on the other. He'd come over with this big set of jaws at your windscreen, Jed would inch in a bit, and it would swing over to him and give him loads of grief. I'd inch in and it'd swing back to me. And on the third time, as Jed inched in and

The convoy prepares to leave Savernake Forest, June 1st 1985. Copyright Alan Lodge.

was about to go for the gate, he just swung the bucket round and went 'Wham!' straight through the roof and through the windscreen. And Jed is just sat there going, 'Wow!'

Seconds later, Jed's leapt out the cab, out through the hole where the windscreen went, and chased off up to this huge machine. And, of course, as he's going up, this landowner has brought the arm in and he's giving it some. Jed's running around trying to get to the cab, and he's following with this bucket affair trying to crush him. I leapt out of the motor and I went over as well, so he had both of us to contend with. And then, as he was having a dig at me, Jed got into his cab round the other side. He's giving him a punch or two and he's got him by the throat, and this huge arm sort of fell to the ground and it's twitching away like a good 'un, as Jed's rattling his neck, and I drove my coach and trailer through the middle of this arm – this huge bloody arm – as everybody else followed in.

The main bulk of the people came together there and we ended up with this quite large convoy. And it was from there that we set out to move down to the Stones. We'd put the word out. We'd been and seen Spider's lot in Bristol and Pikey's lot on the east coast, and our main lump was in the middle of the country, sort of thing, and we'd arranged to meet up on the first large field after Savernake Forest. And of course, Bald-Headed Ray had actually taken Savernake Forest for us, so that's where our main bulk ended up. Later on, both Spider's and Pikey's lot came in, and it was quite a good festival we had going that night.

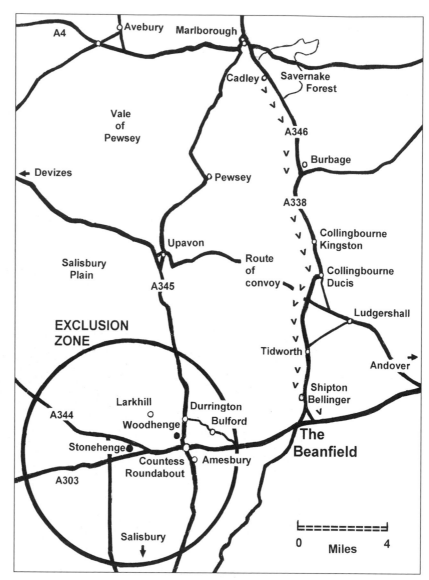

Map showing the route of the convoy from Savernake Forest south down the A338 to the A303, the Beanfield, and the limit of the exclusion zone around Stonehenge, which applied to the 83 individuals named in the injunction. As is abundantly clear, the Beanfield is nearly four miles to the east of the exclusion zone, and therefore well outside the jurisdiction of the injunction anyway. Map by Andy Worthington.

The Battle of the Beanfield

The next morning came along, and it was about half nine in the morning. I was listening to the local radio and it reported that there were 300 hippies actually at Stonehenge, and of course at that I was quite elated and I rushed off and told people. And it's, 'Ali! Ali! Come on, let's go!' We had this huge convoy with this carnival-cum-fairy-type atmosphere, you know – flags waving, Bob Marley on the ghetto blaster. It was wicked. And eventually we all set off and slowly meandered down the road towards what we now know as the Beanfield.

Interview with Phil Shakesby

As we made our way down there, we were about ten miles or so away from Stonehenge, when these two old boys stopped us and told us of these large council lorries that were preparing to dump quite a few tons of grit on the road, along with this wodge of bobbies that were there. Mick, who was my co-pilot, he had another look at the map and he worked out that we could by-pass this huge roadblock by doing a quick left and then a right and then carrying on down the main A303 to Stonehenge. Which is what we did. Well, as we got to that point, they'd already hacked off a large portion of the back end. These hit squads of police had, you know, steamed in from out the junctions, blocked the road, and busily started setting about people and their homes, you know, smashing in their windows and knocking people about like they do.

And we were carrying on. I didn't know any of this was going on, myself. I was in the lead vehicle at the front, as Dale came along on his motorbike. Dale was the outrider. He steamed along and told us, as we were going down the road, what had been happening at the back end. Of course, we knew what to expect at the front end any minute. And sure enough, no more than ten seconds had gone by from Dale telling us, when these riot

Phil, in the hat, attempts to negotiate with the police at the roadblock on the A303 near Parkhouse roundabout.

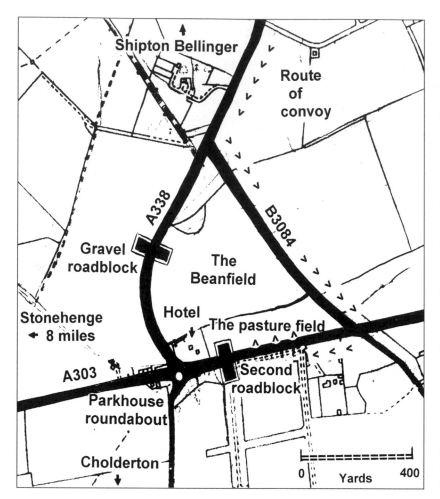

Map of the Beanfield, showing the route taken by the convoy down the A338 from Shipton Bellinger, the gravel road-block just north of the A303, the diversion taken by the convoy down the B3084, and the second police roadblock on the A303, just to the east of Parkhouse roundabout. The Beanfield, and the pasture field – Warner's Field – are contained within the triangle formed by the A338, the B3084 and the A303. Map by Andy Worthington.

wagons came steaming up the road two abreast. There was no way you could go round them. A quick negotiation started with the police, but they weren't prepared to let us go on any further, and in fact we were to hand ourselves in or there'd be bother. Well, we told them there and then that there was no way that people were going to hand themselves in. Then the order was sent out by the high-ranking bobby to arrest all the drivers, and of course this line of riot bobbies had shot out along the side of us and started smashing in the windows.

Well, this chap came up from behind in a flat bed and, by the side of me, rammed into the hedge, and got stuck and reversed out, and then rammed through it again. I thought, 'What a brilliant idea! Let's pull into the field off the road.' So I put my wagon into first gear, which was crawler gear, and made my own hole in the hedge and steamed off through. I'd recently fitted a huge bumper – a really big, heavy-duty sort of fuck-off bumper, you know – and I went and punctured 'x' amount of holes in the hedgerow for people to get through, because they'd already heard what were going on at the back end, and what were going on at the front, as these bobbies had just stormed down, and they were just wrecking homes as they went, you know, smashing in the windows. And people started quickly filtering in through the holes, and people had got chainsaws out and were cutting their own holes in the hedge. And what was the main bulk of us then moved into the Beanfield. At first there were quite a lot of people driving around who weren't quite sure what was what, until we all got parked up and things seemed to settle down a bit.

I was hoping myself that we'd be allowed to leave that field and go to the alternative site. We kept waiting on this Chief Super Duper Grundy, who was the man of the time, and of course he did eventually turn up. I asked him if we could go to the alternative site, and he said, 'No.' I said, 'Well, can we go back to Savernake?' He said, 'No, you will hand yourself in and be processed', and he gave us a deadline as to when we should be doing it. And of course, all this time-wasting that had gone on was so they could build up the forces that they felt were necessary to comfortably outnumber us, and do the same business on us that they'd been doing on the miners.

I mean, the police say there were people throwing petrol bombs and stuff like this. I never actually saw any of our lot throwing petrol bombs. What I did see was quite a few people that felt very intimidated, very frightened after having their homes smashed. And quite a few people had been beat up at this stage by the police and arrested and taken away, and some were still with us that had been beaten up. And people were prepared to resist to a degree, as such. There were a few young ones that were actually having a bit of a running battle with the riot police, who kept coming into the field in full gear – with the batons and riot shields – having a dig at us. I suppose they wanted to know if they could just walk in and do as they pleased.

As I say, there was a lot of time-wasting so they could get their forces together. There was ITN reporters and other such reporters there who had been talking with the police, and the police had informed them that they were going to come in and do the business. These reporters were very concerned for our safety and welfare. You could see by the way they were shaking that things were going to take a very drastic turn for the worse. And sure enough, they did.

When the time came, things were very quiet, and people were just resigned to hanging in the field and hoping that it would all go away. The police came in and they were battering people where they stood, smashing homes up where they were, just going wild. Maybe about two-thirds of the vehicles actually started moving and took off, and they chased us into a field of beans. By this time there were police everywhere, charging along the side of us, and wherever you went there was a strong police presence. Well, they came in with all kinds of things: fire extinguishers and one thing and another. When they'd done throwing the fire extinguishers at us, they were stoning us with these lumps of flint and such.

Assaults in the pasture field.

And in fact, while things had been quiet that afternoon they had been considering whether to use these high-powered single-shot rifles to put a single shot into each engine lock to stop it, because they knew that we'd climb into the vehicles and try and drive off, like you do when somebody's coming at you with a manic set of eyes and a large lump of something. You want to run away from it.

A distressed traveller is escorted off the pasture field, while a vehicle – almost certainly Phil's – burns in the background.

We're charging around, and around and around, and of course as the minutes went by there were less and less of us. And as people were stopping, their homes were systematically broken, and the people were battered and taken away and flung into the riot wagons. It came to the point where there's just Jed and myself left running in the field. Then there was all these bobbies left to deal with us. There didn't seem much point in going on, so I drove out of the Beanfield. I'd been in and out of the Beanfield several times already. You just had to move away from where the main bulk were, and go for where there was less bobbies, you know, because you had less stuff being thrown at you at that point.

There was a dividing line between the Beanfield and the grassy field, and there was a dip where my front wheel went down. As I tried rocking the vehicle back and forth on my clutch, it wasn't coming out, and by that time I'd been surrounded by about 40 policemen. In the same moment, every window in the vehicle came inwards. I'd had nothing broken at that point. It had all been bouncing off the bodywork and some of my windows were Perspex, so all the other windows had been left intact, but in that one instance every window came in.

The Battle of the Beanfield

I'd bolted my doors, and put big coach bolts through them so you couldn't open them, and there were no handles on the front, so they wouldn't be able to get in, but they ripped these doors open with the coach bolts in. How they did it I don't know, but they ripped these doors open. And then this one single riot bobby leapt in and stood on my bed and shouted at Third Eye Jim to get out. He let Third Eye Jim out. He shouted at Mick to get out, and, as he got to the side door, this bobby smashed him right between the eyes with this huge riot stick, and of course Mick flew out the door backwards.

Then he told me to do likewise, and of course I realised as soon as I moved over to the door that he was going to hit me with this stick. Which he did. As soon as I got to the door, sure enough, he went to hit me right between the eyes – the same place he'd hit Mick – so I covered my face, and this baton hit me on the elbow and sent me reeling out the door. And just as they'd got me on to the brow of the field there, because that's where they were taking our particular lot that was left, these bobbies stopped me and forcibly spun me round and made me look. They said, 'See that', and I looked at my home, and there was smoke coming out the side doors. They'd gone and set my home on fire, stopped me and turned me round, and made me look at the flames and the smoke coming out the sides.

Then they turned me back round and whisked me off and bumped me into the riot wagon, where there was a lot of other people that I knew. We've all had the same treatment. I don't think there was anybody in the wagon that hadn't been thumped with a riot stick. And of course, from there it was down to the police cells in Amesbury. They nicked over 400 of us. I heard of one poor kid who'd swallowed his entire stash before they steamed on, and of course the Old Bill sussed out pretty quickly that he's tripping, and they've got him in the back of a riot wagon. They're sitting on his chest and digging him in the kidneys, and threatening how they're going to snuff him out down the cells, sort of thing, and this kid's screaming. Oh, my goodness!

They really went for it that day. I'd never seen the Old Bill lose it so much. And of course, the TV footage of them doing the business went walkies. All Joe Public got to see of the Beanfield was shots of our kitchen knives and axes – so-called weapons – and various buses supposedly trying to run the Old Bill over.

3 Chapter Three
Interview with Maureen Stone
Conducted by Neil Goodwin and Gareth Morris

What is your name and why do you choose a travelling lifestyle?

Well, my name is Maureen Stone – lots of people call me Moz Stone – and I first came on the road in 1984. We received, at Stonehenge, some literature from a guy called David Taylor – he was a member of the Green Party – and he wanted people that could go to Molesworth. We lived in a New Town called Basildon, and it was chock-a-block full of unemployed, brickies, brickies' labourers, and people generally in the construction game that couldn't find any work and that had been going to festivals.

So several of us went to Molesworth, and when we arrived at Molesworth – it was well before the festival started – there were two Quakers called Tim and Bridie – they were nicknamed by us Nice and Tidy, and they were nice and tidy – and we built a chapel out of the runway rubble that had been dumped in the road to stop the people getting in. And lots of other people came, and there was an idea to have the roof thatched, and I think the Bishop of Huntingdon came in and consecrated it or something.

At the same time, there was also wheat being grown – it was only symbolic – but the people were growing wheat for the folk that were out in Eritrea, and lots of the people

The peace chapel at Molesworth. Copyright Celia Kibblewhite.

that were doing that didn't have the money to put in the envelopes to send off to Oxfam or Child Relief, but they had certain skills, in agriculture or building. So yeah, a lot of people from Basildon went to Molesworth, and I was part of that group.

And then, very much later, lots of other people that had come down from the Blue Moon Festival – or was it the Silver Moon Festival? – like Lyn Norriman and all them, they came there, and then later on the people who had been trashed at Nostell Priory came there, and... it's news what happened then. On February 6th, I think it was, 2,000 Royal Engineers, I was told, and 600 armed police came in. The first thing that I knew of it, we were sitting in my bender, which was the best place I think I've had. I've had trailers, I've had trucks, but the best place that I ever lived in was this big, palatial bender at Molesworth that was 60 feet in diameter, had eight huge tarps across it, and a York stone fireplace.

And I heard, 'Ali! Ali! Ali!' at the bottom of the site, and at that point in time I was sitting in the bender with a girl called Punk Cathy, who was my mate, and a guy called Rich and his wife Reik, a Dutch girl, and I heard this 'Ali! Ali! Ali!' going on, and I said, 'Oh', you know, 'someone's having a party.' And they had been at Nostell Priory, and they said, 'That isn't a party, something bad's happening.' I, at that point in time, couldn't differentiate between the 'Ali! Ali! Ali!' of a party and the 'Ali! Ali! Ali!' of 'something really bad's happening' – and it was.

We opened the bender flap up, and we saw this huge ring of lights coming in. Unless you'd been in a situation where you'd seen a war happen around you, you just never saw that many troops. I'd never seen what 2,000 troops looked like. And we were evicted that night, and everybody – the convoy people, the Rainbow Village people – just became one and the same then, and then it became 'The Convoy', because a convoy, after all, is just a group of vehicles moving up the road, that's what a convoy is to me. It's a convoy of vehicles, not people that you can classify as all being the same, with the same view in mind. It's a load of vehicles moving up the road with a load of people.

Did you see Michael Heseltine at Molesworth?

No, I only saw him on 'Spitting Image'. I just saw the puppets. I still even didn't know what he looked like until sometime later. I never saw him, no. I saw all the troops. At the point when the troops came in my bender it was where they were running the perimeter line round, so they burned my bender, and so that was just the end of that. I was doing a massive land squat on MoD land. They gave me an hour to move off – I couldn't possibly move off in an hour – and so they burned what I lived in. Other people got longer, but they weren't on the perimeter line.

It was very different then from the Beanfield. I reckon all the squaddies must have been on orders not to talk to us, because at one point, where I lived, they were in chainsawing a young hawthorn grove, and I'd gone up to some young squaddies and said something like, 'What the bloody hell do you think you're doing, cutting down this lot in the middle of the night?' and they wouldn't talk to us. That was the thing that the women noticed all the time, that they would not speak to us, the army lads wouldn't speak to us. The police would hurl loads of abuse at you, but the army lads wouldn't speak to you, so we reckoned that they must have been on orders not to, because... well, at one point I had shouted at them, 'Northern Ireland made it easy for you', and I think it did, because prior to that troops that had gone out of this country had gone out to fight somewhere else in a war – be they Koreans, Germans or whatever; Japanese – but all of a sudden the army were being told not to relate to women that might look like your mum or your sister. So yeah, I think Northern Ireland made it easy for them.

Did you come into contact with troops in any other situation?

No, only that massive amount of them, somewhere in excess of 2,000. I don't know how many millions it cost to get us off of Molesworth, and then Cruise missiles never even got based there – I mean, they did at Greenham – but at Molesworth there was 150 people, some cats and dogs and a goat, and it cost the Cambridgeshire rate-payers – or everybody that pays their taxes, I suppose; I don't understand all the finances a lot, but everybody that pays their taxes pays towards defence – something like £2 million to get us off a bit of derelict ground. And that's all Molesworth was. There was no army base, there was nothing, there was just hundreds of acres of ground going to waste, and in 1984 a handful of people went there and grew wheat for Eritrea.

Who came up with the name Rainbow Warriors at Molesworth?

There was a girl from Nostell Priory – she's a New Zealander, she's a great friend of mine. Her name's Bev – I hardly knew her there at all – and she had come from Nostell Priory, and at that point in time there were lots of people living there that had come from council houses like me, or they were travellers that had been on the festival circuit, or they were tipi-dwellers from Tally. There was a great, broad spectrum of people already there. So we all looked round at each other, and when the travellers came in from Nostell Priory that had been trashed... I think it would be fair to say that there was snobbery there in a small part, that some people said, 'I don't know whether we need these people here', but the vast majority of people, like me, sat there and said, 'These are exactly who we want here.' These are the people that I looked at when I went to Stonehenge the last time and thought, 'I'd love to be them.'

And I was really glad – I was not glad that they got trashed – but I was really glad when they come there, and I could show them – like Phil Shakesby – that we could say, 'This is the free food kitchen, and if you want any food it's free, and if you want any blankets there's this and that', and I think it was one of the best places that I lived in... I mean, I've lived at lots of other good places too, but I think Molesworth was a place where people

Children on a
dragon parade at
Molesworth.
Copyright Celia
Kibblewhite.

waited just to meet other people. In a way, it was a gathering point, and for sure that was the point in time that the powers-that-be pushed what they called 'hardcore convoy' out of the peace movement. I wasn't even part of the peace movement then. I was like somebody from a nylon tent the year before and wanted to be part of it, that's what I was.

What were your plans for Stonehenge in 1985?

I've told you a bit about Molesworth. When I was at Molesworth there was a young woman there called Jules, and I was present at the time that her baby was born, which was Phoebe, and I was very honoured to be asked to be the grandmother – the godmother – of this child. I said 'the grandmother' because Jules used to say I was her honorary mum, and I was Phoebe's honorary grandmother, so it was quite an honour for me to be asked to be this child's godmother, and to go to the naming ceremony. I'd only ever watched it from the outside once before, and I wanted to be part of it, and I thought it was a great honour to be asked this. So basically, at the end of the day, that's what I was going to Stonehenge for. I was also going to Stonehenge for the festival, and to run a café, and have a good time the same as all the other people, but first and foremost I was going to name Phoebe Stonechild at the Stones.

What was the café about? How was that set up?

It was all on the basis of a free food kitchen. This was our dream. It never happened, but a guy called Rasta Mark and his woman called Pauline, another guy called Soldier Bill, and me and Len, we'd all come from Basildon New Town, and we had this idea that we'd run a free food kitchen at Stonehenge. So we got lots of donations from other stalls, and if people had money they could pay for the food – which lots of people do actually – and if you didn't have any money you could just drop in whatever you had. So – because we weren't vegetarians, you see, and lots of it was vegetarian – we'd run a meat and vegetarian one, with perhaps chicken stew, pizzas, baked potatoes in their jackets with cheese, and as much tea or coffee as you could drink.

So that was our dream. It didn't ever come off, because we never got there, but I think if we had it would've been really brilliant. And amongst us there was also lots of musicians, so there was lots of music that was going to go on, and there were people that were excellent craftsmen, like Len, who could do wood-carving and leatherwork. So there was going to be workshops incorporated in all this, and that's why we had so many tarps and crockery.

You had a good idea that the festival was going to go on?

We travelled in hope that it would, yeah, otherwise... If at any moment in time I knew what was going to go down, that we were going to get trashed like that, beaten up and everything smashed up... If anybody had told me that at any point in time, for sure, well, I wouldn't have gone. I might have said, 'Well, I'll stay here' or 'I'll leave my children in Savernake Forest.' Maybe Len might have gone out on a bus with other blokes, maybe it would have been worse, I don't know, but we were a long way away from the solstice. And this is what has been asked in court all the time: did we go with the intention of getting onto Stonehenge on the 1st of June? Well, actually – personal – I never thought we would get to Stonehenge that day, but I thought we might find somewhere to park up, something would be offered to us, something would go on, and at the end of the day the worst way round would be that we wouldn't be able to get that near the Stones, but people could still go on for the ceremony. And at that time – I don't believe it now – but then, five and a half years ago, I believed it, yeah, because we travelled with such hope. We still was also frightened of getting trashed at the same time. People were still thinking, 'Will it be alright?' It wasn't blind fanaticism or anything, but people travelled with hope.

What was the scene like when you left Savernake and travelled down?

The day before I'd lost my vehicle – the steering had gone – and then one of my best friends, Abbey, who Kelly was going to travel with... They had packed up this huge picnic lunch together, and at the last moment I had a really bad feeling about Kelly going with Abbey, and said so, and Abbey said, 'I'm glad Kelly isn't going to come with me, in a way', and she went with someone else. And the hold-up before we got to Savernake... I knew that there'd been a dreadful accident, and then when I found out it was Abbey, to tell the truth I was really distressed that night in Savernake and most of the next day, because I was still trying to find out what hospital Abbey was in, and things like that. So that was the worst thing, if you like, as I travelled on to Stonehenge, because Abbey was going to

The convoy on the road from Savernake Forest. Copyright Alan Lodge.

be part of the naming ceremony. She had been around me and Jules at Desborough airfield, and she was a lovely young girl, really accommodating and friendly, and just... you really liked her, and all I had found out about Abbey was that she had these dreadful facial injuries, she had had her legs trapped, and I had heard that her hand had been laid open to the bone.

So actually I didn't travel all that happily onwards. I thought loads about Abbey, was quite sad about that, but still I was aware that it was a total carnival atmosphere. And I was still wanting to go to Stonehenge, because I didn't feel it was right at that time for me personally to stay in Savernake Forest. I had thought about it, though. Lots of women in the Rainbow Village talked about staying within the forest, and that it was safer. A girl called Rainbow Jo, she was actually the only person that I ever spoke to, apart from Sid Rawle, that said, yeah, she'd stay there, because she was very close to having her baby, and didn't want to travel onwards. And I totally understood that, and that was the end of that, really, and then I made my decision to go onwards. But yeah, I think it was a carnival atmosphere, and happy, hopeful people.

As you were travelling down, did you come into contact with the police at all?

I can't remember properly. I think I did. I think they wrote down that I had black hair and green eyes and several silver rings and bangles, but I never ever spoke to any police officers, and they never spoke to me. I can remember a time that my friends Reik and

Rick came over to us for a bit to stay in our truck, because maybe what they were in weren't entirely legal – and we weren't entirely legal either! – and waited until it all died down a bit and nobody was writing anything on the forms again. But lots of the time the police actually weren't asking people any questions. They were standing by the side of the road, ticking things on clipboards off. So, no, I was never actually told 'breach of the peace' or anything like that.

But you knew there was an injunction?

Oh, yeah.

But that was a civil injunction.

That was a civil injunction, and I knew that I wasn't a named person on it, and I didn't consider myself to be a servant or an agent of any other that was on that list, so – maybe it was naïve to consider that – but that was how I looked at it. I looked down the list; my name wasn't on it. I knew that I'd gone to Stonehenge in '84, and there'd also been this same thing going on, and I thought the same thing would happen. I thought that people would get on site, that there was so many people that wanted it. It seemed to me... I mean, as we drove through Wiltshire and Hampshire – in and out of the borders, because you did quite a bit – people were waving to us. People were stood outside watching us go by like a carnival. Nobody was hurling abuse, sticks or stones or anything. As we went past, most of the children were waving to people in the pubs, and the people in the pubs waved back, and that's what we saw. It was all 'Whoo! Whoo! Whoo!' like that. It was alright.

What was the first time that it got really heavy, when you could see that the police were going to make a move?

I think it was when we got up to the roadblock, which we didn't see. We never saw the roadblock. I saw a washing-up bowl, a kettle, somebody's washing rack, and some kitchen utensils – I think a pair of kitchen scales as well – scattered across the road, and I knew something had happened from the people before. I knew that they had gone on that fast, and things had fell out, that something had happened that they then moved very quickly, because if you drop a kettle you get out and pick it up again, or if you drop your washing-up bowl you need it. If something happens, like the door flies open and that flies out, you stop and pick it up and put it in again. I saw tat over the road that you wouldn't leave, and I knew something had happened further on, and it wasn't so very far, maybe another 50 or 60 yards, before then we saw what had happened to the vehicles in front.

And there was police. And there were smashed-up vehicles. And they weren't just smashed-up vehicles, they was Kitchen Jim's, who I'd had a cup of tea with the night before, and had a smoke with, and listened to some sounds with. It was his home. It

47

Police with shields at the roadblock on the A303 near Parkhouse roundabout.

wasn't someone's smashed Cortina, or their little runaround car, it was someone's home smashed up, and I took great notice of this. There were other vehicles in front of that, there was lots of policemen, there was a great gap in the hedge, and there were vehicles and caravans and people that I knew in on the field, so I pulled straight in with them. I didn't go up to the line-up and ask what had happened. I could see what had happened. There were no occupants, there were smashed-up buses and vehicles, and lots of policemen. There was a gap, and lots of friends in there, so I went straight in where my friends were.

So you knew that they'd been trashing the vehicles?

Well, you could just see it straightaway. There were no occupants. By that time, obviously, Jim and Helen and everyone like that... I didn't know Helen Reynolds very well then, but I knew other people's vehicles, like Kitchen Jim's that, as I say, I'd been on the night before. There was no question that you would just draw up next to those smashed-up vehicles and get out. You would of course try to get in where – obviously something bad had happened to them – those people have got away. I'm going to get in there, where the other people who haven't had that happen to them are.

What happened when you got into the field?

When we first pulled up onto the B-road, we weren't aware that there was gravelling and gritting lorries. We saw the trashed vehicles, we saw the people in the field, so we pulled straight in, and we got as far away as we could from what looked like the pigs up at the top end, and where people were going up then to negotiate with them. We got as far away from that as we could, 'cause that was always a good place to be, as far away from that.

And we got out, and we had so much stuff packed in the caravan, we couldn't run anything out of there. We had loads of wood with us, so we got it outside and done an open fire. We were cooking chips, chapatis, tea, coffee, and just generally talking to the other people that were around us, finding out what they thought. And in a way – I know it was probably stupid – but us lot were well away from the negotiating area, and so we were still talking to each other with hope. Every now and again, someone would go up there and say, 'It's well bad up there. Do you want to go up there?' and come back again.

It wasn't until Shirley come up to me – and I was well into the chips and chapatis by then – and Shirley, Terry's girlfriend, come up and said, 'Moz, they've got one of my puppies. I've got the matching puppy here. I just want the puppy back, 'cause I'm frightened that if I walk up to them on my own, they're going to grab hold of me and arrest me, so if you come with me you're...' – perhaps she thought I was older and more sensible, and they'd take more notice, which I thought might be true as well – so I went with her.

And when we got there, the riot police were holding the puppy up by the scruff, and just shaking the puppy, and saying, 'Come on, if you want it, here', so we got well up to them, within reaching distance. The pigs stepped back into the long line of officers, and said, 'Here you are, if you want the puppy, come and take it. You've just got to give this officer your name.' So we stepped in, and then we realised, behind this one line, how many lines... They were massed like a block of Roman troops. The lane was just chock-a-block with layers of them. So we said something inane like, 'Can we have our puppy back?' and they said – into a talking brooch! – 'We have two women prisoners. Bring up the dog-handling units for two dogs.' And we said, 'Whoa, hold it, we're not women prisoners, leave it out. I've got my children still back in that field', and went to step back into the field, when all these officers said, 'No, you can't.'

At this moment in time, further down the line, the same batch of officers had started throwing things at Lin Bin's trailer, so Lurch and Lin Bin were hurling abuse at the people that were hurling lumps of flint at Lin Bin's trailer. And Lin Bin had noticed what had happened, and had said to Lurch, 'Look, that's Moz and Shirley there', and started shouting – fighting abuse, I suppose, nearly as good as what the riot pigs were chucking at them. Me and Shirley just stepped smartly back into the field, and fucked off back to where we had come from, without the puppy. But that was nasty, dangling the puppy up, then 'Here you are, here you are', and then bringing it in. They could just have put the puppy in an RSPCA van, and then we could have picked it up when we got out, or something. But it wasn't that. They were being nasty. They knew this 17-year old girl wanted her puppy back, and it was just part of their bastardry.

Police invade the pasture field while a musician plays on.

And loads of stuff like that must have gone on all day with other people, but that was just a little bit of what made me realise how many officers were there, because up until then I didn't realise. So I went back and told Len how many officers were out there. He believed me shit-hot. We took more notice of the helicopters then. We took more notice, maybe, of things going wrong out on the negotiating front, because things weren't going wrong by anything anyone was saying at our end, trying to negotiate, there was just this brick wall. I think then, by about five o'clock in the evening, I knew it was going to go badly for us, but I didn't think that badly. I thought we were all going to be arrested, and probably all our trucks were going to be impounded.

When they came in at seven o'clock, we had just got into the vehicle moments before. We didn't actually know they were coming in at that moment, but it was almost like intuitively we got in the vehicles, we knew they would be coming in soon. We got in, and we just watched. We weren't going anywhere, you know. It was an old truck that was only pulling our caravan out of courtesy. It was Ed's truck. We had lost our towing vehicle. It had struggled along at ten and 15 miles per hour, and coughing and spluttering, so it weren't going anywhere. There was no point in trying to drive into the Beanfield, there was no point in trying to get away. I don't even think we probably had very much fuel.

Clearly distraught, a woman and child are escorted off the pasture field. Copyright Tim Malyon.

So we just sat in the vehicle with the children, and watched hundreds... They said 207 run in, didn't they? Well, I don't believe that. I was at Molesworth, and I saw what 2,000 police and troops look like. I think there were hundreds and hundreds of policemen running into the field. And when they descended on us, we had maybe 40 or 50 officers slamming their way into a totally stationary vehicle, saying, 'Open up!' Len couldn't pull the door open, because they had dented it in so much – it was on sliding runners – so it didn't work any more, because they'd dented it in so that it couldn't slide open. Afterwards, Ed said to me that they had beaten the door right off, and he never did find it again, but that's neither here nor there; it's just what Ed said about his vehicle.

Len and Ed were ordered out, and they got out. I, at that point in time, already had slung everything that looked like... a knife, a saw, anything that looked dangerous, I had thrown it into the back with the children, and was standing in front of the children. All the time that the officers were banging on the sides of the vehicles, I'd never heard so much noise, with the helicopters... You could hear people that you knew screaming. You couldn't see them, but I could hear them. And there was fucking loads of it going on. I could hear someone screaming for her husband. I could hear loads of people...

Bobby was still crying. Kelly had got to the point that she wasn't crying anymore. It was like something really strange had happened to her. She had become incontinent; she had lost control of her bladder. I picked her up and tried to get out the door. As I looked out the door, a riot policeman had swung a club, and I'd said something like, 'Don't hit her, she's only a child' – something like that – and he said to another officer, to the side of him, 'I thought she was holding a dog', and I think it was because Kelly had really long hair, it was like hip-length hair and it was hanging over my arms, so maybe he thought I was holding a Red Setter or something, but he nearly fucking hit her. He was a Rizla paper away from swinging a club in and hitting her.

But he wasn't my arresting officer. Another one was, and he never said, 'I caution you', or anything like that. He just said to me, 'Are you part of the same family?' because he had seen Len and Ed getting dragged away by four officers, and there was still about 40 officers standing around this stationary vehicle. The vehicle that was next to us was Chris and Sheila's, which was a big bus called 'Dawn Treader', and on the side of it they had something like 'Live without walls and fences', and I think, as the riot pigs had run in, they must have thought we were heavy duty, because we had things like 'Live without walls and fences', you know, on a bus near us. And anyway, the riot policeman that took me off afterwards said that he was a Ministry of Defence policeman, and Len's arresting officer actually called me by my nickname, Moz. I asked him how he knew, and he said, 'You're the people that built the chapel at Molesworth, aren't you? I'm a Cambridgeshire Ministry of Defence policeman.' I mean, I never said that in the evidence. The judge wouldn't even let me say what really happened to us.

When we got into the holding bus... In my evidence in court it was stopped several times, because I related the story of this young man that was beaten – brutally, continually – in the aisle just next to me, while the rest of the people on the bus, mainly who were festival-goers... but Ribs was one of them, which at the time I never knew Ribs, and he was sitting in the front of the bus, and was aware that Ed Myers, Len and me were having a go about this youth being beaten. He was taken out unconscious at Lyndhurst. Kelly thought he was dead, actually, but why wouldn't she? She was only 12, and seeing all that fucking violence she thought he was dead.

And then when we got to Southampton police cells, I was queued up with the other women. We asked for toilet facilities, and food and drink for the children, and we weren't given them, and I got locked up in the cells with two other women, so there was five of us – me, my two children, and two other women – locked up in a cell that was probably designed for maybe two people. There weren't any mattresses or blankets, there were just two wooden benches on either side of a very small cell with an open toilet – a very dirty open toilet, but there you go, it was only a police cell.

And then in the early hours of the morning, probably about five o'clock in the morning, I had social services come in with a form that said that Jules, James and someone else – I can't remember the name; maybe it was Maggie Festival Services – that these three people in Savernake Forest would be guardians for my children. Well, of course, I recognised Jules' name straightaway, and so I signed a form letting Bobby and Kelly out into their care, as their guardians – and they were taken straight into care, and kept there.

And I got given a receipt back through the cell door, where I had signed 'Maureen Stone' and then it was taken round to the men's cells and he signed 'Len Stone', and then at the bottom of it also came out 'Bev Riley', who had signed for Maev, which signified to me that they were juggling lots of bits of carbon copies about, because why would 'Bev Riley' be on 'M. Stone and L. Stone' for Bobby and Kelly Stone? Why was 'Bev Riley' on the bottom of it? And I looked at this receipt, and then when I looked at it carefully it said James, Jules and the third name, and then stamped on it was, 'Or at Seagarth Children's Home, Southampton.' Now there is no way that I would sign a document signing my children over to the Seagarth Children's Home in Southampton, but that's where they were taken for 72 hours, and kept under quite severe lock-up, where they were escorted to the toilets, they weren't allowed out, and my 12-year old daughter was severely bullied by 17-year old girls who said, 'Your mum will never get you back, you little hippie slag', and clouted her quite a bit.

Why are you suing Wiltshire Constabulary?

One of the reasons that I'm suing the Wiltshire Constabulary is because I'd like to see the people that were at the level that made the decisions about what happened to the people on the Beanfield... They had no regard, I believe they have no regard for anybody in this country, and I don't care whether it's my sister who's a nurse in Wimbledon, or my mum that worked in Woolworth's, or me, from a Basildon council house, I think these people have got no consideration for the people that live in this land, and I'd like to see bastards like that squirm, because loads of the time – and I'm not being bitter here – loads of the time you end up seeing some poor sod in the dock squirming, and just for a change I'd like to see these people answer some serious questions about what they did.

4

Chapter Four

'Stonehenge '85: Souvenir Issue'

Written and compiled by Sheila Craig.
Originally published by Unique Publications, Glastonbury, 1986

The Convoy', The Ridgeway, near Wantage, July 1985: Who are the heroes of Stonehenge? Can it be the 520 arrested, the majority of whom broke bail by staying within the 25-mile radius? The people who came from all over the country to help with transport, food, money or just moral support? The people who organised gigs to raise money and drum up support for the convoy? In reality, there are no heroes of Stonehenge. There can be no heroes. People who fight for the right to live in freedom are not heroes. They are taking the only path open to them. When the basic rights of individuals are taken away, there are no options: conform or be pushed under. There is no 'Peace Convoy': it is a conglomerate of free-thinking people with vastly different religious, ethnic and social beliefs, who put Truth above all else. When the use of the law restricts personal freedom, it's up to you – and only you – to say enough. The time has come to stand up for yourself and your personal liberty. After all, it's your future.

Sheila Craig, Glastonbury, May 1986: The newspapers described it as a 'battle.' We experienced it as an attack. Of course, in one sense it was a battle – of ideas and ideology – but Rainbow Warriors are warriors of the spirit and do not carry arms. We went in our vehicles with our homes on our backs, and we didn't just take our families, our animals, our beds, our books, our clothes, our pots and pans; we took with us the warm fires, leafy hedgerows, and smoky logs crackling under the stars. For Stonehenge is more than a festival; it's a way of life, a celebration of a way of living all year round. For many, it's as much a part of the annual cycle as solstice is to summer. Is it really possible to stop the solstice sunrise?

Afterwards, to add insult to injury, the police confiscated our axes and our saws and other domestic implements, saying they were dangerous weapons, although to me it seems symbolic of the way in which the authorities are trying to undermine the survival of the travelling movement, which, behind the 'dirty hippies' propaganda, they find politically threatening. Well, we never got our axes back, or our saws, but we still have the stars, the hedgerows and the crackling log fires. Every man, woman and child who was there that day has a unique story to tell. This book puts just a few pieces of the jigsaw together – and tells the story of just one convoy – but I hope it gives some idea of the picture as a whole. It is written out of love, not bitterness.

Dice George, 'Karelia', 1vi85: On a sunny stony Saturday summer afternoon in high spirits we left the forest. I was in the middle. I was forced into the grass field. On Radio One I

STONEHENGE '85

A Collection of Material to Commemorate 'The Battle of the Bean Field' June 1st 1985

Edited by Sheila Craig

Solstice Sun
On a riotshield
Bloodsacrifice
Returns

The ritual
Of the baton blow
Where the shattered
Van
Now burns

The people
Dragged bleeding
Through the
Daggers of glass
Victims of evil
That now
Comes to pass

The tourists stop
and the tourists
See
The Holocaust
On the A303

— ZIN

The original frontispiece of Sheila Craig's booklet 'Stonehenge '85: Souvenir Issue.'

heard that they were trying to negotiate a peaceful settlement. I played my flute. I lit a fire. I made tea. I was sitting in my bus when police paramilitary charged. I said, 'I surrender.' I came out of my bus with my hands on my head. They hit me on the head. I rolled into a ball. They hit me some more. They interned me for two nights, then they cautioned me and charged me with unlawful assembly.

Sally: They were charging straight towards us with their shields and truncheons. I was standing outside the truck with the children and yelled, 'Don't be so stupid. What do you think you're doing?' It had an effect. The ones nearest us lowered their truncheons and just herded us off. From the road we could see our friends and their coaches being beaten up. It seemed unreal, like watching a film.

One of the Beanfield's more iconic photos – proud, defiant and unbowed, an injured traveller is arrested and escorted off the pasture field. Copyright Tim Malyon.

Lin: Whether it was a body or a bus didn't seem to make any difference. The windscreen caved in simultaneously with an iron spike coming through the driver's side window. If I hadn't instinctively drawn away as the windscreen broke, the spike would certainly have gone through my skull. I left the driver's seat as a policeman was coming through the windscreen, flailing his baton wildly, and shouted to them to stop as I had three babies on board. But they took no heed until the ITN camera crew arrived. We — myself plus nine-month old baby and 14-year old son, two other mums with tiny babies, and two pacifist men from Molesworth — were led away bruised and bleeding to the waiting riot vans.

The Earl of Cardigan: I saw a policeman hit a woman on the head with his truncheon. Then I looked down and saw she was pregnant and I thought, 'My God, I am watching police who are running amok.'

George: We had the windows bricked and I was covered in shattered glass. One of the bricks hit me on the head, and my head started to bleed. It was odd thinking that the forces of (dis)order were throwing bricks at us. When that happens, you don't think about the political ideology of non-violence, you just think that some bastards are out to get you.

Ben: Well, after the Beanfield the fear has gone. Once you've lived through something like that it makes you fearless, doesn't it?

Nell: There's only one winner in the end and that's peace. Violence and hatred will only burn themselves out in the end.

George: Maybe the convoy culture is not the same as yours, but everyone should have the right to live as they want. Repressive societies cannot tolerate travellers. Remember, the Nazis went for the travellers first as well.

The build-up: Rainbow Fields at Molesworth and on the Road

Sheila: There was never really any question of not going for it. Of course, we each had our moments of doubts and fears, but — the sum of the parts being greater than the whole — we were being swept along by a shared vision, a shared intent, a common purpose. All winter we'd been looking forward to Stonehenge — summer, light at the end of the tunnel, a time for ritual, ceremony, celebration, a gathering of the clans. The festival was also a chance to make some money, running a café, doing a stall, and a time for unwinding from the pressures of life on the road.

Life had not been easy that year. As well as the normal pressures of survival — food, wood, water, keeping warm, being persecuted and being moved on — a lot of us felt as though we'd been living in a war zone. Not only our vehicles, but also our psyches were in a pretty battered state after being evicted by government troops from Molesworth nuclear base, and hounded ever since by the ever-angry warlords of the state. The pressures only served to make our spirit stronger, and threw us closer than we'd ever lived before. It was a time of caring, sharing, learning and coping with our fears. Even at Desborough, where sickness struck and the end of the world seemed nigh, I heard angels singing, heavenly choirs. And still we kept on laughing, dreaming, plotting, scheming, outwitting the authorities every time. Our preoccupation was always, 'Where next?' — finding a suitable site to move to after each impending eviction.

In March, we held our own Rainbow Fields Free Festival at Polebrook airfield, near Molesworth, at Easter. All the time, Rainbow Fields on the Road was expanding, joining and being joined by other travellers and other groups we met along the way. More and more, we were becoming part of a greater convoy, a greater whole. In April, when the injunction was presented to us at Sharnbrook, it was difficult to take seriously. It seemed meaningless, almost comical, just a bit of paper, a patch from an already crumbling wall. So the festival was banned, but we were the festival. It didn't seem to make a lot of difference, especially as we seemed to be banned anyway, wherever we were, whether it was a disused airfield in the middle of nowhere or a site right beside the Stones — although, even at the 11th hour, we trusted that we would find an alternative site and go through the 'normal' legal eviction of 28 days, even though admittedly that was not always what had happened.

Sharnbrook lay-by, where the convoy was presented with an injunction in April 1985.
Copyright Alan Lodge.

If people ask me, what is the connection between Molesworth and Stonehenge, I say: I am, she is, he is. Ever since Molesworth, we had been locked in conflict with the authorities, hounded, hassled, persecuted and refusing to disband. What happened at the Beanfield seemed a logical culmination of events, the iron fist behind the soft kid gloves that handled us when we were living in the public eye at Molesworth. Yes, it's true to say we lost touch with the official body of the peace movement, living where we were living, on the edge and beyond the back of beyond, and yet out there we were right on the front line, meeting the full weight of the war machine head-on. Rainbow Fields on the Road still had all the magic of Rainbow Fields at Molesworth, but now our motley, little, ragged-trousered band was being subjected to heavy police harassment and surveillance, frequent individual arrests, being filmed daily by helicopter and buzzed by fighter jets. This was no local policing but a nationally coordinated action, the police working in cahoots with the Home Office and the Ministry of Defence. After the miners' strike, the special policing squads – we called them the 'A' team – turned their attention on us. And as well as attempting to demoralise us, one of their functions seemed to be to spread alarm among the people, treating us like dangerous terrorists. Once, in Corby, the police surrounded the whole of Sainsbury's when we went to do our shopping.

It was life in the raw, experiencing ourselves and one another in our true nature – no trimmings, the aluminium stripped off, the sides of coaches laid bare. None of the protection that society usually has to offer, none of the safety of brick walls and television, no hiding place, no lies. Our eyes were fully open to the state of the world. And when it came to the crunch, we were not just making a nice symbolic gesture. Our non-violence – or otherwise – was put to the test for real.

The first 'official' fair of the year – the Tree Fair at Long Marston, near Stratford-on-Avon – was banned as well, called off at the last minute because of police pressure on the

Convoy vehicles preparing to leave Long Marston airfield, May 31st 1985. Copyright Alan Lodge.

landowner. The fair, organized by Green Deserts, was to have raised money for re-foresting in Sudan. The message we received was that if we attempted to go there would be police waiting for us with rubber bullets, so, not wishing to be intimidated, we went anyway. The only problem on arrival was Womble's windscreen being smashed by a farmer's JCB. So we held our own festival and were joined by many hundreds of people, including the handful of friends who'd stayed behind at Sharnbrook lay-by and had been evicted by hundreds of police the next day. It was an excellent week. The sun shone, and a baby was born to Sue and Curly.

On May 31st, the great snowball rolled south to Wiltshire, past the border police and then on to Savernake Forest. That was the day that Abbey had her accident. While travelling in convoy, the van she was driving crashed into a car coming the other way. We all stopped and waited in the tree-lined road while ambulances and rescue vehicles rushed past to cut her free. We were shaken up by this, and it seemed a bad omen. It was evening by the time we reached the forest. Kitchen Jim and Phil had gone ahead to 'take' the site and our spirits were raised again, having actually succeeded in getting past all the police lines en route and arriving at the forest. The convoys from Yarmouth and Bristol and Wales arrived, and all through the night there were shouts of 'Ali! Ali! Ali!' as different convoys from all over the country rumbled in.

The Battle of the Beanfield

Cosmic Martin: It was a beautiful summer's day. The vibe around camp seemed electric, enhanced by the beautiful forest area owned by the Earl of Cardigan. Everyone had travelled from all over the country and congregated at Savernake Forest to prepare for this moment. There were rumours that the police didn't want us there – 'there' being Stonehenge, our next port of call. Full of high emotion, joyous spirit and common intent, we proceeded to line up our vehicles. The convoy of Rainbow People went forth into history.

Sheila: It was an epic ride, the biggest, most magnificent convoy ever, stretching and snaking its way over the Wiltshire Downs ahead and behind as far as the eye could see. When we passed through villages, people stood outside the doorways of their houses, smiling and waving at us. There were three men, two women, two children, three dogs and one cat on board our bus. Dreadlocks Julie said, 'They're going to trash us', but, being an optimistic peacenik/peace activist type of person, I said, 'No, they wouldn't dare.'

George: There were hundreds of colourfully painted vehicles, which stretched back as far as I could see. The slow convoy, not travelling more than 20 to 30 miles an hour, was followed by a police helicopter above us. The first encounter with the police was when they blocked the road with a few tons of gravel, so we turned off just before the roadblock. We travelled down the narrow road for a mile and then turned onto the A303, the main London to Exeter road, which passes Stonehenge. The road was blocked with two lorries full of gravel, and behind them police. I thought, 'This must be the edge of the exclusion zone.'

Sheila: The police began attacking the leading vehicles, smashing windows and arresting the occupants, which caused everyone else to break through the fence into the neighbouring field. At the same time as the front vehicles were being trashed, the police also attacked from the rear, smashing up the last coach in the line. Up to this point, no one had done anything to break any laws or to provoke the police in any way.

Dice George: When the convoy was stopped, I could hear the sound of breaking glass and shouts and screams and 'Ali! Ali!'s and sirens, but it was round the corner and I couldn't see, and I wanted to be there but I had to stay at the controls of my bus, waiting. That was the scariest.

The first serious assault on the travellers – and their vehicles – at the roadblock on the A303 near Parkhouse roundabout.

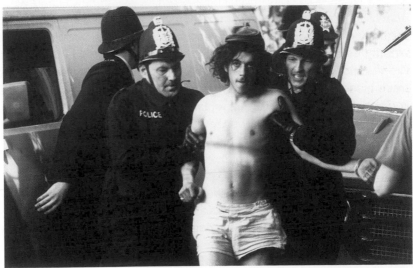

The Battle of the Beanfield

Cosmic Martin: I noticed policemen running amongst the traffic jam on the road, smashing windows. Six officers were in my mate's crew cab van. I didn't think they should be bundling him off for sitting in his van on the Queen's highway. When I told them this, they told me to get lost or I'd be for it. The next thing I know, I turn round and there's eight policemen with truncheons raised, charging at me from a gate, so I legged it.

Bruce Garrard: Police radio control ordered extra riot vans (PSUs) to cut across MoD land to 'deal with' the back end of the convoy. 'You know what to do', they were told. This was before the front of the convoy had even reached the first roadblock.

Alan Lodge (Tash), Festival Welfare Services: I had got out to take some photographs, when, by some vehicles a little way in front of us, I saw a squad of about 20 policemen running back down the convoy. Some officers smashed five or six windscreens of the stationary vehicles and the occupants were arrested, some dragged through the broken glass. People who saw this – including myself – were fearful of the level of violence used by the police in making arrests. They responded by returning to their vehicles, and some drove off the road through a hedge into an adjacent field. About 80 vehicles had done this when the police formed up on the top edge of the field, dressed in their riot kit and getting ready to charge. All the vehicles in the field then drove around, and the police, being entirely on foot, withdrew back to the road.

Sheila: The bus I was on tried to get through the open gateway, but it was a long bus and a narrow road, and we got wedged between the gatepost and a tree. A crowd of police, with truncheons raised, were charging up the road towards us, so we just had to move. Chris drove on, and one of our enormous side windows caved in against the tree. It gave Ali a bit of a fright, as he was standing next to it, but that was only the first sound of breaking glass we heard that afternoon.

Alan Lodge: I was directed to a number of head injuries that had resulted from the initial conflict on the road. All of these head injuries that Mo and I dealt with were truncheon wounds to the back of the head, and some people were quite distressed. From then on, the situation grew yet more tense. Police reinforcements were brought up, wearing one-piece blue overalls (without numbers), crash helmets with visors, and both full-length Perspex shields and circular black plastic shields. They formed up behind two police PSUs that had crashed into the hedge earlier. There was some stone-throwing and stick-waving from people in the field, and a stand-off situation developed, with sporadic outbursts of violence.

Sheila: We could see the skirmishes at the entrance of the field. When we saw people throwing stones and waving sticks around, some of us ran up to the top of the field and surrounded them. 'You're just playing the same game', we said, and tried to calm them down.' After a while, things quietened down. People dispersed around the field, which was like a big bowl, and put the kettle on. Our bus was parked down at the bottom of the

A traveller with a severe truncheon wound to the head is stretchered off the field by an ambulance crew. Copyright Alan Lodge.

field, next to a fence leading to the famous Beanfield, though at that point we didn't know how famous it was to become. It did feel odd, sitting on the grass on that beautiful bright day, when all around the edge of the field were solid lines of police with helmets and shields glinting in the sun. Ali and I made daisy chains, and Chris and Dave played guitar. All around the field, people were doing similar things, and further up the field I could hear someone playing flute and Music Martin on the accordion. As time went on, it was fairly obvious what was going to happen. I began to feel real panicky, and Julie and I spoke about escaping to the woods with the children. The trouble was, we could even see helmets sticking out between the trees in the woods. What helped me was being given a good talking-to by Jules, resplendent in her purple spangly gown, and Rich, with his sardonic Brummie wit and raffish smile. Then Dale came along. 'Some picnic', he said, cool and calm.

George: There was a strange calm for a few hours. Some people tried to talk to the police, but we were listening to the police radio, and the chief cop said he wasn't interested and he wanted us all arrested, but to keep us talking until the cops had enough reinforcements to attack us.

Sheila: From the beginning it seemed like a trap that had been well-planned. The message filtering through to us at the bottom of the field seemed to be: leave the bus (our home), leave the field on foot and be arrested, or stay in the field with the bus and be arrested. So we stayed put, all the time the helicopter hovering low overhead and booming instructions in a loud, distorted, Big Brother voice, 'Calling all personnel...' By then a lot of us just wanted to get in our vehicles and leave peacefully, but that was not being allowed.

The Battle of the Beanfield

Alan Lodge: There was no middle ground to be found, so, with others, I attempted to organise a meeting with Assistant Chief Constable Lionel Grundy, who was in charge of the operation. This took about 90 minutes. During this time I saw a number of other injuries. One man I was shown was on the ground, semi-conscious, with a truncheon wound to the back of the head. An ambulance was called, and I assisted the attendant and helped convey the casualty through the police lines. The ambulance crew were initially apprehensive about their safety, but assurances were given.

Bruce Garrard: The Assistant Chief Constable was told at 4.12 pm that people were prepared to leave the field peacefully. He replied that this was not negotiable, and issued orders to arrest everybody. On being told that there were insufficient numbers of police to do that, he ordered his men to prevent any vehicles from leaving the field until reinforcements arrived, and he himself flew down by helicopter to brief PSU commanders before the final assault.

Alan Lodge: It was early evening before we were able to meet Assistant Chief Constable Grundy. The tone of the meeting was, 'Do what you're told, or else.' He reiterated that people should leave their vehicles and be arrested. I met him again a little later, and attempted to reason further with him, but Mr Grundy then threatened to arrest me for obstruction if I persisted. Police were now massed in large numbers and obviously getting ready to charge.

George: Just before we were charged by the police, we heard on the radio that they were about to charge, so we started our bus. From here on I can only say what I saw and what happened to me. The police entered the field and we drove away from them. All the vehicles that were not moving were being trashed, and the occupants dragged out and

Preparing for the final assault: a group of police officers advances into the Beanfield shortly after 7pm.

arrested. We then drove into the next field, and tried to keep away from the rampaging cops. Slowly, more vehicles were stopped, and the occupants dragged out, covered in shattered windscreens.

Debbie: I was struck by a brick thrown through the windscreen. There were hundreds of police, about 50 round every vehicle. The police were ultra-heavy. They smashed every window in our bus. The boys tried to get off the bus peacefully and were beaten rather badly.

The Earl of Cardigan: I shall never forget the screams of one woman who was holding up her little baby in a bus with smashed windows. She screamed and screamed at them to stop, but five seconds later 50 men with truncheons and shields just boiled into that bus. It was mayhem, no other word for it.

Nell: I was on the Judgement Day bus. We were in the first field. They all came on us. We drove into the second field, the Beanfield. Then the bus stopped. I thought John had stalled it, but we'd run out of diesel. So I grabbed the three dogs, another coach turned up, and I jumped on it with the three dogs. The guy in the coach jumped out, then we got out as well when we saw Blue Lake was being trashed. By this time we were well and truly surrounded. We stopped running around and sat waiting for them. They grabbed me and grabbed Terry, and he said, 'Oh well, we'll be in the cells together.' One of them hit me in the ribs with his truncheon. 'Lie still', he said, 'or I'll put your head in.'

Reik: When the police came down the hill, we wanted to be inside our truck and moving. Jules was standing there with Phoebe in her arms. We picked her up and drove into the Beanfield to get away. I was just driving round and round, I didn't know where I was going. Then suddenly we were surrounded. We said, 'Let's see how many windows they trash', and sure enough they did the back and the front with me still sitting in the driver's seat. Then they tried to do the side window of the truck, but it was Perspex and the truncheons just went 'boing!' and bounced back. It was quite funny really.

Terry and Shirley: In the Beanfield, Terry shouted, 'Don't touch her, she's pregnant!' Actually, she wasn't — well, she was, but they didn't know it at the time — so when the baby came along they called him Rikki Bean.

Cosmic Martin: I bumped into a friend, Lin, who owned a luxury coach/home. She invited me on board for a coffee, so we sat and had a chat while the kettle boiled. Tarot, her young baby, slept, and her other children played. The next thing, I look out of the window and there's loads of Old Bill swarming down the field around vehicles, smashing windows and dragging people off. Lin jumped into the driver's seat and we headed off into the Beanfield. I grabbed the kettle and turned the gas off. Everyone realised that there wasn't going to be a compromise, so they headed the only way they could, into the safety of their homes and away from the maniacs. Halfway up the field, we noticed a woman clutching a baby, running our way. We stopped and picked her up and set off again, driving in circles like hunted prey. Other vehicles crossed in confusion and everything was spinning. The lady handed me her baby, who can't have been more than nine months. Standing near the front of the coach, I could see clearly that we were done for, so I advised Lin to stop and switch off, so as to alleviate the situation, which she did. Six officers with riot sticks surrounded the front of the coach and started smashing the front windows. Glass flew everywhere. I handed the baby back to her guardian and noticed one officer go round to the driver's window, where Lin was still seated, and smash it with his stick, then the big window directly behind that, where her baby slept, oblivious. I shouted, 'Peace, peace, there's a baby on board', and proceeded off the coach, where I was arrested. The next three days I spent in Portsmouth cells, eventually to be bailed out with a 25-mile exclusion order on Stonehenge. The rest is history, but sometimes I wonder at the wisdom and understanding of people. I shall pray for their souls.

Moz: Lenny lying on the ground and me standing there saying, 'He's not violent, don't hit him, this is my home and these are my children.' It was only an act, really. I knew there must be one of those 40 cops who would listen and I would get through to him. He could just possibly realise suddenly that this could be his mother or his sister talking to him. Nah, it wasn't non-violent. I was just trying it on really. It was just a blag, and, as it happened, it worked. But it's where you're coming from, isn't it? In true non-violence you're coming from love. Well, that's not where I was coming from!

Sally: From the road I could see Womble's bus. He wasn't going for it, but he wasn't exactly not going for it either, driving around with his head down and the police throwing missiles at him. Then I saw the police swarming round our truck. I grabbed Alice under my arm and ran back into the field and shouted, 'Oh no you don't!' They stopped, but the truck had been damaged when we finally got it back again.

Sheila: Julie and I lay on the floor with the children at the back of our bus. Chris, Roddie and Dave were at the front of the bus, not going anywhere. We'd already decided to stay put, taking the third choice in the guiding life principle of fight/flight or acceptance. There was no one in the driver's seat and the engine was switched off. I was doing all the protective things I could think of, like visualising the bus bathed in golden light, at the same time spinning my mantra around the children. Police surrounded our bus and shouted, 'Open the door.' The passenger door was locked. Roddie was gesticulating, about to embark on a pacifist 'Won't you please talk to us' rap. Julie yells, 'Open the fucking door', and he does. We were told to get off the bus, which we did, with our arms up in surrender, then we were escorted off the field in our little gaggle.

George: We were finally stopped and all dragged out. I was dragged out of the vehicle, and two cops jumped on me and told me that if I moved they would kill me! I was then dragged off, with one trying to dislocate my shoulder and the other almost breaking my wrist. I was asked if I had ever had a broken wrist, because I was soon going to have one.

Cowering travellers are rounded up by police during the final assault in the Beanfield. Photographer Tim Malyon was forced to run soon after the policeman in the bottom picture spotted him. Copyright Tim Malyon.

Sheila: As we passed the fire engine, a group of five or six policemen stood back as the first flames took hold. Minutes later, what I presumed to be a gas cylinder exploded. The fire engine is no more.

Bruce Garrard: Altogether, 520 people were arrested and dispersed around police cells throughout the south of England, including Bristol, Portsmouth, Plymouth, Yeovil and Southampton, and charged with unlawful assembly.

Custody and care orders

Sheila: We were led onto the road to wait in a line with the others, standing for hours in the baking hot sun. Flanked by police on all sides, the line grew and grew, other friends and other families all being herded in their little groups. It felt as though we were waiting to be taken to the concentration camps. Many people with bleeding faces were dragged along and bundled into riot vans. Others were carried off on stretchers to waiting ambulances. At last it was our turn. People in the straggly long line were taken away by the busload. Climbing onto the big gak shiny vinyl police bus was a far cry from the bus – our home – that we'd left in the field.

On the bus we each had a police officer sitting next to us. I asked mine, who was Ministry of Defence, where we were going and he said he didn't know. Only the driver knew, and he was getting instructions from the radio. I wondered if the Big Brother helicopter in the sky was masterminding things. From the beginning it had felt as if the whole affair was being conducted by remote control, toy soldiers just following instructions. The children were by now getting tired and grumpy, and hungry too. Ali said, 'I don't like being arrested', and I said, 'Neither do I, but at least we're still all together.' It was a long journey, the atmosphere relaxed, and the police had taken their hats and visors off.

It was ten or 11 at night when we arrived at Aldershot. The tall police building looked grim and sinister. Even more sinister were the officials standing outside to greet us, wearing surgical rubber gloves. Women and children were last off the bus, even though by then the kids were very hungry and desperate to go to the toilet. Eventually, they were brought a biscuit and a cup of water. We weren't allowed off the bus, but had to wait over an hour while the men were processed first.

Then it was our turn to be processed – fingerprinted and photographed – each with an arresting officer. It must have been after midnight when we were finally locked up. Dreadlocks Julie and I were in the same cell with our children – Ali, four, and Emily, one and a half – and Jake the Spirit of Albion cat. The cell was cold and there were no blankets. At last we were given a blanket, and the children curled up asleep together after their incredibly long ordeal.

A couple of hours later, a social services visitor came and said the children would have to be taken into care. We said, 'What, now? After all they've been through? Couldn't they at least wait until the morning?' She said the law of the land blah-de-blah-de-blah. Unless we provided a custodian immediately (in Aldershot? At three o'clock in the morning?), they would have to be taken to a children's home: 'If you don't sign this piece of paper placing them voluntarily into care, then we will have to place them forcibly into care, and then it will be harder for you to get them back again.' So we woke the children, all sad and bleary-eyed, and told them they had to go.

Refuge in Savernake Forest

Reik: They arrested Rich and took him off, leaving me and Jules standing there with the baby. Another cop showed up. He didn't seem to know what to do with us, so he said, 'I'm not looking.' We ran into the woods and hid. We could hear the sound of policemen's boots scrunching. Jules was feeding Phoebe the whole time to keep her quiet. Gradually, we met other people who'd been hiding, crouching in nettle banks or lying in ditches, some who'd been there for hours. We crept through the woods and came to a cornfield. There we met a farmer, who was friendly. He said, 'There's a lot of police about.' I don't think he knew what had been going on. We asked him if he would give us a lift to Savernake Forest, and he did.

Savernake Forest, after the Beanfield. Copyright Alan Lodge.

The vandalised interior of one of the travellers' homes.

Sheila: Meanwhile, back in the forest, Sid's beard had ignited when he heard the news. Jules returned to find him with his face badly burned and bandaged up, and many children crying for their mothers. That's when she and Sid and other previous 'go-for-it's, who this time had stayed behind in the forest, stepped in to play their part, running the massive rescue operation. Rainbow Jo, Mike, Sally, Jim and Jan worked through the night, contacting lawyers, press and police, trying to trace lost, injured and arrested persons and find out what had happened to our vehicles, nursing people suffering from shock, and trying to get the children out of care (though the authorities did not consider them suitable guardians).

Over the next few days, as people were released, the forest became more and more like a refugee camp: people made homeless by the loss of their vehicles, without food or money or possessions; roaming, homeless dogs; and wounded people hobbling around on crutches, with their heads in bandages or their arms in slings. It was thanks to the compassion of the Earl of Cardigan that we were allowed to stay in the forest, a safe refuge. The police wanted to take further reprisals, but he would not allow them on his land. Volunteers from all over the country turned up to help. There was a first aid post, an information tent, and a free food kitchen. We might be anarchists, but when it comes to the crunch we know how to organise. Release lawyers worked tirelessly round the clock, giving legal advice and helping to trace missing persons. On the Sunday, a few people were released – mainly mothers with young children – and returned to the forest. The full damage to our vehicles was beginning to unfold.

Lin: At about 2 am on the Sunday, I was given permission to collect my bus from the trashing field, and went with a police escort to do so. However, the vandals had been working well, and I found my home to be wrecked to such a degree that it couldn't be driven.

Frank Jackson, 'Monochrome': Paraffin poured on children's beds; oil poured over the interiors of buses and caravans, in one case the contents of a chemical toilet; beds and furniture wrecked; guitars and other musical instruments smashed; money missing; personal effects ripped up (letters, paintings and photos); wiring ripped out; ignition keys missing; windows and interior panels smashed. One woman found her caravan in this state: a candle had been laid horizontally in the middle of the floor and set alight, but luckily it went out without setting fire to anything. A pot of stew had been tipped over, the gas cooker ripped out, and the two doors pulled off their hinges.

Lin: This is the first time my home has been attacked in such a way by the police, but for many of my travelling friends it is the third or fourth time in the last 12 months. Each trashing just makes us more determined, with our strength and spirit, to carry on doing what we believe is right, and what is our right.

In the field opposite the Stones

This section looks at the activities around Stonehenge on June 1st, which received very little media coverage. Further detailed information on these events, from the police viewpoint, can be found in Chapter Eight.

Dawn, Green Gate, Greenham Common: I went to Amesbury on May 31st with some friends in order to be ready to set up the campsite for Stonehenge '85 on June 1st. We were determined the authorities could not possibly succeed in banning the event. For me personally it meant far too much to even consider the idea. I've been going to Stonehenge for the last six years. That was my first taste of real peace and love and anarchy in practice, and ever since, although I've heard occasional stories of heavy scenes at the festival, I can honestly say I've never seen any, and it was the beginning of a totally new experience of living for me.

The Battle of the Beanfield

I was part of that happening in the field opposite the Stones later in the afternoon of June 1st when about 200 of us managed to get in and sit down and start to think maybe it was as easy as that. For about 15 minutes I actually thought we'd cracked it, that the festival was on, because, if your motivations are right, opposition just melts away.

This daydream was destroyed when suddenly police reinforcements arrived, and before we knew what was happening the charge took place and 'hippies' were running everywhere trying to escape, trying to get off the ground (we'd all been sitting down), while people in uniform held them down, tripped them up and, literally, bashed them, all the time saying we had to move, get out of the field.

Stonehenge 1985 was the third time in a year that the convoy had been trashed. It was the revenge of the state for all the times that people have got together to celebrate freedom or to act against the state. It was a lesson to those of us who won't be told what to do and how to live and how to think, and it's one we ought to start thinking about before it's too late!

In the cells

Pixie: So now they've got me. A young policeman about the same age as me stands beside me, embarrassed. He hasn't been on the field yet, but witnessed his elder parading me in a very distressing manner down the road into his custody. He's apologising! Pah! If he cared, he'd remove these fucking cuffs that are chewing my wrists to pieces. He's frightened! He won't look at me, can't, 'cause I'm angry at this humiliation. I've got to smoke a cigarette from a woman's fingers, 'cause she's the only one allowed near, and my fingers are too numb to feel. Oh, but I can feel my wrists! The large group at the roundabout is separated into buses and Transits. We sit there, eight of us: four men, four women, separated by mesh. They've moved the cuffs so my hands are in front of me at last. I really want to hug Kathy.

Amesbury police station, late afternoon. There's dozens of pig vans going back and forth from this small car park. Our van is backed up to an open garage. We are taken out one at a time, interrogated and strip-searched in these cold empty garages. It's like the Gestapo rounding up the Jews! Processing over, I'm pushed into an open garage containing maybe 20 men, a good number of which are bleeding from the head and cradling arms, ribs, legs. My wrists seem pathetic in comparison, but they hurt. We wait. We wait a bit longer. It's bloody cold, and still we wait.

A few of the younger men are taken away and there remains maybe ten to 15 men in T-shirts, in an open garage at night, bleeding, with four or five blankets and half-a-dozen chairs. We hassle for water, threaten for water and better conditions, but still nothing happens, except the continual stream of derogatory jokes from the well-clothed pigs with cups of tea! I began to become aware of what was happening: we were being singled out. The older men were better-known figures from travelling groups I had encountered. The younger men I had met on site. One thing we all had in common: we were leading drivers on that convoy in the Beanfield.

We grouped together to try and comfort each other, to use what little strength we had left to change our immediate problem. It was difficult to concentrate on anything as the night drew in and the cold settled on concrete floors and walls. The older men went about keeping our spirits up, remembering previous similar attacks and how they overcame them in the end, directing our energies towards the oppressors rather than at ourselves. I had watched men leave one or two at a time and tried to convince myself I was next, but they would be replaced by one or two other new arrivals, latecomers who would leave again shortly after. I found myself one of ten men who were to remain under scrutiny for another ten days.

At 4 am we get a handful of rolls and biscuits provided by the CID who seem to have more about them than the inspector. It's mostly meat and few of us actually eat anything, preferring that the few women there eat. By the time I and 12 to 14 others are escorted to a waiting bus the sun is rising. We find ourselves driven to Bristol, where we are distributed around several police stations. I and five others are the last to disembark. We've missed breakfast and, after another strip-search, we are given a cell each. I close my eyes and get the first sleep in a very tiring 28 hours.

I wake a couple of hours later to a plate with a half-defrosted cheese and tomato pizza and lettuce (two pieces of) and a cup of tea. I can't get back to sleep for indigestion. By afternoon I'm nodding off when the door opens and I am rather degradingly hustled through procedure into the back of a black maria. I'm stuffed into a box two feet by two feet by five-and-a-half inches. I can just sit upright on a hard bench. I am aware of six other boxes the same size containing the people I came with. There is no ventilation. We sit there for a quarter of an hour and are then driven roughly back to Amesbury. Again we are left in the sun for maybe an hour or two before we are taken into the station.

None of us sleep, as we have to share the blankets and the floor is cold! We revert to ripping the cover off the mattress. It is now Monday morning. I know this 'cause the glass in the wall has gone grey from black. I am put in the back of a Transit van. Again it is just light as we are driven to Salisbury police station and deposited in a large detention cell. I kick and bang that door until eventually we are given two blankets each and allow ourselves some sleep. Not long, though, as breakfast is served – egg on toast – and the court opens.

One by one they leave. I don't know their names, couldn't even speak as such, I'm so tired and disorientated. I'm all on my own and it does not help hearing them return from court with bail. I enter. I sit. I stand. I sit. I stand and am told very coldly that the police have as yet insufficient evidence and, due to crimes I appear to have committed, my application of bail

Impromptu press boards at Savernake, revealing the anti-traveller bias of most of the media. Copyright Alan Lodge.

is refused. I didn't even get the chance to speak! The police solicitor was the only one who spoke and he spoke against me. I was given ten days in custody of Salisbury police station.

Court orders and carnage

Sheila: On Monday we were taken to court in Basingstoke (others to courts elsewhere in the country); again, taken by bus and handcuffed to each other, dangerous terrorists, police escorts with flashing lights leading the way; again, waving to people, this time our wrists in chains. After many hours we were charged with unlawful assembly and most of us released on bail. The bail restriction in our court was not to go within 15 miles of Stonehenge or even enter the county of Wiltshire. ('What is the law of this land coming to if a woman and child cannot travel freely in their own country?' – solicitor in court).

Most of us immediately broke bail by returning to the forest. Oh, the feeling of homecoming after being released, the feeling of euphoria! Breathing the fresh air, the smell of bluebells, the sweet, sweet smell of the earth, being reunited with our friends, our family and our children. All this in a beautiful forest to beautiful reggae music provided by the Rastas and some beautiful vibrant sinsemilla. The atmosphere was festive, golden, mellow.

Most of our buses were still in the pound but we all rallied round and helped one another keep body and soul together. Friends miraculously appeared from far-flung places – Tony, Ros, Monika, Albion Dave. Donations came pouring in, and local people turned up with van-loads of food, clothes and pet food. There was a dedicated RSPCA volunteer, who, even in the wee small hours of the morning, was to be found beavering away helping people to discover the whereabouts of their missing, confiscated animals. (Some dogs left in the hands of the police had been put down, others were badly kicked or beaten). Words are not enough to thank all those who came to be of service.

Then came the rain, people spending days huddling together under tarps and other makeshift shelters. And as people went to the pound to try and retrieve their vehicles, the full extent of the damage began to take its toll. Vehicles had been wrecked inside as well as out. The police had systematically vandalised our homes, many beyond repair. Those that were still drivable came limping, one by one, back to the forest, others had to be scrapped, others towed in. It was a scene of metal carnage.

Dice George, 9vi85: When I got my bus out of police 'custody', my knife was gone, my wood-axe was gone, my blankets were gone, my jacket was gone, so much of my hard-earned tools lost or stolen. 'There was lots of confusion, things got put in other vehicles', they said. So did they have no orders? Are not police paid to protect our liberty and justly acquired property even if we're dirty gypsies?

The battered remnants of the convoy prepare to leave the refuge of Savernake Forest. Copyright Alan Lodge.

Lashed by the wind and rain, travellers watch musicians perform at the reconvened Solstice Celebration at Westbury hill-fort. Copyright Alan Lodge.

Solstice

The Guardian: Led by an ancient yellow-and-black striped bus, like a battered banana, the Stonehenge festival convoy trundled out of Savernake Forest last night and plunged the Marlborough area of Wiltshire into a huge and exotic traffic jam. About 100 of the travellers' mobile homes, with stove chimneys sticking out of side panels and heads poking from sun roofs, left the town at 3 mph on the A4 west towards Avebury.

Sheila: Next stop was the White Horse Hill at Westbury in Wiltshire, a very steep, ancient hill-fort on the edge of Salisbury Plain. Here at last the festival did get underway, with a stage and cafés, in spite of being in a state of siege for much of the time. Police sealed off the lanes and prevented people who left the site from returning, which made it almost impossible to fetch food or water.

The Guardian: As the swollen ranks of hippies hoping to celebrate the summer solstice at Stonehenge settled in for an evening of rock and roll and waited for darkness, an uneasy calm descended on the Wiltshire countryside last night. It resembled Nottinghamshire during the tense days of the miners' strike.

Jules: There we were at Westbury, couldn't get any water onto site, and there were helicopters flying in to pick up newsreels, though it was only film of all of us staying put. The press were really goading us to go to the Stones. The world press were there in their hundreds. When I opened the top door of the truck it was like being part of a Punch and Judy show. Moz and Martin leaned their heads out and said, 'Anyone seen the President's brain?' We told them what we thought of the state of the world, but all they seemed interested in was whether I was going to take Phoebe to be named – as if they wanted to see her get her head bashed in or something.

The Lone Ranger

Chris: Solstice eve on Westbury hill-fort. Wind driving rain across bedraggled benders and battered buses. Roving newshounds, hungry for another bloody confrontation to report, sniffing around, asking, 'What's happening?' The usual confusion. People hunting down generators for the bands wanting to serenade the solstice in. Got a blim?

I'd driven over from Glastonbury, where some Rainbow Villagers and other refugees from Savernake had gone. Since February my bus had been trashed three times, I'd been arrested and held twice, and my child taken into care. I'd been hurt, frayed, disillusioned, but I was determined to go to the Stones for the solstice as a gesture that my spirit would not be broken.

It became obvious by midnight that no one was going to Stonehenge. I pulled out on my bike down the long, steep hill. The rain mercifully eased off for a while. Stoned and exhilarated, I was fuelled by the wild night air and a spirit of adventure. A couple of times I passed little groups of vehicles pulled in on side-roads. I swished along the wet road, with no lights on my bike, wondering if these were police waiting for a convoy that would

Stonehenge off-limits. Copyright Alan Lodge.

never arrive. The operation must be costing the state a small fortune, better spent on sites for travellers.

About an hour before dawn, I reached the last roundabout on the A303 before Stonehenge. I was questioned about who I was, where I was from, and told that I could go no nearer the Stones or I'd be arrested. I was curious as to what harm a lone cyclist could do to the sacred monument up the way. I'd gone too far to be deterred. I pulled off to the left at the roundabout, a side-road that goes to the rear of the Stones. I left my bicycle in a field of rape, which, after the violation of June 1st and what was happening now, seemed a bitterly appropriate crop. By now I was soaked and knackered after my night ride. I dragged myself across the hill, avoiding a police sentry, and emerged on a slope overlooking the Stones.

Arc lights flashed on the henge, breaking through the dark gloom, and I guessed this was the signal for the media to film the solstice dawn. Or were they searchlights? I felt no magic. The place seemed dead, surrounded by a web of razor wire, guarded by authorities blind to mystery. A few gentle spirits had managed to pick their way across the landscape, but there was no real sense of celebration. I felt cold. The sun hid his face. The Stones were barred from their own people – no real ceremony, no communion, a pilgrimage to a place made empty and sterile by control. The tribes were scattered. The festival, the rainbow and the solstice were celebrated in our hearts, not round the Stones. Summer 1985 was a damp squib.

Recuperation

Jo Staranka: The weeks following the trashing were ones of slow recuperation in the full glare of the national press. We moved from the relative seclusion of Savernake Forest to the wind-swept heights of the Westbury White Horse. Ironically enough, the land there proved to belong to English Heritage (who 'own' Stonehenge) and the MoD. Three frenetic days in the High Court in London saw Sid Rawle, Brig Oubridge, Lin Lorien and I win the case for a possession order on the land. Interestingly, the MoD, who took out their order against 'Persons Unknown', sought to bar us not only from the White Horse, but the whole of the Larkhill and Imber ranges. A week after the convoy left the White Horse, Cruise came out and headed for Imber, next door.

The wet and muddy solstice came and went, seeing Stonehenge surrounded by police and press only. Once people left the White Horse, they split up, some heading towards the south-west, others north to Cannock. It was not until early August that we came together for the first of the series of court hearings stemming from June 1st. This was the pleadings: the police dropped the 'Unlawful Assembly' charge, which was not going down too well with the miners. Most of us now face 'Obstruction' charges only.

5

Chapter Five

Interview with Nick Davies

Conducted by Neil Goodwin and Gareth Morris

How did you become involved with the convoy in 1985?

I was working as a reporter at *The Observer* in London, and there were all these stories about how the police were going to try and stop the convoy getting to Stonehenge, so I decided that the best way to cover it was to travel with the convoy, because if you don't get inside a story like that the police try and lock you out. So I discovered – maybe through Don Aitken – that there was a bit of a convoy down at a place called Wick, near Bristol, and I drove down with a photographer on a Friday afternoon and talked to the people there, and they said that I could get in one of the buses with them and travel along with them that night. So I did.

And then you went on to Savernake from there?

Yes, we travelled up from Wick to the forest on that Friday night. It was dark by the time we got there, and I didn't really know where I was. About the first person I met as we came into the woods was the Earl of Cardigan, and he was standing there looking rather bewildered, as all these people came in from different directions. We settled there in the woods overnight, and I spent the night just wandering around talking to different people about what was going to happen the next day. My feeling at that stage was that the police were highly likely to try to prevent the convoy getting to Stonehenge, and that it was highly likely there would be violence. And I was worried, I suppose, that people in the convoy didn't seem to be aware of this, and that they were really rather over-relaxed about the whole thing. This was ironic, because later on the police wanted to claim that the convoy was armed to the teeth, and that Savernake Forest was the site of some kind of council of war at which a great strategy was being hammered out. It just wasn't like that. There were a lot of people playing guitars and sleeping.

Part of the emphasis of the police defence in this case has been on the organisation of the convoy, that it was some sort of organised entity with a common will. How ramshackle was it? How organised was it?

The whole essence of the convoy is that it is disorganised. The nearest person there is to a leader is Sid Rawle, but all that really amounts to is that Sid is a very good talker and rather likes talking, and therefore people like journalists or politicians latch onto him and talk to him. He's a nice guy, but I don't think there's anybody in the convoy who actually acknowledges him as a leader. And in the background here, I think that the police are not

79

necessarily lying. I think their problem is that they're ignorant, and they had virtually no solid, reliable information on this group of people at all. They were relying on rumour and really very dishonest newspaper reports. There may have been points where they really believed they were up against some kind of army that had hand grenades and machine guns, but if that's so then it's a very bad failure, because the police are supposed to be able to gather intelligence. But they did fail. They really didn't understand the people they were dealing with.

Were you aware of the meeting between senior police officers at Trowbridge in February 1985, and if so, what do you know of that meeting?

I wasn't aware of it at the time that it took place, but I later became aware that really the whole of the Wiltshire establishment had sat down to decide what to do about the convoy, and this involved various landowners and the County Council and the police and their solicitors. And it was a question really for them that they didn't want these people coming into Wiltshire and occupying the area around Stonehenge, but there wasn't really a law that enabled them to keep the convoy out. So it was a question of taking advice to find some kind of legal cloak to throw around the operation which they wanted to launch. So they came up with this business of the civil injunctions to justify all that then happened, and it seems to me still highly questionable whether what happened was really lawful.

Staying with the injunctions, there's been mention of a character called Les Vaughan. What was his involvement with the serving of those injunctions?

You have to understand that Les Vaughan is a fascist, and that's not just a rude word that you throw at somebody. I mean, he's a leading member of an extremely heavy, well-organised, covert fascist group in this country, and that's his politics, and that's been his life. He was working at this time as a private investigator of a rather lowly type in Salisbury, and one of the jobs that he had was that he worked as a paper-server for the firm of solicitors who were hired by the County Council, and therefore he became involved in, first off, the business of gathering the names of individuals in the convoy upon whom these injunctions could then be served, and secondly – and illegally – he was, it seems, trying to set the convoy up in some way, in that a number of people that I spoke to made signed statements to the effect that Vaughan had been trying to give them weapons. I published that story in *The Observer*, and Vaughan complained about it and said it was untrue, but the legal action which he launched to sue us collapsed at an early stage, and it's my honest opinion that Vaughan was trying to get arms to the convoy, so that it would then justify the police violence.

Could you describe what happened to the back of the convoy on June 1st 1985?

On that Saturday morning, the convoy started moving out of the forest. I had a bit of bad luck, in that I'd been with them all night, but at the point when they left I was in Swindon trying to put some rolls of film on a train back to London, and it took me several hours of walking and running and hitching lifts to catch up with the back of them, but I finally succeeded. I was travelling in a vehicle about four from the back, and behind the convoy there was a line of about six police vans travelling along, and the convoy was stopping and starting every time a vehicle broke down, you know, the way it does. And at one point a vehicle – say, about eight from the end of the convoy – broke down, and the rest of the convoy travelled forward without realising that its tail had been left behind. After a few minutes, while they were fiddling around with the engine, trying to get it going, a young boy came running back from the front vehicle in this rear portion towards the other vehicles in the convoy, shouting that the police were about to bust them, and that they'd heard this on the police radio.

And at that point, sure enough, officers on foot came running down both sides of the vehicles, shouting and leaning... And what they did with my vehicle was that they came up both sides, tore open the front doors, pulled the keys out of the ignition, and then pulled the driver out of the front of the vehicle. His wife, or girlfriend, who was in the passenger seat, was also hauled out, and I was left in the back of this little van with their two children, who were aged about eight and ten, and who were extremely frightened. And it was rather sweet, because the boy, who, as I say, was about eight or nine years old, started rummaging around in the kitchen cupboard at the back of this van and pulled out a little frying pan to defend himself against the police, and I said, 'Just put it down, calm down.' There was nothing he could do. He wanted to save his parents who'd been dragged off screaming.

Police apprehend a fleeing traveller during the first assault on the convoy on the A303 near Parkhouse roundabout.

The Battle of the Beanfield

A few minutes later, the policemen came back into the van to get us. They came in with their sticks raised, and they were obviously highly agitated, and I was afraid that we were all going to get hit, so I made it very clear that we were not a threat to them, and tried to calm them down. We were taken out, and I was arrested for a minute or two, but I produced my press card and explained that I was an outsider, watching. And so, while everybody else from this portion was bundled into the vans and driven off, I was let go, and I then had to walk another mile or so to catch up with the rest of the convoy where they'd stopped.

Nothing precipitated this act by the police at the back?

No, the convoy was just driving along the road. They didn't do anything to specifically break the law or to provoke the arrests. It was simply that they were isolated from the rest of the convoy, and so they were a vulnerable target. I know that the police tried to make out at the trial that these rear vehicles had been driven across the road as some kind of roadblock to cut off the police at the rear, which was bizarre, because what actually happened was that the police themselves, having taken these vehicles over, drove them across the road, because presumably they were frightened that the convoy might come back or something. But it wasn't the convoy drivers who moved the vehicles. It was the police who did it.

What did the travellers do when in the pasture field?

Once they were in, the main thing that happened for hours and hours was that there was just this stalemate, this long wait. Most of the people who were among the travellers in the field were rather anxious, because they could see they were surrounded by police. One or two people tried to drive their vehicles out through the Beanfield and couldn't find a way out, so they were just stuck there and surrounded. After a while, two or three people came across to me, where I was standing on the fence between the Beanfield and the grass field, and asked me if I would help them to negotiate with the police, because the police wouldn't talk to them. So, it's a little bit of a problem for a reporter, because you're supposed not to get involved in the story you're covering, but on the other hand it seemed crazy not to help if I could.

So I went into the field and across the other side and started to kind of liaise between the travellers and the police. For two or three hours, really, we were putting up various suggestions of compromise, and the officers on the ground there would go away and check with headquarters and come back and reject them. So, for example, at one stage the travellers said that they would simply abandon the idea of going to Stonehenge, and leave, and the police came back and said, 'No, that's no good.' So then they suggested, 'Well, we'll not only leave, we'll head north out of Wiltshire under police escort.' And the answer came back, 'No, that's not good enough.' So they said, 'We'll head north as far as you like. You can escort us to Newcastle if you want to. We'll just, you know, reverse out of here and go wherever you want.' And the answer came back, 'No, that's not good enough.'

Interview with Nick Davies

Lionel Grundy, the Assistant Chief Constable of Wiltshire at the time of the Beanfield, who was in charge of the police operation on the day.

And eventually this dreadful man, Lionel Grundy, who was then the Assistant Chief Constable, arrived on the scene and made it quite clear that there were to be no negotiations, and that everybody in the field was to be, what he called, 'arrested and processed.' Somebody – it wasn't me – said, 'Well, that's crazy. If you had a couple of football hooligans in a football stadium, you wouldn't arrest everybody in the stadium just to get at the hooligans.' But he wasn't interested in making any distinction between those he alleged had actually committed offences, and the rest. He wanted everybody. And the way that it actually finished up with the negotiations with him was that he gave the convoy half-an-hour to think about it, and we were supposed to go back to say whether we were just going to surrender. Some ten or 15 minutes had passed and the police started buckling up their helmets and picking up their shields to come into the field, so that the half-hour time period was never permitted.

So, from the police position, there was a certain inevitability about what happened at seven o'clock, would you say?

Yes, and there's two different interpretations on it. The most lawful one would be that the police genuinely believed that the travellers had committed offences and that they all had to be arrested. The other – which I was picking up from the kind of foot-soldier policemen – was that they were extremely angry with the convoy, that they'd had enough of them over the years, and that this was their chance to get in there and crack some heads. That was something that the policemen were saying explicitly. One officer warned me to stay out of the field. He said, 'My lads have been putting up with this lot for 11 years. They've had enough of it, and there's going to be some heads cracked in there today.'

The Battle of the Beanfield

The final assault on the Rasta Bus: 'They just crawled all over that vehicle, with truncheons flailing, hitting anybody that they could reach. It was extremely violent and very sickening.'

Given the ferocity of police attacks on certain individuals, do you think that targets were chosen in the lull beforehand?

On the whole, the police tactic was that if it was moving they were going to hit it. Anything that moved, they went in on it. The nearest thing to a specific target they developed was the Rasta Bus, which was bigger and faster than any other vehicle, and remained free right at the end of the battle. The Rasta Bus had provoked the police simply by refusing to be arrested and refusing to be stopped, so when it finally did slew into another vehicle and came to a halt, every officer in the field, it seemed to me, came crowding in on it. They were like flies around rotten meat, and there was no question of trying to make a lawful arrest or anything else. They just crawled all over that vehicle, with truncheons flailing, hitting anybody that they could reach. It was extremely violent and very sickening. And it was at that point that my photographer, who was trying to take pictures of it, got arrested, and I myself got threatened and told to leave. In fact, there was a senior officer who came up and said, 'Come on, lads, calm down. Don't give the press a field day', because he could see us there. What they were doing was not a legitimate police operation; it was just bullying.

Do you believe that, at seven in the evening, the police were reasonable in their belief that members of the convoy still held the common purpose of establishing a festival at Stonehenge, by force if necessary?

At that stage it would be quite unreasonable to hold that belief, since the convoy had made it clear explicitly, repeatedly during the day that they'd given up, they'd abandoned the idea of going to Stonehenge in the face of police force. That Saturday morning they'd set out to go to Stonehenge to have a festival, there's no question about that, but there is

The victim of one of the most brutal police assaults of the day, witnessed by Nick Davies (in the picture on the right). Copyright Tim Malyon.

a question about whether they'd be prepared to use force to get there. I guess the truth is that some of the people in the convoy would have used force, but a lot wouldn't because they're not into fighting, they're pacifists. But by seven in the evening, everybody was frightened off. They didn't want to go down the road any more to Stonehenge, they wanted to go back to safety away from the police. So it's a quite unreasonable belief.

How would you describe the manner in which the police carried out the arrests at seven o'clock, and are there any specific examples which spring to mind?

This was the most undisciplined police operation I've ever seen – and I have quite often been in riots, and I have occasionally seen individual police officers blow it, but I have never seen an entire police operation run riot like that. It wasn't a matter of law enforcement, it was a collective act of bullying, and it really shocked me to see it. It really upset me personally, as well as making me feel outraged as a voter and a taxpayer that policemen I pay for could behave like that. When it comes down to specific incidents, it was in fact the overall violence that was most upsetting. The attack on the Rasta Bus was the most violent single incident I saw, and I've still got this very, very clear picture of some particular guy, who's about 18 years old, wearing a brown kind of bomber jacket, trying to climb out of the window to escape the police violence, and kind of sinking slowly down onto this sea of policemen with their sticks beating him. I saw his tooth chip as he went down, he was going, 'Oh no!' and it's really clear, that picture. He wasn't attacking the police, he wasn't armed, he wasn't able to do them any damage at all. He was simply trying to get away from them and they beat the dirt out of him.

Do you have any criticisms of the portrayal of travellers by the mass media?

The mass media's a joke, generally, and particularly where the travellers are concerned. There are two factors at work. One is that, individually, reporters are scared of the convoy. They're afraid they're going to get mashed up or raped if they go close to them. So you've got ignorance. And the second thing is that, on the face of it, the convoy looked like a good story. What makes them a good story is that they fit a kind of cliché from Hollywood – they're crazed hippies. And if you put the ignorance and the cliché together, you stick with the cliché, you see, because you don't go close enough to them to see that they're not crazed hippies. But it makes good copy.

And on the particular occasion of the Battle of the Beanfield – so-called – the police told them to stay down the bottom of the hill, out of the field, and the reporters agreed, which

Visored police in uniforms without identification numbers.

was crazy. The police had no legal right to keep the reporters out of the field, but they allowed themselves to be herded like sheep away from the field, so that they didn't see what went on. So then, when the police came down the hill afterwards and gave them a lot of complete guff that fitted into the clichéd image of the crazed hippies, they bought it. And the next day, what the police didn't tell them they invented for themselves, so you've got all this stuff about petrol bombs being thrown, which just didn't happen. It's a fiction, but it all goes to shape public opinion. In a way, you look at them and they're just a joke, but it becomes a pretty dangerous joke when prospective jurors and voters and people who should be angry about what happened get fed this kind of nonsense.

Given the press that were there who were going to cover the incidents, what methods did the police use to protect their anonymity?

The main thing that the police did was that they didn't have ID numbers on their riot jackets. And that was surprising, to put it mildly, in that during the miners' strike a year earlier there'd been a lot of complaints about the police in those big public disorder situations not being identifiable, and the Chief Constables and the Home Office had given all kinds of reassurances, on the record and officially, that that would never happen again. And yet here we were, with five different police forces involved, and I would say that 80% of the officers were not identifiable.

What do you think of the trial verdict?

It's difficult for me to say, because I wasn't sitting through it, but if you get away from all the fine detail of the legal argument, and exactly who said what to whom in court, and get to the bottom line, what happened in the Beanfield was an outrage. It should not have happened in a civilised society. And the people who did it – that's to say the police – appear largely to have got away with it, and so that's wrong.

Given that the whole operation, from June 1st 1985 to the present court case, could have cost in the region of £9 million, how do you feel that this money could have been better spent?

Well, it could have been better spent on not being spent on this operation in any way. One of the big lies at the bottom of all this is that the people of Wiltshire didn't like the convoy. That isn't true, in my experience. My family live in Wiltshire and did not want the police chasing these people out of the county. It isn't even true of the people who live close to Stonehenge. On that Saturday, as we were driving to the Stones, people were not hiding in their houses in fear, they weren't throwing rocks at the convoy to get them out of Wiltshire, they were waving. It's just a typical piece of undemocratic behaviour that the Wiltshire establishment regarded these people as a threat, but the ordinary people, who are paying the poll tax and who have funded this expensive operation, didn't actually share that animosity towards the convoy at all, yet they end up picking up the bill for it.

Chapter Six

Interview with Kim Sabido

Conducted by Neil Goodwin and Gareth Morris

How did you become involved in the Beanfield incident in 1985?

I became involved because I was a reporter on duty at the weekend, on the Saturday, when my news desk had some sort of prior notice that, despite the injunction taken out by English Heritage and the National Trust preventing the convoy from gathering at Stonehenge, that they were likely to proceed down there, so I was asked by my news editor to go with a camera crew down to Stonehenge, or try and tag along with the convoy before it got to Stonehenge, to see what materialised.

So what sort of time did you get there, to the Parkhouse roundabout?

Yes, we got to the Parkhouse roundabout when the convoy itself... We'd been following right at the end of the convoy, at the tail end of it, and we'd been speaking to various groups from the convoy as we went down, as we approached it. We got to the Parkhouse roundabout and left our car there and then walked up – I mean, we saw some of the preliminary skirmishes with the police before we walked up – to be told by the police that we could go no further, and that's when we took a decision to come back, walk slightly back away from the police roadblock, and climb over a barbed wire fence and up the side of the Beanfield to get into the field itself.

After you got into the field, you interviewed travellers and people that were sitting in their vehicles. What was their reaction to being contained in the field at the time?

Their initial reaction was that they didn't quite know what the police had in store for them or what was being planned. Initially they wanted to gain access to Stonehenge and they wanted to proceed to have their festival. There was a mixture of worry amongst a number of them about what was ahead, what might happen, and others were fairly nonchalant and fairly laid-back about it. In the initial stages they were quite happy. It seemed to be quite a merry gathering at that time. That was before the first initial talks with the police across the fence.

The police alleged in the trial that the people, once they'd been contained in the field, still expressed this common purpose to go to Stonehenge, using force if necessary. Would you agree that their belief was reasonable, that members of the convoy still had that intention, when ACC Grundy actually came to the field to negotiate?

Interview with Kim Sabido

Once they had made contact with the police and once Grundy had started talking to them and they'd gone away and discussed the prospects of the day, I think the feeling was that they wanted to be allowed to go, to leave the field peacefully, to take their vans and all their belongings with them. It was then and the next stage of negotiations, when Grundy then told them that they couldn't take their vans and all their belongings with them, that tension mounted considerably. I think at the stage you're talking about there was a general feeling amongst the people in the field that they just wanted to get out without any trouble.

So when it came to the arrests at seven o'clock, after the negotiation, how would you describe the manner in which the police carried out their operation?

Well, as a reporter who's reported from Northern Ireland and seen a lot of police riotous confrontations and in Liverpool during the Toxteth riots, I've seen a lot of civil disturbances, in which the police have been confronted by large groups of people and have had to deal with it in different ways and the consequences of that. And I've seen people being killed in Northern Ireland and I've seen a lot of people being killed in the Falkland Islands, but the way that the police behaved in the final stages of the Beanfield, and how they confronted people and their property in the Beanfield was, I think, one of the biggest shocks of my life, more shocking than any deaths I've seen in a war zone, simply because the police are a civil force, supposedly carrying out a civil duty, and

Police advance on coaches in the pasture field, while, in the background, other vehicles flee into the Beanfield. Copyright Alan Lodge.

following an injunction taken out by English Heritage and the National Trust they were supposed to try to, perhaps, prevent the convoy getting to Stonehenge, but there was no way that I could accept that they could use the force and the manner that they did, by moving in...

It was almost like a scene from *Zulu*, where you had a whole line of policemen banging their shields, moving slowly, progressively up the field, smashing any vehicle or anybody in their way. And one of the scenes that sticks out in my mind was when they had smashed all the windows of a van and they were pulling everybody out of it forcibly – by their hair, most of the time – and one woman had a baby in her arms, and they grabbed hold of the woman by her hair and started to grab the woman out backwards from the van. And we were filming this and at one stage a senior police officer shouted, 'The cameras!' and they stopped for a second and looked, and then someone with a shield pushed the camera and covered the camera with a shield, so that you couldn't see any more of what was happening, and that happened on several occasions.

For a civilian such as myself watching this – slightly detached, because I wasn't part of the convoy, I'm not a member of the police force – I was watching it in a detached sort of way, but I was rooted to the spot for a second, because I was so shocked by what I was seeing. It was like a scene from Rome between gladiators and lions – or not even lions, between gladiators and people who were thrown into the pit to try and fight them... It was barbaric, and I couldn't quite come to terms with seeing police officers acting in this way, because, as I said, I've reported from a war, and it didn't affect me that way, because people were there to fight, they were there to kill each other, and the pros and cons, everybody knows about them in a war, and it wasn't such a shock. Seeing civilian police officers treating women with babies in their arms, people who weren't armed as far as I could see, who were just trying to get out of this field, and they were being beaten – in some cases almost senseless – by police officers wielding batons, was a total culture shock to me.

As you've described, the police operation that day could be described as a kind of semi-military operation. How do you view the use of these tactics in this country, and the fact that there's been an increase in this kind of operation? What implications do you see for democracy?

In a simple phrase, I'm appalled by it. I was appalled then, and I still am, because, as I said, they're a civilian force, paid for by the British people to maintain law and order. What they did then was a divergence from maintaining simple law and order into what was almost a semi-paramilitary force. I've seen the army, together with the UDR in Northern Ireland, acting in that way, but then perhaps they would say there's a justification for it – I'm not sure – but there's a completely different scenario in Northern Ireland, because they're faced with people with guns and bullets. There were no guns and bullets at Stonehenge [the Beanfield]. It was a civil matter that they were dealing with, and ordinary people

Police restrain a female 'prisoner' in the pasture field.

they were dealing with – members of the public – and yet the police acted... to me they acted like a paramilitary force, and from talking to a few policemen, listening to what they were saying to one another, they intended to act that way. There seemed to be a preconceived idea of how they were going to act towards the convoy. Some were heard to say that they'd had enough of the convoy from previous years, and they were going to make sure that it didn't happen again, and they were going to give the people in that field the feeling that they didn't want to come back, and that meant using their truncheons, and using every means at their disposal.

The Battle of the Beanfield

So, as I said before, it was like a scene from *Zulu*, where you saw, at a certain stage, a cohesive force, armed with batons and shields, moving forward in a pre-planned way to inflict as much damage and physical harm on some people as they could, and I think that's a terrible outcome for civil life in a democracy. And I think the South African government, as it was before, would have loved to have shown films of that to the people of South Africa, to say, 'Look, this is how life has to go on in democracies in the northern hemisphere, so we're not so bad.'

The police were alleging... One of their excuses they used for the method of operation was that people were – particularly in the field – they were using their vehicles as kind of battering rams and threatening the lives of police officers. You were walking around the field with a camera and you were getting in the way of a lot of things. Would you say that that was a reasonable accusation from the police?

I think, looking at what they said in that way, I would say that the police were running around after all these trucks... the vans and the trucks were trying to get away, they were trying to escape from what they'd been involved in, and escape from what was happening to their vans and the people in them, and therefore that sort of terror or scare tactics... they were running around like a headless chicken, in a way, they didn't know where to go and they were just running around, trying to stop being attacked by the police. And in that way, policemen running around with riot shields and batons in the middle of a large field, chasing them, they were going to get in the way of them, because they were running away, they were trying to get away, and therefore a collision between a van and a policeman who was chasing after a very fast-moving vehicle was inevitable. I don't think they were planning to knock policemen down. I didn't get the impression that they were planning to try and knock policemen down, although I'm sure, as would be natural in that situation, with a frightened animal – because they were acting like frightened animals – they were just going to try and drive through, and if anyone got in their way then they'd have to get out of the way. And you saw that in a lot of cases – policemen having to throw themselves out of the way of vans. I saw that, certainly, but I'm not sure there was a premeditated intention to run the policeman down. It was just the policeman was there, that van wanted to get out, and therefore the policeman had to jump for it, and I got no impression there was a deliberate ploy to try and kill or harm the policemen.

What about what became known as the Rasta Bus, one of the last ones to be stopped? How would you describe what happened?

I think by that stage the police had made that their main target. They wanted to get the so-called Rasta Bus, and they wanted to smash it and they wanted to get everybody out of it. It seemed to be the focus of all their attention at that stage, and they went for it – as they'd gone for a lot of the others – but there seemed to be more vengeance in their attention on it than had been paid to some of the other vehicles and some of the other people. So that was the focus of their attention at that stage, and they were out to get it.

Interview with Kim Sabido

After you'd finished shooting the events in the field, what was the fate of your tapes?

Well, once the tape... we had to go to an 'inject point', where HTV had a van, and we edited it and then sent it down a landline back to London. We had to go to two, because the first one was broken and it took a long journey to get there, but all the material was just fed down straightaway – all the whole lot. We did send an edited version, but we sent the whole lot down first, so that they had it, and then I put my voice down on a separate track, and sent that back. When it came out, they'd actually put someone else's voice – a reporter back in London – on it, and they edited it themselves back in London.

And at that time, after we'd finished that, and we'd left that point to go back to the Beanfield to see what was happening, the cameraman actually said to me, 'That's probably the last time you'll see that footage', and I said, 'What do you mean?' and he said, 'It'll disappear', and I said, slightly naïvely, I suppose, but I thought that that would be very unlikely... And he said, 'Well, it's happened before, and, because it's so controversial and it involves the police, certain figures at ITN will see that coming in and will make sure it's never seen again by anybody else.'

And when I got back to ITN, during the following week, and I went to the library to look at all the rushes, most of what I thought we'd shot was no longer there, and from what I've seen of what ITN has provided since then, it disappeared, particularly some of the nastier shots that were taken at the Battle in the Beanfield – of the woman being dragged out by her hair, that I know was filmed. We filmed that happening, because I was standing there when it happened, and I was there to hear the police officer shouting, 'The cameras! The cameras!' and the big baton coming in front of the camera, and our cameraman being dragged down from the bonnet of a car, because he was filming things he shouldn't. Well, all of that has gone.

Would you say this was a form of self-censorship on ITN's part?

Yes, as far as it didn't just disappear, it was a conscious decision of somebody at ITN to make sure that film disappeared from anybody else's hands – or from anybody's hands – once they'd seen it. So as far as I'm concerned, that was a form of self-censorship. It wasn't a role imposed by the police or it wasn't ITN reacting to what they feared would be an order from the courts. My understanding of it, as it happened, was that ITN decided to do that before it came to the police making an order, or for the courts being brought in. They decided to impose their own self-censorship, and make sure that the more controversial aspects of our filming would no longer be seen, and would not be available to anybody again, and it was a conscious decision by ITN to do that.

7

Chapter Seven

Interview with the Earl of Cardigan

Conducted by Neil Goodwin and Gareth Morris

How did you first hear about the proposed events of June 1st 1985?

I was telephoned late on Friday [May 31st] by a policeman who put a rather strange request to me. He said he was on the tail of a small number of people, who he thought were coming into Savernake Forest, and would I please issue an instruction, or an order, or some such, to the effect that the whole of the forest was shut? Would I declare it shut and close the whole thing down? Whereupon, if those people – about half a dozen in number, I understood – came into the forest they could then be arrested. I explained to him that that was virtually impossible. People can wander in and out of the forest where they will, and therefore I couldn't physically do it, even if it made sense. And of course, given that on Bank Holiday Mondays and the like, the forest often holds thousands of people, I couldn't for the life of me see how six people coming into the forest could be any kind of a threat to law and order. If they behaved badly when they got here, then the police could presumably deal with that – they are used to dealing with much bigger numbers. So I said, basically, 'I don't see the threat, but more importantly, if there is a threat, I can't shut the forest. It hasn't got a door on the outside, or a moat around it. I'm afraid I simply can't help you with that.' And that was the end of my first advance warning.

Did you act on this advance warning? What did you think?

I couldn't act on it, because, as I said, it was an impossible thing. You can't shut a forest.

Sorry, when I say 'act', how did you respond to the call? Did you seek more information?

After that phone call, I thought not much more about it, and went down to Marlborough that night, where I was going to be having a meeting with the mayor in Marlborough Town Hall. Six was such a tiny number that it was just of no consequence. I got on down to Marlborough, where I was shocked to see something like a hundred vehicles progressing in a convoy through the high street, and sitting on the tail of those vehicles was another large number – 40, 50, 60; I have no idea, really – of Ford Transits, each one with ten or 12 policemen in it. I had never seen this many policemen in one place at one time before, least of all Marlborough High Street. I briefly stopped, out of curiosity, as one does, to find out what on earth was going on. I didn't learn much about it, because no one was very keen to discuss it, and I was a bit short of time anyway. So we parted, and I went on into my meeting. Then at about 11 o'clock at night, I came out of my meeting, went back to the forest, and discovered that, while I had been in my meeting, all of that convoy, with the police still on its tail, had forcibly entered the campsite on the edge of the forest, which was administered and run by the Forestry Commission, and were camping there for the night.

Did you go to Marlborough police station the next day?

The next day I certainly did go to Marlborough police station, and had a number of conversations with a number of officers, talking about what was happening, because later that night before, and all of that Saturday morning, I had, of course, made it my business to try very hard to discover what on earth was going on. And when I went down to the police station – on more than one occasion, from memory – in late morning, they were, of course, keen to know what the mood was in the camp, who was doing what, who was going where. And so, to the best of my knowledge, I told them.

In the court case, they have mentioned several times petrol being placed into containers in Savernake Forest. Can you tell us a little bit about what you might have seen in there?

I'm afraid my memory of that is very hazy. I don't believe, five years on, that I actually saw it happening, but I'm fairly sure that I did hear one of the convoy members claiming that he was going to be doing it tomorrow. And I think, when the police later asked me what was happening up there, I may well indeed have said that some of them had been putting petrol into milk bottles, but I don't think I actually saw it. It was just a reported threat.

The most significant conversation that I can remember now having that Saturday morning was with one particular policeman, who told me something very unusual. Basically, he told me that, regardless of what happened that day, every single one of the people – all 500-strong or whatever – was going to be arrested before the end of the day. He even went so far as to tell me where and how this was going to happen. He said he didn't want it to happen in Savernake, but he wanted to arrest them all down in open country – in particular, by implication, near the Stones, where there was a lack of tree cover – because he didn't want anybody to escape. He wanted every single person to be captured. He told me that he was going to be using a helicopter for this, in order to make sure that all the stragglers were bagged as well, and that again was another reason not to do it under the trees of Savernake, but somewhere out on the more open edge of Salisbury Plain, where they could all be captured. And he also told me that, by the end of the day, I could take it from him that every single person would be arrested, and so it proved.

Could you describe the events you witnessed on the day?

So, at about one o'clock, from memory, the convoy formed up in the campsite at Savernake, and headed out onto the road, turning left in order to go south down towards Stonehenge. The journey took a very long time. We constantly stopped every mile or so, long stops of perhaps 15 minutes at a time. It took almost the entire afternoon — at least that's my memory — to get ten or 15 miles down the road. The atmosphere I've often described — and we've seen clips on the television of it — was carnival-like, really. There was music playing, there were flags flying, and not a policeman to be seen. The only policemen were in the helicopter that occasionally flew overhead. I was not quite sure of the reception I would get from the convoy if they knew who I was, so I was in complete anonymity, on a motorbike with a friend [John Moore], and we stuck fairly close to the HTV television film crew who were there, for we reckoned that professionals like that would know where to be to get the best news; an intelligent place to station themselves. We reckoned, if we stuck fairly close to them that would probably be for the best. So, sticking close to the big wagon, we went all the way south as far as what has now become known as the Beanfield.

The first I knew — that we'd arrived, as it were — was when the convoy came to a sudden halt, after turning off a side road to join the A303. I could hear shouts from the head of the convoy — for I was with HTV, some ten or 15 vehicles back from the front — and I ran up to the front after a while, having parked my motorbike. Once we got up to the roadblock, there were about six policemen in ordinary dress — ordinary police uniform — and they were having an exchange, for want of a better word, with a similar number of travellers. The two positions were quite simply, 'Get out of the way, we're coming through', and 'No you're not, this far and no further.' This went on for a short period of time. It has to be said, in the interests of fairness, that quite a few of the people who came up to listen to this conversation were carrying things that could have been

The calm before the storm: Lin Lorien and baby Tarot look at their reflections in a policeman's shield, shortly before the first assault on the travellers on the A303.
Copyright Tim Malyon.

Reaching an impasse: early negotiations going nowhere. Copyright Tim Malyon.

interpreted as weapons. One of the travellers was carrying a pitchfork, and one was carrying a length of wood, which could have been used as a weapon, although he was not using it as a weapon at that time. Before long, there was quite a huddle around the police – or rather, in front of the barricade – of people trying to tell the police to get out of the way, and the police saying that they weren't going to be allowed to proceed to Stonehenge, and 'Why can't we go to Stonehenge?' and 'What's it to you if we go to Stonehenge?' and endless variations on that theme.

Eventually, it was clear that something of an impasse had been reached, and I remember a vehicle coming up from the very back of the convoy – it came up on a little grass verge – overtaking all the parked cars. It got right up to the front of the convoy, and suddenly, with no warning that I could see, did a right turn and went smartly headfirst through the hedgerow at the side of the road and ended up in the field, leaving something of a hole in the hedge right in front of the police roadblock. Once that first vehicle had got into the field through the hole, the next vehicle tried to go through, and, from memory, that vehicle also got in. At about this time – either just before the second vehicle, or just after – the police realised that, with this hole in front of the barricade, if they didn't do something about it, one by one every other vehicle on the road was presumably going to play follow-my-leader and go straight into the field.

In order to prevent that, the police moved up one of the Transit vans that was just behind the barricade, moved it up with a deliberate intention also, it seemed to me, to park the vehicle across the hole, thereby blocking it. As they started to roll the vehicle up towards the hole, the next convoy vehicle – be it number two or number three – was just starting to go through the hole at the same time. I seem to remember that it was a large motorcoach. They both went for the same hole simultaneously, but it seemed to me, standing right beside it, that the police were just a fraction too slow. If they'd moved literally two seconds earlier, they would have got there before the bus. Sadly, they were just too slow to prevent the bus getting through, but the two vehicles collided right in the mouth of the hole, and the bus, being five times the size, went on through the hole, leaving the front end of the Transit extensively damaged.

That incident was – or seemed to me to be – the cue for the police to take a very different view of proceedings. Up until then, it seemed to me that it had been little more than sort of push-and-shove, and no one had done anything too outrageous, but, understandably, the police thought the damaging of their Ford Transit was putting us into a totally different ball game, for want of a better word, and the attitude of the police present changed, instantly and dramatically. What happened thereafter was that the police who had been in ordinary police uniforms seemed to all stand to one side, and out from behind the barricade – where we previously hadn't been able to see – came quite a number of police in a very different manner. They had their police helmets secured with a chin-guard and strap, implying they were going somewhere where there was some risk of those helmets being dislodged. They were all in sweaters. Each man carried a drawn truncheon, and they came out 20- or 30- strong, or so it seemed to me, and started to work their way down the line of vehicles.

Their tactics were to surround the front of each of the vehicles in turn, and my most vivid memory, I think, is the terrible noise of them drumming their truncheons on the sides of the vans. If I had been inside, as some were, it would have been very frightening. They were shouting, 'Get out! Get out! Get out!' loudly, and lots of them shouting it all at once, and in particular, 'Give me the keys!' People were being told instantly to take the keys out of the ignition, give them to a police officer, and to get out of their vehicles. I must stress that it must have been very frightening to have been inside those vehicles at that time, surrounded by men banging on the outside of your vehicle. The other thing that they were doing was banging on the windscreens of the vehicles, and some of the windscreens managed to survive this treatment, and many of them didn't.

As they worked their way down the line, it was noticeable that the police fell into two categories. When they came to each vehicle in turn, with some of the vehicles the occupants were given what one might describe as a reasonable chance to respond to their instructions. There was a brief pause between the instruction being given and their vehicle being damaged, in which they had time to comply. Not a great length of time, but there was some time before your vehicle was smashed up, your windscreen was put in, or whatever the thing was. With some of the other groups, it seemed to me that the smashing up of the vehicles, and the instructions to 'Get out! Get out! Get out!' and hand over your keys, were given absolutely simultaneously, and therefore there was no

The assault on Helen Reynolds' vehicle, as described by the Earl of Cardigan.

possible chance to understand what was being shouted at you, and to respond and comply, before your vehicle started disintegrating around you, with your windscreen broken in, and your side panels beaten by truncheons, and so on.

This operation went on, vehicle by vehicle, for quite a number, starting at the head and working back towards the tail. I was standing on the bank, right at the edge of the road, and eventually, the line of police having dealt with the occupants of the first few vehicles, reached a vehicle which I was quite close to, which again was instantly memorable, because it clearly, in some early life, had been a county ambulance, with the glass place where they put the word 'ambulance' over the windscreen, and the joint double doors at the back –straight, and with windows at the side, it was an ambulance, or had been. And it was very striking, when the police got up to that vehicle, because the very first thing that happened – long before any conversation had taken place between the police and the driver of that vehicle – was that a policeman rained an enormous blow on the windscreen. I mean, the man brought his truncheon right back over his shoulder, and gave a colossal blow to that sheet of glass, which to my amazement didn't chip, didn't crack, didn't do anything. The man's enormous blow just bounced clean off it, as though the windscreen had been made of rubber. I was standing next to John Moore on the bank at the time, some 20 or 30 yards away from the scene, and I remember asking him if he had seen that, because it was the most extraordinary thing. I remember thinking, 'Gosh, if I ever have a new car, I should like my windscreen to be made from whatever that one's made of', because the blow just bounced clean off.

Then, unfortunately, this ambulance fell into the second category – as evidenced by this great blow on its windscreen – of being one of the vehicles where the destruction of it started long before the occupant had a chance to comply with the instruction. The destruction of the glass in the side windows and the attempted destruction of the front window happened simultaneously with the shouts of 'Get out! Get out! Get out!' and the banging and the crashing and the shouts and cries of people, and the whole chaotic scene. I can only guess what reaction this produced on the occupants. From where I was, I was aware that there were two girls in the vehicle, in the front seats, and immediately the police started smashing up their side windows. Some of them turned their truncheons round, so they had a bit that was just sticking out of the back of their hands, and sort of stabbed the windows, which exploded inside, breaking the glass. The side windows having now been broken, one of the police reached in through that broken side window – the passenger window – and grabbed a handful of hair. I couldn't see clearly into the vehicle from where I was standing – I was some little distance off – but it was clear to me that he had hold of the top of her hair, and was pulling her vigorously. She, of course, was screaming blue murder, not wanting to be pulled, because what she was being pulled through was a window that had been broken ten seconds earlier. There was broken glass everywhere, and there was what looked like an attempt to pull her out of that window that was framed with broken glass. She was screaming badly that she didn't want that to happen, and she was pulling one way and the police officer was pulling the other.

Eventually, the police managed to get the back doors to the ambulance open – or they came open themselves, or whatever – and managed to climb in through the back doors of the ambulance. And there came a point where one of the policemen who had climbed in through there appeared to have hold of the driver – or the person who was being pulled by her hair – round the middle and was holding onto her body. And briefly, it seemed to me, the policeman inside the ambulance was unaware of the policeman outside the ambulance, and they were both pulling in different directions, with the occupant's hair and the broken glass being what they were both pulling in opposite directions, which was not very nice. The policeman on the outside then realised that his colleague inside the van had actually arrested her, or got hold of her, and released his grip, whereupon the policeman inside the ambulance took her out through the back. She was arrested and taken away, and I didn't see her again that day.

After the ambulance and the head of the convoy had been dealt with, the police then retired back behind their barricade – or at least those that had smashed up the vehicles – but the effect of what they had done produced total panic in the ranks of the convoy, and everyone tried very hard to get their vehicles out of the line on the roadway, and get them into the field at all possible speed. I suppose, if you'd been vehicle number 20, you could have seen what had been happening to the first 19 vehicles in front of you, and the knowledge that you were likely to be the next vehicle smashed up would have been rather frightening, in all probability. Anyway, some vehicles then made fresh holes in the hedge. About halfway along the hedge there was a gateway, and quite a few vehicles went through the gateway, but by various means all the remaining vehicles ended up in the field. I can only speculate why they went in there. Some probably went in there because... just follow-my-leader... others probably went in there to avoid destruction, as they saw it, and others probably went in there with a view to getting round the roadblock. But for whatever reasons, all three lots of vehicles ended up parked in the field. They immediately got off the road and went down to the far end of the field, as far down to the bottom end of that field as possible away from where the police were. They having departed, and those occupants in the vehicles they had smashed being taken away into custody, the police then had control of the whole of the roadway, and fairly rapidly it filled up with police.

There then followed a long period of inactivity, really. The police could see that the convoy wasn't coming out of the field, and they – the police – made no attempt to go into the field. With the convoy vehicles parked down the far end of the field, there was then the start of a very long stand-off period, when for long periods of time virtually nothing happened, other than groups of the convoy who came up to the fence line, and spoke, shouted, discussed, argued, whatever, through the hedgerow – them on one side, the police on the other – what the options were now. Could they go back to Savernake? Could they go down to Stonehenge? Are we coming out? Are you coming in? – and endless permutations thereof. That's what most of them were doing. Occasionally, certainly the younger members of the convoy would taunt the police. There were offensive remarks being made through the fence, and there was, from time to time, some missile throwing. It was of a relatively trivial nature, though of course, if one of the missiles had hit you, you wouldn't have thought it so trivial. But it was just small sticks and stones that they found lying around the field that were being thrown at the police. The police by that time were appearing in the road in full riot gear – the helmets, visors, full-length see-through shields and riot truncheons – and were protected, as long as they kept their shields up and about them, which they did. So the occasional stone coming over the top, or someone chucking a bit of wood over the top of a tree... I don't want to minimise it, but I don't think anyone thought they were at risk of life and limb at that moment.

One particular person was very noticeable at that time. He was wearing a green motorcycle helmet but with no visor – the whole of the front of his helmet was exposed. And he had a high-powered catapult, and occasionally he would come up and approach the police lines – where I and the rest of the press and others were hanging around, watching through the fence – and would fire his catapult in our general direction, which used to keep hitting the plastic shields of the police, and there'd be a loud sort of 'ping!' beside me, and the stone would fall to the ground. With the sole exception of him – who we all tried to give quite a wide berth to – what was going on there was relatively trivial, and indeed from time to time more senior members of the convoy would come up to the stone-throwers and tell them off, tell them to stop, lead them away, and generally tell them not to behave in that fashion. But that was very much a fringe activity.

Most of the people were coming up to the fence and trying to have a more sensible contact with the police, trying to discuss the various options that were open to them. The police demeanour throughout all of this was, 'We are in no hurry at all. No, we are not about to come onto the field. There is no panic, we've got all day. This is what the position is, and you have a simple choice, but don't give me a snap answer now.' The police seemed to be saying, 'Go away, talk amongst yourselves, we'll still be here when you come back. Come back and tell us how you feel.' And it was very striking to me that the police seemed to be in no hurry at all. Indeed, they said they had all the time in the world, and it was for the convoy to have a long, hard think about what they wanted to do, and then come back and tell the police about it. If one had to try and summarise the negotiations, they were spasmodic. There'd be a little group of two policemen and perhaps six travellers who'd start discussing it, and then that'd break up and then 20 minutes later there'd be a different group of people 50 yards further down the hedgerow and they'd get into a conversation.

I became aware, when I was standing there watching all of this, that what was happening there was the key to the whole day. I was frustratingly out of earshot, and I very much wanted to hear what was going on at the negotiations. I therefore thought the sensible move was to move into the field, not only because that would give me access to the negotiations, but because I also felt that it was only a matter of time before the police started looking around themselves in the road, and then they would see the three or four civilians that were standing there, and sooner or later we would be invited to move along there, absent ourselves, leave the scene, and then I would probably never discover how this thing had panned out in the end. And yes, due to natural inquisitiveness, I was quite keen – without breaking the law – that that shouldn't happen, and that I should be able to continue to watch what was going on. As the missiles were being thrown from the field into the road, of course those of us standing in the road without shields were at some small risk, and therefore of course by going into the field we also took ourselves out of the rather limited line of fire. So for all these reasons, we eventually moved from the road into the field, and were able, with other members of the press – in particular Nick Davies, I remember – to get right up to the negotiations and indeed to stand as close to the police and the travellers as the participants themselves, and actually mingle with them and hear at first hand who was saying what to whom, who was making what suggestion, and so on.

Having heard half a dozen of these impromptu groups and gatherings discussing the options, it slowly became clear what the police position was, which was a very simple one. They considered that from that moment, exactly as I had been told in Marlborough earlier, everybody in the field should consider themselves as good as arrested. In particular, no one in the field was going to be able to absent themselves, nobody in the field was going to be able to get in a car or bus or whatever and go back to Savernake, and nobody was going to be allowed to proceed nearer to Stonehenge. They were all detained, if not yet physically. They were totally surrounded by the police, and they were sort of in the bag, and it was only a matter of time before they were physically taken away. The choice the police were making then was very simple: 'you come out, and when you come out, as we have said, you will please come up to the nearest police officer, who will...' – I think the euphemism for it was, 'want to ask you some questions' or something, but I think we all knew, or they said that they all recognised, that that meant they would be arrested, while they worked out who was going to be prosecuted for various offences and who was not. The option therefore was that everybody had to come out of the field, and if that didn't happen the time would come when the police would go into the field. But those were the only two options, and, as I said, I discussed it endlessly with Nick Davies and others at the time, I paid close attention to what was going on at several of these meetings, and anyone who says that the police had other options available, or were making other options available to the convoy other than, 'You are all arrested. Are you coming out, or are we coming in?' is, in my opinion, wrong, because the police's position was crystal-clear to me and to all the others who were in earshot.

Not much happened apart from these sporadic negotiations, for want of a better word, until just before seven o'clock, when I was in the field quite close to where the main negotiating had been going on, and I was able, from my vantage point, to look down into the road, and I suddenly noticed that all the people – all the police, that is – were being told to stand up from where they'd been sort of lying in the hedgerows all afternoon, [and were] dusting themselves off, putting on their tunics, straightening their ties and generally getting ready to make a significant move.

And on the stroke of seven, because I remember asking Nick Davies what the time was, the police entered the field in about four different places all at once, from beside the A303, where the convoy had been parked, and started to trot and jog all the way down to the bottom end of the field, where most of the vehicles were parked up. It seemed to me that this move caught the convoy by surprise. A lot of people had been out of their vehicles – making cups of tea, playing with the kids, walking dogs, discussing their predicament, and half a dozen other things – and they were not able to get back to their vehicles before the police arrived, and were sort of caught out in the open, and these people were immediately arrested by the police. Most people then jumped up into their vehicles, as best they could, and started driving them around in a circle. I was told later that this was a traditional defensive move, the idea being that if everyone's rumbling along at ten miles per hour in a circle, there's nothing the police can do to stop them and arrest them.

The police then stopped the vehicles, one by one, as best they could. The means employed was to hurl enough missiles at it to call it to a halt. They threw all sorts of things at the windscreens, and presumably many drivers, when their windscreen exploded around them, rapidly came to a halt, whereupon the police were able to climb up the steps into the buses, arrest the driver and all the occupants, and lead them away to detention. As time went on and they had weeded out those that were going to stop at once, and they were left with those that were not going to stop at once, the police used more and more frantic methods to stop the remaining buses. They threw their truncheons. Policemen took off their helmets and hurled them at windscreens. One large flint, about the size of a grapefruit, was picked up by a policeman and hurled through a windscreen, which exploded. They used their round black plastic shields... some policemen were using them like a frisbee, holding it on its edge and flicking it out

Desperate resistance: protected by a helmet, a traveller shelters behind the wheel of his van, which has had its windscreen smashed and its bonnet beaten.

of the back of the hand through pre-broken windscreens to try and hit the driver and bring the vehicles to a halt. Some policemen indeed even unbuttoned the fire extinguishers that some of them wore chained to their legs – or chained to the outside of their shin – which is a steel container, and they would unchain them from their legs and hurl them through windscreens – anything to stop the drivers driving their vehicles. And by these tactics, one by one, all the vehicles were brought to a halt, drivers arrested, occupants arrested and taken away.

So having moved in at seven, for the next quarter of an hour or so it was pretty much mayhem in that field, with these buses careering round, and the police slowly bringing them, one by one, to a stop, and then arresting the occupants. All sorts of little tiny flashes of memory particularly stick out. There's one particular teenager who was led past me at one point with an enormous cut on the top of his head – I don't know how he got it – and he was led past me screaming 'No no no!' and the blood was just running down his face like a waterfall. He was to feature next morning on the front page of quite a few newspapers, and as he was led right past me – and the fact that it was such a young person screaming like that – obviously I remember that very vividly.

There was another scene, again at the height of the battle, for want of a better word, when one policeman broke away from the main action and ran up towards where John and I were hovering on the edge of it, watching, and we thought this was another occasion when a policeman would come up to us and try and arrest us, thinking we were part of the convoy. That had happened a couple of times before, but on each occasion we'd been able to persuade them that actually we were nothing to do with the convoy, we were just onlookers, and that policeman had then gone back and left us alone. So when this latest policeman came up to us, we assumed this was more of the same, but he wasn't coming to see us, and he trotted past us, going up to one of the many empty buses that were littering the field, just behind us. Just as he got up towards the bus, he saw, lying in the field, which was now littered with the contents of many of the vehicles, a large mallet – a hammer – about 18 inches long, that was just lying discarded in the grass and had fallen out of one of the many vehicles. He rushed up into the bus, up the steps, and, with half a dozen amazing blows with that mallet, reduced the dashboard of that vehicle to powder. Then he came out of the vehicle, flung the mallet back down on the grass where he'd found it in the first place, and went back to rejoin the struggle. I remember looking at John, and saying to him, 'What an extraordinary thing. What was the purpose of that? That bus was not even occupied, much less threatening anybody, or driving in anyone's direction. Why on earth did he feel the need to do that?'

The battle then continued and, one by one, all the vehicles were taken away. Eventually there was only one bus left, which everyone has now christened the Rasta Bus – brightly painted, horizontal stripes down the side – and though the police eventually got all the buses to halt, there was this one bus that was left, and it defied the police's most frantic attempts to bring it to a halt, driving round the field in increasingly frantic ways. As the

Police rounding up the occupants of a coach during the final assault in the pasture field.

police initially couldn't stop it, they tried all sorts of things, including, at one point, getting into one of the other buses that had been abandoned, and trying to ram this one remaining bus with the vehicle that they'd commandeered. It became something rather like Starsky and Hutch, or one of those American films that's always got a good car chase, but this was sort of a bus chase, a coach chase, with these two machines, like demented elephants, careering around the field. Whenever they came alongside each other the sides would bang together; they would try to push each other out of each other's way. It was an amazing sight in a Hampshire field on a Saturday afternoon. Both drivers, of course, were only concentrating on the job in hand, and I and all the police who were on foot had to keep well out of the way, because there was some risk, if you were just wandering around the field aimlessly, of finding yourself in the path of these two vehicles, who had only eyes for each other.

I suppose that brings us onto the question, that I've often been asked, as to whether the drivers of these coaches were actually trying to drive at the police. I've always said that, in my opinion, from what I saw, the answer to that question must be no. There were that many police in the field that day that if any one of them [the drivers] had wanted to hit a policeman with his vehicle he could very easily have done it, therefore I've

**Close-up of the
photo opposite.**

always rejected that theory. We all had to get out of the way of vehicles during the course of that day. Certainly I did. If there was a policeman chasing after a bus and it was careering across the field and I was in its way, I never felt that that driver was trying to hit me. He was just fleeing, and I was in his path, and as a pedestrian it was down to me to get out of his way, which was very easy to do, and I and all the police did exactly that. I understand the police said that the driver of the last vehicle was pretty close to being able to be charged with driving his vehicle at the police, and, if any of them could be, I suppose it would be him.

The Battle of the Beanfield

Anyway, eventually even his vehicle, for reasons unknown, did come to a halt, and the police were then able to totally surround it – all of the others having been taken out of action – to climb up into the bus, and to arrest all the people in it. Unfortunately, that last bus had been the one that had been keeping them going longest, and briefly, when the police got into that bus – in my opinion, from close range – they briefly lost the control that they'd held that afternoon. All their pent-up frustration and adrenalin of the afternoon was vented on the occupants of that last one bus, and the violence that was shown to the occupants was appalling. The truncheons were rising and falling on their bodies like no one's business. It was – very briefly – very ghastly to see.

Apart from what happened to that last bus, I suppose the single incident that distressed me the most that day was very close to the end, when a woman was seen at the front of a bus that had just come to a halt; that had been brought to a halt by the tactics I've described. She immediately picked up her baby, which was behind her, and stood up in the front of that bus, and shouted to the police that – though she realised that she was now going to be arrested, and, you know, the game was up and the bus was going to be taken on by the police – would they please come in with a very high degree of caution, for want of a better word, because, as she said when she held the baby up, 'Look, there are babies on this bus, so come on in if you must now, but have a care', basically. And as she stood there by this large sheet of glass, holding the baby up, a missile from the back of the police ranks hit the windscreen, which exploded into a hundred pieces, and the woman and the baby were both covered in broken flying glass. And that was as appalling a thing as I shall ever see.

Thereafter, that being almost the end of the battle, most of the people were taken to the roundabout and put into buses and, by all accounts, taken to prisons and police stations the breadth of southern England. John and I watched that briefly, but the whole operation was now winding down, so we wandered back to the field before starting to go home, and were surprised to see that the police were going through all the vehicles that they'd insisted were left behind... For many people earlier that day had said, 'If we come out of the field, we must bring our vehicles with us', for fear of them being broken up like happened once before in similar circumstances, I was told, but they were told, 'No, the vehicles must stay.' And when the vehicles and the people had been separated, we saw the police searching the vehicles, which we watched closely for some time. Many of the vehicles were open, and the police were able to just walk in and inspect the contents, but some of the vehicles had been left shut, or locked, and some of the police methods of gaining entry to those vehicles were unorthodox, to put it mildly. If they couldn't get in, they broke in.

By then the whole thing was winding down, so eventually we found my motorbike and went home.

8

Chapter Eight

Excerpts from the police radio log, June 1st 1985

Abbreviations used:

Kilo: (Kilo Control) Police Control room supervised by Assistant Chief Constable of Wiltshire (ACC) Lionel Grundy until late afternoon, when he left by helicopter to supervise events at the Beanfield.

BW1: (Bravo Whiskey 1) Ground forces supervised by Superintendent Burden.

HC1: (Hotel Charlie 1) Helicopter Unit (Chief Superintendent Denning).

WH1: (Whiskey Hotel 1) Chief Constable (of Wiltshire – Donald Smith).

Hotel: (Hotel Control) and Rom. (Romeo Control) Other – unidentified – Police Control rooms.

AM: Amesbury police station, Prisoner Handling Unit.

PSU: Police Support Unit vehicle.

RTA: Road traffic accident.

PDF: Unidentified; perhaps something to do with 'Public Disorder.'

All other abbreviations (e.g. A1P, D1B, JS5, SO2) refer to individual police units.

1214	909	Have you had a report of possible movement [from Savernake Forest]?
	Kilo	Yes, confirmed.
	909	For your information... forming up inside the forest and movement imminent.
1214	HC1	We're over the site now and filming. There is a line of some six vehicles, headed by a blue coach, which has moved out onto the road and they appear to be starting...
	Kilo	Confirm there are five in the line at the moment.
	HC1	Yes, confirmed. Five in a line and there is beginning to be a tail-back along the main road from the junction with the picnic site. Some sort of police presence should be available for traffic control.
1217	Kilo	Can you say the sex of persons in the vehicles which have left?
	JS5	We're sort of tied up at the entrance at the minute. Majority male and female [sic]. They've got pedestrians in the road blocking it and letting all convoy vehicles out of the picnic site. About 20 have gone to the road so far.

1222	A1P	Location: the Fork, Stonehenge. We have detained approximately seven or eight persons in possession of a PSV single-decker coach, which is mobile with us. Instructions please regarding disposal of the coach. I have an officer who can drive it if necessary.
	Kilo	Suggest at this stage you take it to AM.
1234	D1B	I don't know whether you are aware, but it would appear from what we have here there's a lot of holiday traffic caught up with convoy, which may cause problems with any future plans of ours.
	Kilo	Your comments noted. We are trying to get it stopped at the A4.
	D1B	Appreciated, but there is a lot of traffic which is mingled in with convoy vehicles and to try and sort of... trying to weed them out at this stage seems highly unlikely. As I say, there's obviously going to be problems later on.
	Kilo	Yes, your comments noted.
1245	SO2	The situation on the road outside the site is that the traffic is stopped in most directions. The convoy are still forming up but not all their vehicles are on the public road. We are doing our best with traffic. We need a motorcyclist to get some of the members of the public, who are stuck in the middle of the convoy, going in the same direction out when the opportunity arises.
	Kilo	Yes, your comments noted, but we have no motorcycle.
1250	SO2	Without being absolutely precise I think it fair to say they are on the move. At least 50 vehicles have gone from the site. They are still coming out but the general movement is about 20 miles an hour south.
	Kilo	Roger.
1252	Kilo	Are you aware the leader [Phil Shakesby, presumed by the police to be the 'leader' of the convoy] is in the black coach?
	BW1	No, I was not aware of that. One vehicle has broken down just in Savernake. We shall probably overtake it, but the main bulk of the convoy – 50-plus vehicles – is now heading south from Savernake towards Burbage.
	Kilo	Did you get that message about the black coach?
	BW1	Would you repeat?
	Kilo	The leader is in the black coach, for your information.
	BW1	I take it the black coach is in fact leading the convoy?
	Kilo	No, we don't know what location that is. The leader is in that coach though.
	BW1	Received.
1255	D1B	Is it possible for anyone to check the site at Savernake? We are behind the

convoy now, but I understand there was some vehicles still left in the site, and I am a bit concerned about what might come up behind us later.

Kilo   Yes, noted. We will get that done in a minute.

1308   SO2   Approximately nine vehicles have joined the rear of the convoy. Information from a motorist in the opposite direction: the convoy appear to be blocking the road deliberately outside the garage at Cadley. On the other hand I suppose they might just be getting diesel or something.

Kilo   Confirmed they were trying to get fuel.

SO2   Your message received. Could you ask DM to check the picnic site to give us some idea of how many vehicles are left and how many people are left up there?

Kilo   Confirmed there are eight coaches and approximately 12 vehicles still at the site.

SO2   Your message received.

1309   WS17   Can you tell us where the convoy is now to prevent us getting trapped between them and our own troops?

Kilo   The convoy is stationary at Cadley.

WS17   Roger.

1315   BC35   I have just come past Stonehenge Fork about half a mile towards Longbarrow [roundabout]. There's a group of three vehicles and about eight to ten hippy types stopped by the side of the road.

Rom.   Roger.

1318   BC35   I was directed by an officer from Longbarrow roundabout. I'm on the A303 west of Longbarrow roundabout. There's about 50 hippies there, about 24 walking towards Longbarrow roundabout.

Kilo   Inform Longbarrow roundabout.

1319   C2B   I am informed by the Forestry Commission, who have got their spotters out, that there are ten persons with one motorcycle and a blue VW van on the track which runs between last year's site and the Stonehenge car park.

Kilo   Roger.

1324   SO2   The convoy are rearranging themselves at the rear so as to leave a red coach, ACE 126, as the last but one vehicle. We noticed when this one went out. It had upwards of 20 men in it.

Kilo   Roger.

1326   Kilo   For your information there is a red coach, which is next to last of the convoy, containing 20 hardcore members.

	BW1	Received.
1330	BW1	Can you tell me, please, the location of the prison vans?
	Kilo	At present AM.

| 1336 | AM12 | For information of PSU sited Countess roundabout: there are about 70 hippy types en route from Amesbury en masse to their location. |
| | Kilo | Roger. |

| 1338 | A2B | Message from Dorset PSU Commander: all the hippies who were lying about Amesbury appear to have moved off and are now near Countess roundabout. |
| | Kilo | Roger. |

1340	C5P	Reference your last: a crowd of about 150 to 200 have just crossed the bottom of the A303 and they are going up towards Bulford. Standby 1, we'll check in case they try to make it up the north side of the field.
	Kilo	Roger.
	C5P	It appears they are going up the north side up towards the top of the field, the top of Stonehenge Fork.
	Kilo	Roger.

| 1345 | A2B | In excess of 100 persons on foot have just left Amesbury passing the Druid's Lodge en route to Stonehenge. |
| | Kilo | Roger. |

| 1346 | C5P | The main group of about 2-300 are now approaching and are roughly halfway up the hill towards Stonehenge. They have been warned. They say they intend to make for the stones and whatever the consequences will be worth it. |
| | Kilo | Roger. |

1351	Kilo	Location [of the convoy] now?
	HC1	We are between Collingbourne Ducis and Collingbourne Kingston, stationary at the moment. Heading the convoy is what appears to be a number of press and TV vehicles. The head of the convoy proper varies between a blue breakdown vehicle, a light blue Transit type and blue coach.
	Kilo	Roger.

| 1356 | HC1 | They have now turned right into Collingbourne, still A338 towards Leckford crossroads. In front of the convoy is one or two motorcycle outriders and a number of press vehicles, approximately nine, and leading |

the convoy is a TV camera vehicle, a blue and white Volvo.

Kilo   Yes.

1357   XSS1   Mobile en route to Marlborough, about ten miles out of Marlborough. This is the vehicle with all the PSU equipment, shields and helmets etc. We have had a request from one of the PSUs following the convoy into Marlborough to liaise with them re: issue of equipment. However, two other of our PSUs have been deployed elsewhere. Can you tell us where you want us to go with our equipment?

QJ   The only thing you can do at this stage is to follow down the A338 to Collingbourne Ducis towards Andover.

1359   Kilo   Can you get Mr Burden to the telephone?

BW1   He is with me now. Go ahead.

Kilo   This is the ACC [Grundy]. When you stop these people you are aware that we have had information that they have... they possibly have inflammable material on board. What I want you to do is stop each one of them and be very specific in the advice that you give them. You are to tell them that the Stonehenge Festival is cancelled, as we have previously discussed in the terms of the Order, and tell them to go away. However, in view of the information we have received, I want every one of those vehicles searched with a view to finding out if there are any dangerous weapons or such material on board. Any instances there will be dealt with as a breach of the peace, as you are aware. However, those who are prepared to turn away must be told to move right out of the area. Is this understood?

BW1   Received. I take it they need only be told once.

Kilo   Roger.

1404   HC1   [Message to Kilo] For your information... the first one to seven vehicles would appear to be the smaller type, not too many personnel. The vehicles seven through to 15 would appear to be the personnel carriers and the ones to concentrate on.

1406   Kilo   Location now?

HC1   We are entering Tidworth. The head of the convoy is stationary, allowing the remainder to regroup. The convoy in total stretches back approximately to Leckford crossroads.

Kilo   Yes, keep us informed.

1411   Kilo   As soon as the convoy shows signs of moving and in which direction let us know for the deployment of Gravel 1 and 2.

HC1   Yes, understood.

| 1416 | Kilo | Instructions are: the gravel is a last resort. Use PCs with hand signals and, if possible, slow signs before the gravel. |
| | BW1 | Noted, that's understood. |

1420	BW1	What you are suggesting, not to dump the gravel is not, I suggest, not practicable. I recommend we dump the gravel. If you require a police officer to give a hand signal, then he can be the other side of the gravel dump. We can't do what you are suggesting fast enough.
	Kilo	This is the ACC [Grundy]. Do exactly what you have just said, because that was the intention. I don't want the gravel to be the only means of stopping. In addition to the gravel I want clear signals given on the convoy side of the gravel.
	BW1	Yes, all received. Have I now permission to dump gravel on this road?
	Kilo	Hold it at the moment. We will give you a direct instruction. At the moment the lead vehicle has broken down in North Tidworth or South Tidworth and everything has come to a halt. So just hold it for a minute.
	BW1	All received and clear. All I require please is just a 'go' for the dumpings and it will be carried out.
	Kilo	Understood. That will be done.

1424	HC1	The convoy is past the crossroads heading south A338 Leckford crossroads.
	Kilo	Yes, confirm towards Parkhouse.
	HC1	Correction, apologies, towards Parkhouse.

1424	BW1	Message received. Kilo from Bravo, Kilo from BW1, message received.
	Kilo	Yes, operate Gravel 1.
	BW1	Confirm go.
	Kilo	Go. Confirm go.

| 1425 | HC1 | [Message to Kilo] We have a motorcycle outrider now approaching Shipton Bellinger. If he gets anywhere near our ground unit they suggest they may attempt to take him out, because obviously intending to return and report. |

1425	Kilo	If possible deploy a Range Rover to stop the motorcycle in front of convoy.
	BW1	Confirm you require a motorcycle at the front of convoy stopped.
	Kilo	Yes. Prevent him going back.
	BW1	All noted.

| 1428 | Kilo | How far into the village are the convoy? |
| | HC1 | We are immediately ahead of a motorcycle outrider which is now approaching the gravel. We are some 200 yards in front of the head vehicle. |

Excerpts from the police radio log, June 1st 1985

1431   Hotel   Confrontation is imminent. Have you got any ambulances standing by?
        Kilo   Yes, confirmed.

1432   HC1   [Message to Kilo] They have turned left, turned left prior to the road block. They are now heading to the A303 north of the road block.

1434   BW1   Confirm turned left?
        Kilo   Yes, they've turned left. Would you go up the A303 to Thruxton Farm which is first left and block the road?
        BW1   Noted. First turning right at Parkhouse, vehicles turning right towards Parkhouse.

1435   Kilo   [Message to HC1] Confirm there are two out on the A303, heading towards Parkhouse on the A303. Will you instruct ground units to block the A303 completely on the Hampshire side of Parkhouse?

1435   BW1   Can you confirm they are turning right towards Amesbury?
        BW3   Yes, confirmed.
        BW1   We need men to block the main road on the roundabout.
        BW3   Roger.

1435   Kilo   [Message to C5P] Stop all eastbound traffic A303.

1436   MC2   Can we have all traffic stopped westbound A303 from Countess?
        Kilo   Also westbound.

1437   HC1   [Message to Kilo] Head of convoy stopped just Hampshire side of the crossroads. The convoy trails back then on the A303, then the minor road, then back onto the A338. Can we get something or some unit to the rear of the convoy on the A303 Hampshire side?

1437   Kilo   Make attempts to deal with the rear of the convoy, as many vehicles as possible.
        SO2   We are in range but we are a long way north of Shipton Bellinger.

1438   BW1   [Message to Kilo] Can you say... have all the convoy turned left, or are there any still approaching the barrier?

1438   HC1   We are just checking the whole of the convoy now. We appear to have them back through Shipton Bellinger, and the tail end appears to be towards the end of Tidworth.
        Kilo   Are there any approaching the barrier?
        HC1   Negative at this stage. They are all leading up towards the minor road,

Early stand-off between travellers and the police at the roadblock on the A303 near Parkhouse roundabout.

turning left and then turning right onto the A303. Now we are with the tail end of the convoy, which has been blocked off by PSU following, which is just Parkhouse side of Tidworth.

Kilo   Roger. BW1, did you receive that?

BW1   Yes, all noted, thank you.

1440 HC1   It looks as though the tail end of the convoy has tried to block the road to our PSUs. We are returning now to Parkhouse crossroads and can see a number of Peace Convoy vehicles going across country trying to use fields to gain access to the various roads.

Kilo   Roger. BW1, did you receive that?

BW1   Yes, all noted and monitored.

1443 D3B   [Message to Kilo] 10/1 with six prisoners en route to Amesbury.

1444 Hotel   [Message to Kilo] Can we have an ambulance please to Parkhouse crossroads? Let's employ a Hampshire ambulance. He might not be able to get around this side.

1445 HC1   Below us are the wooded areas of the A303. A number of Peace Convoy vehicles and certainly one police unit involved in an RTA. A number of Peace Convoy vehicles are now in a field to the north of the A303 adjacent to the crossroads.

Kilo   Roger.

Excerpts from the police radio log, June 1st 1985

1446   BW1   Superintendent requests permission to use shields [and] riot gear. Missiles being thrown.

Kilo   Authority given.

1448   BW1   Urgently required, please: prisoner handling equipment.

Kilo   Roger.

BW1   Thank you. Enquiry please: where are the prisoners to go?

Kilo   Amesbury.

BW1   Noted.

1450   HC1   The convoy is now entering the field in more numbers. Vehicles are continually driving around the field. Several police officers could only gain access on foot. We are blocked off with vehicles. From Mr Denning: this is clearly in Hampshire. It is stressed that we allow them to enter the field, and, should the owner at our request then assist or request them to leave, we have a suitable breach of the peace situation, which we could contain in the field and deal with.

Kilo   Yes. Roger. Agreed. No policemen on foot to enter field.

1452   SO2   I have got a bit of bother with three PSUs at the rear of the convoy. We have some prisoners on their way into AM.

Kilo   Yes. How many?

SO2   Two Transits have gone. I can only make an estimate, possibly 15.

Kilo   Yes. Roger.

1500   BW1   Can you confirm that Amesbury can handle the prisoners at this stage and do not require further assistance?

Kilo   Extra men sent to AM.

1502   BW1   Please inform AM there is one prisoner Transit en route with a motorcycle escort. Very violent prisoners, very violent.

Kilo   Roger. Being done.

1503   HC1   To update you... they have breached entry into the field from several directions and are currently tearing down fencing on the B3084 side of the field to make a further entry/exit. If they start leaving the field by that particular route they have reasonable means of gaining an escape route to Andover.

Kilo   Roger.

1504   Kilo   Can you say how many vehicles are in the field?

HC1   Approximately 60 in the field. The tail of the convoy is now contained very close to the field with the PSUs behind it.

One of the earliest arrests at the roadblock on the A303 near Parkhouse roundabout.

	Kilo	Roger, all received.
1505	BW1	In view of the last message from HC1, do we deploy in the minor road, the B3084?
	Kilo	Endeavour to contain the field. Endeavour to contain the field.
1507	A5A	The situation at Rollestones crossroads all in order. Numerous persons on motorcycles turned back [presumably a contingent of Hell's Angels, who were also attempting to approach Stonehenge]. Resuming back to Longbarrow.
	Kilo	Roger.
1507	HC1	It is obvious that a number of the convoy are arming themselves with sticks and staves and they are breaking through the hedge.
	Kilo	Roger.
1508	Kilo	Can you advise best tactic to contain in this field?
	HC1	Standby.
1510	HC1	From Chief Superintendent Denning, a message as follows: containment possible with PSU vehicles and personnel on each corner of the field. Foot personnel to be deployed along A303 edge and the B3084 edges. From

what we've seen above, and obviously ground crews can see and have seen, clear circumstances involving a breach of the peace. No better opportunity to take positive action on this, bearing in mind suitable numbers of personnel required, and the back-up of prisoner vehicles for somewhere in excess of 200 persons. Understood?

Kilo Roger.

1511 BW1 Can you contact Kiwi Reception [in Bulford MoD Camp] and get them to send the Luton van loaded with protective clothing and riot gear to the scene?

Kilo Roger.

1513 BW1 For the information of Mr Burden, who is now with me, will you please repeat that last message in entirety?

Kilo The best way of containing in the field: PSUs on each corner, foot patrols along the A303 and B3084. The fences are down and they are arming themselves with fence staves. Three Hants PSUs en route to you under the command of Chief Superintendent West.

BW1 Are you giving me permission to go into the field yet?

Kilo Negative. No.

BW1 In that case, with your permission I am going to try and talk my way through this. I accept that when they come out they must be arrested for breach of the peace, but if I can talk them out that will be better.

Kilo Yes, agreed. There are more personnel coming from Amesbury to support you.

BW1 Yes. Now listen, one thing I can't do from here, because I don't know the road block situations, is deploy the personnel to the other four corners. I cannot deplete my personnel from here. I do not wish to. Now would you please deploy PSUs as they are coming to the scene from the other side of the road blocks.

Kilo Yes, your request noted.

BW1 The trouble is, I have got two roads blocked off along which I would love to push personnel.

1514 D1B Regarding the shields: are there any shields en route for the Wiltshire personnel? Things are a bit aggressive and we request shields as urgently as possible.

Kilo We understand the shields are at Parkhouse.

D1B Yes. Whoever has got them, can you direct them to the east corner junction A303?

1518 Kilo For your information, there are 36 trained PSU personnel from the MoD. Would you please consider whether you wish their assistance?

Helmets and
shields ready for
allocation.
Copyright
Tim Malyon.

	AA4	Yes, I will check on the situation here and call you back.
	Kilo	Yes. Roger.
1522	BW1	Receiving urgent.
	Kilo	W1, go ahead.
	BW1	We have an impasse situation here where if we are not careful they are going to start to win. The signs are they are starting to make petrol bombs inside [and] my men on the road are being stoned from within the field. We are just having to stand there with shields and take it but I don't like the way the situation is going. Did you receive so far?
	Kilo	Yes, go ahead.
	BW1	I feel at the moment, while I have sufficient manpower here, we are going to have to make a judgment to go into that field to stop it.
	Kilo	Act according to circumstances. We are getting MoD to you.
	BW1	I need as many uniformed personnel, for appearances if nothing else, so I can make a great show on the road before we go in.
	Kilo	Yes. Roger.
1524	Kilo	Have you any personnel you can send to Parkhouse?
	A5P	Yes, I have got myself, a Sergeant and first call PSU.
	Kilo	Yes. Fully equipped?
	A5P	We have got all our own personal protective equipment.
	Kilo	Yes, make all haste to Parkhouse.
	A5P	Roger.
1533	BW1	Message from Mr Burden. Standby. We will eventually have to go into the field, quite obviously. All I would like you to do is to tell me when we have

got the other PSUs in position. They are coming from Hampshire on the other side of the field, and also I would like to have MoD PSU, and then we will really take the lead from you, I feel, from the helicopter as well, as to when we go in.

Kilo   Yes, received.

BW1   The one big problem is, we are going to have to come back through the vehicles. I know the risk. I have weighed the risks. We are going to have to deal with the situation as and when we come to it.

Kilo   10/7.

BW1   The problem is, once we get in the field we are going to have to combat moving vehicles. Have you any suggestions as to what we could do? The only obvious thing, of course, is vehicles which we can ram them with.

Kilo   Your comments noted. Standby.

BW1   Bearing in mind... we can combat the petrol bombs and sticks but not the moving vehicles.

Kilo   You should have an amount of spikes with the PSU equipment. There are four sets of spikes – correction, five sets of spikes – en route to you from Kiwi Barracks to deal with vehicles.

BW1   Five sets of what?

Kilo   Spikes.

BW1   Noted. I don't know whether they will be any good in the field.

1543   BW1   Just getting information that it looks as though they may be trying to break out into another area. They are spreading petrol over the field in preparation to set fire to it.

Kilo   Yes, Fire Service have been alerted.

1551   BW1   Can you get HC1 to check on the Salisbury side of Parkhouse crossroads? Persons are on the move, believed to be hippies making their way from the A303 diagonally across to the A338.

Kilo   Roger.

1601   A5A   I don't know whether you are informed of this but part of the convoy is making its way across the field [the Beanfield] from the field they were in.

Kilo   Confirm in which direction.

A5A   Cutting across the field in the direction of Countess, cutting across to the main road.

1605   HC1   Reference your last: the triangle which is bounded by the A303, A338 and B3084 is split into two fields. The convoy in its majority is centred in the field on the A303 side of this triangle. Currently 12 vehicles have broken through from that field into the field on the north i.e. Shipton Bellinger side. They are obviously making attempts to find a route out on this side i.e.

Shipton Bellinger and Andover. We have no police personnel to prevent them at this stage.

Kilo   Roger.

1606   Kilo   Can you move down to the triangle formed by the A338, B3084 and A303, and deploy your units along the A338 and B3084 to contain them in the triangle?

SO2   Message received. At the moment I am blocking the exit from the field into the B3084 road. If I move from here they will undoubtedly try and come out from this road.

Kilo   Yes. Roger.

1608   Kilo   Can we have some personnel on the triangle formed by the A338 and the B3084? The A303 would appear to be covered, the A338 and B3084 not well enough. This is according to HC1.

BW1   Yes, noted, thank you.

1610   BW1   Is the ACC still there?

Kilo   Yes, send.

BW1   I just ask, at the request of the people in the field, to open up negotiations along policy lines I had. However, I promised to meet them again at 1615 hours, when they are going to tell me whether as a group they would be willing to come out peaceably from the field. This is obviously on a condition that no festival will take place and they are not to go near Stonehenge. Is this negotiable?

Kilo   [ACC Grundy] No, the position now is that, from the information you have given us, they have committed a series of offences, and as far as I am concerned they are to be arrested as soon as you or Chief Superintendent Illman tells me that you have adequate resources to go in there and deal with them as efficiently and with as little trouble as possible. Now the position is that I am waiting for you to tell me that you have this mass of resources there. Understood?

BW1   Yes, all received. Any further suggestions on meeting the mobile vehicles inside the field?

Kilo   Have the spikes arrived with you? That's one point. That's all part of the information I require you to relay to me. In terms of the dialogue with the people, then you can meet them and talk with them, but you now know my objectives. Understood?

BW1   Yes, Sir. I can tell you know that we leave no alternative but to go into the field and a confrontation situation... [message lost]... mobile large vehicles with officers on foot... [message lost]... our own vehicles of some sort or another.

Kilo   No, at this time I'm not saying go in on foot. I want you to tell me when you have got sufficient Transits to go in and it is possible with the vehicles you may be able to stop them. Now consider this, consult with Chief Superintendent Illman and come back to me. Understood?

BW1   Yes, received, and for the information of Control we are still awaiting drink here and in this heat it is imperative.

Kilo   Yes, this should have come with the spikes. Understood?

BW1   Yes, alright, just arrived. Thanks very much.

1617   Kilo   Can you bring Mr Illman and Mr Burden to the vehicle?

BW1   Standby. Is this urgent?

Kilo   Yes.

BW1   Go ahead. Superintendent Illman [here].

Kilo   [ACC Grundy] The situation now is that, as you get sufficient resources, I want you still to report to me. However, I want you to contain the situation to try and prevent vehicles leaving the field, maintain them inside the field in a stand-off position... The chopper at present is down being refuelled. When it comes on again it is to come to Headquarters, pick me up, then I'll come down and together with you assess the situation. Understood?

BW1   Yes, all received.

1632   D2B   For your information, we are en route to Amesbury with four prisoners.

Kilo   Yes. Roger. When you get there can you query them, whether they can handle any further prisoners or whether we should consider Salisbury?

D2B   Yes, confirm the alternative to Amesbury.

Kilo   The first alternative is Salisbury.

D2B   Yes. Roger. Will do.

1633   SO2   Message for BW1: in the B3084 I now have six PSUs – two and a half from Avon and Somerset, one from Thames Valley, two and a half from Wiltshire. In the junction with the A303 there are two other PSUs, making eight in all along the B3084.

Kilo   Yes. Roger.

1646   G1   We have information that there are 15 peace-type vehicles travelling A303 from Andover towards our location. Could we have instructions whether to let them through our road block and join the others on the site or prevent them from entering on the A303 junction B3084?

Kilo   The instructions are: they are to be advised that the festival will not take place and they are to be turned away.

G1   Roger. Willco.

1650   JS5   You have about 200 persons walking up the old Amesbury Road direction of Stonehenge.

	Kilo	Roger. Understood.
1650	Kilo	Have you sufficient personnel at your location to contain these persons making their way from Amesbury?
	A2P	I have 30 personnel here. How many people are meant to be coming towards our location?
	Kilo	The number is between 100 and 200.
	A2P	Yes. Roger. Is this a confirmed figure? We had something similar earlier, which didn't come to anything.
	Kilo	Yes, it may be the same again. I think it's the same crowd that have been milling about out on the Countess Road and on the A303 at the roundabout earlier on.
1657	AM12	Are you aware that a couple of hundred hippy types [are] converging from Stonehenge Road area towards Stonehenge?
	Kilo	Yes, is this to Stonehenge Fork?
	AM12	Yes, en route to Stonehenge Fork.
	Kilo	Yes. Roger. Is it a definite 200?
	AM12	In the region of 200. I'm not going to count them.
	Kilo	Where are they now?
	AM12	They are about halfway up the road towards the A303 just past Home Farm.
	Kilo	Yes, understood.
1702	C5P	We have just had a report from other members of my PSU who had to get transport up by members of the public. It would appear they are grouping at various points along the A303, where my PSU are stretched, and behaving threateningly.
	Kilo	Yes. Roger. Standby.
1706	Kilo	I understand large number of persons approaching you on the A303.
	A2P	Yes, they haven't come over the ridge or into sight yet.
	Kilo	Oh, I understand they are all over the road just out of your sight.
	A2P	We have approximately 40 officers here at present awaiting their arrival.
	Kilo	Yes. Roger.
1708	Kilo	When you get to the roundabout, turn right A303 signposted Exeter towards Stonehenge. You will come up behind a group of approximately 150 marchers all over the A303 marching towards Stonehenge Fork. Will you follow behind them? There are other officers in front to prevent their entry to Stonehenge.
	QLX1	Yes, noted.

Excerpts from the police radio log, June 1st 1985

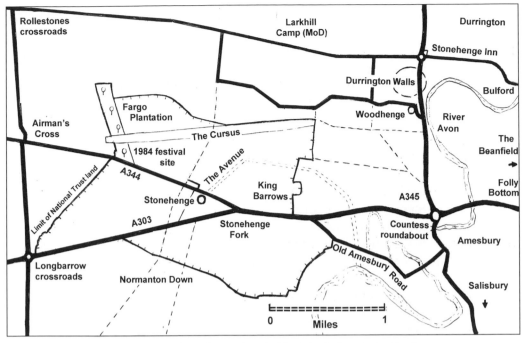

Map of Stonehenge, showing the various places where incidents took place during the day.
Map by Andy Worthington.

1711	TO1	As you appreciate, I am at Stonehenge Fork with two PSUs. Approximately 250 of these hippies have climbed over the fence at the top of the hill and are in the field adjacent to the road. No problem at present but some assistance would be required.
	Kilo	Assistance is en route coming up behind them.
	TO1	Roger.

1721	Kilo	Will you send half a PSU to Cadley Garage where there are groups of hippies causing problems on the Savernake Estate cutting down barriers. There is only one Forestry worker with them. Understood?
	SO2	Half a PSU to Cadley petrol station.
	Kilo	Confirm, problems with barriers being cut down.

1722	TO1	I have still no back-up at the monument. They are making for their original [festival] site. We are endeavouring to cut them off but lack of personnel prevents this.
	Kilo	Roger. Understood. There are units en route to you. They should be with you very shortly.
	TO1	If they could come to the monument car park I will deploy from there.
	Kilo	Roger.

| 1724 | Kilo | Things are getting out of hand at Stonehenge. Can a PSU be released from your location to Stonehenge car park? |
| | BW1 | Yes, noted. I'll try and get one sent. |

| 1725 | Kilo | 20 motorcyclists have just left Amesbury for your location. May cause problems. Understood? |
| | TO1 | Yes, thank you. |

1725	Kilo	There are units en route from Devizes of Avon and Somerset. When they arrive at your location would you direct them to Stonehenge car park. Understood?
	C1B	Sorry to trouble you. Let me confirm that when Avon and Somerset reach my location I have to direct them to Stonehenge car park.
	Kilo	Yes, confirmed. It's four or five Transits.
	C1B	Roger, will do.

| 1728 | Kilo | There is some sort of problem at the roundabout. This is a request from BW1. |
| | HC1 | Noted. |

| 1730 | HC1 | [Message to Kilo] The problem appears to be centred on the roundabout of the A303 towards Countess Road. There are approximately 15 motorcyclists of the Hell's Angels type and a number of the Peace Convoy types on foot running away and moving away from Countess roundabout, and there is a number of police officers, a considerable number of police officers deployed on the ground. |

| 1730 | C5P | I am a bit concerned now about the safety of the officers on the road checkpoints. Three of them on the A303, the Bulford turn-off, have just been driven out by a number of motorcyclists who have gone off into the distance, but presumably [are] by now at Parkhouse, and they have also tried to force one of the Transits off the road. With your agreement I'll redeploy back to Countess with a full unit. |
| | Kilo | Yes. Roger. Agreed with the redeployment. |

1731	BW1	I was monitoring your message from HC1. He was in fact correct in all points. The motorcyclists have now gone back up the canal. Instructions are that, if you can spare it, a PSU be sent to the junction with the Bulford road, where some assistance may be required with these Hell's Angels.
	Kilo	We are withdrawing our men back from that junction, back to Countess Road. We have no other PSUs at the moment.
	BW1	Where are the Gloucester ones?
	Kilo	They've been directed to Stonehenge where there are problems.

	BW1	Noted, thank you. Have we got possibility of rustling up more?
	Kilo	Yes, there are more en route from Dorset, probably in Salisbury at the moment.
	BW1	Noted, thank you.
1735	HC1	We've dropped both our passengers [including ACC Grundy] for the conference at Parkhouse. We have instructions we are now going to Stonehenge to monitor situation there.
	Kilo	Roger. If on the way you see the motorcyclists and their intentions will you let us know?
	HC1	By all means.
1736	TO1	All units have now arrived, pushing these people back across the fields to where they entered it on the A344. At the moment they don't seem to be getting any nearer the stones. I'll let you know the situation later.
	Kilo	Roger. HC1 will be overhead shortly to monitor the situation.
	TO1	Yes, all received. Thank you.
1737	HC1	Some of these motorcycles, some 20-plus in numbers, now heading down London Road, Amesbury, past the NAAFI towards the town centre.
	Kilo	Roger. Understood.
1742	HC1	We are now overflying the group of some 350 persons who are currently moving back towards Amesbury, the car park side of the monument in the field, and approaching the Fork and continuing towards Amesbury, being shepherded by police personnel. Apparently looks to be no problems with them at the moment.
	Kilo	Roger. Understood.
1746	HC1	Can you get further units, particularly vehicle units, up to Stonehenge? All the personnel have been shepherded onto the A303, just Amesbury side of Stonehenge Fork. A number of scuffles taking place between police officers and arrests made. There are no police vehicles at the scene and they will be required.
	Kilo	Roger.
1746	Kilo	Up to the A303, vehicles required urgently.
	MC4	Roger.
1747	BW1	Can I have an immediate update on whatever vehicles, heavy plant vehicles, are available [for Parkhouse]? Provisions have been made. The Assistant Chief Constable requires a complete update on all those vehicles readily available to us at this position from this area.

	Kilo	Roger. We will come back to you.
1752	HC1	There would appear to be sufficient police personnel in the location here now to contain the situation. A number of scuffles still taking place and arrests being made. The majority are making their way still down the A303 towards Amesbury and have just reached the turning down the old Amesbury Road towards the town centre.
	Kilo	Understood.
1755	Kilo	Standby message for you. Reference the heavy plant: we are getting the list together. About 25 in the county. We will come back to you with a more exact list later.
	BW1	Standby.
	Kilo	Further to that message for the ACC, there may be some delay in getting these details.
	BW1	There cannot be any delay. We must have vehicles, we must have heavy vehicles, we must have them urgently. Will you contact please Wilts County Council, see what they can do? I would suggest you also contact anyone else in the area who may be able to assist – Sergeant Williamson at Kiwi Control.
	Kilo	We are dealing with this, but delay may be in getting vehicles to you.
	BW1	Yes, we appreciate there's bound to be some delay. As soon as you can.
1758	C1P	[Message to Kilo] For your information: report of passing motorist – unknown quantity of persons in grass behind Longbarrow Wood, hiding when vehicles go by. Unknown quantity.
1801	A5B	Location Longbarrow.
	Kilo	Message for you: reported by a member of the public, persons in Longbarrow Woods adjacent to your location. Can you deal?
	A5B	We are at the moment tangled up with traffic diversion.
	Kilo	Will you deal when you can?
	A5B	Roger. Willco.
1803	A2B	I'm walking with the party down the A303 towards Countess. Is there any process as to how we should deal with these people when we get there, or where are we going to leave them?
	Kilo	Stay with them until they disperse into manageable groups.
	A2B	Yes, received. This may take some time.
	Kilo	This is appreciated. Perhaps we can wear them down by arresting them.
	A2B	Yes, received. Standing by.
1813	TO1	As stated earlier, unless instructed to the contrary, I intend to try and split

these people up into small groups and head them towards the A345 up towards Marlborough. As you appreciate, the A303 is taboo [and] Amesbury itself has enough problems with the people that are there this afternoon.

Kilo   Yes. Roger.

1815   Kilo   There are a number of hippies coming towards you on foot, if you have any means left to divert them up the A345 towards Durrington.

C5P   We have them in view. There are two other police mobiles, but they are interspersed with bikers.

Kilo   We don't want them to go into Amesbury, sooner they went Marlborough way.

C5P   Roger.

1815   TO1   We have got problems at Countess roundabout. We may need some help down here rapid.

Kilo   Roger. What sort of trouble have you got? How many are there there?

TO1   We are endeavouring to stop them. We are getting difficulties here.

Kilo   Yes. Roger. Try and contain it for the time being. We'll try and get someone out from AM.

TO1   We've only got about a dozen blokes down here at the moment.

Kilo   Yes, we are trying to get someone to you.

1820   BW1   What is the situation at Countess?

Kilo   Extra men required.

BW1   For what purpose and how many?

Kilo   We have about 200 to 300 causing problems, motorcycles interspersed. Trying to divert them towards Marlborough.

BW1   Hell's Angels is this?

Kilo   Yes, some of them.

BW1   Yes, standby.

1825   TO1   Further to my last, we have about 150 pedestrians at Countess roundabout milling about doing nothing untoward at present. They are on the grass verge on the eastbound carriageway. Have you any thoughts on which direction we ought to shove them?

Kilo   Yes, north or inside. We have two coming towards you from Parkhouse.

TO1   Roger. I will advise them to disperse in small groups, otherwise we will arrest them.

1832   Kilo   There is more heavy plant coming to you [at Parkhouse], estimated time of arrival 30 to 45 minutes. And can you keep us up to date with the ACC's conversation with the occupants of the field?

BW1   Yes, as soon as I know something I will relay it to you. Can you tell me what plant is expected at that time?

Kilo   A Scammell and a Matador, both heavy recovery units, and one other heavy recovery vehicle. Also a ten-ton lorry and a JCB.

BW1   Yes, noted. Standby.

Kilo   Also the two remaining gravel lorries.

BW1   Yes, noted.

1839   DQ27   Convoy of 12 vehicles heading [north] from Cadley towards [Savernake], for your information.

Kilo   Roger. DQ27 standby.

1841   BW1   What is the situation now at Countess?

Kilo   They are still dealing. Everything's in hand.

BW1   Noted.

1842   DQ27   We have monitored this convoy of vehicles into Savernake Forest, just outside Marlborough.

Kilo   Can you confirm they have gone back to picnic site or farther up towards Cadley?

DQ27   Picnic site just outside the Marlborough boundary.

Kilo   Roger. Received.

1848   SO2   There is a great deal of vehicle movement on the site [pasture field and Beanfield] and a lot more people getting into their vehicles.

Kilo   Roger. Received.

1856   SO2   There are now ten-plus coaches and about 20 other vehicles moving in the field. They are forming up in a circle, going round and round. I am virtually certain they are going to rush a gate in a minute.

Kilo   Roger. Thank you. Received.

1856   TO1   Could I have redeployment for 9A, 10A, 11A, 12A and 13A, the Avon and Somerset [PSUs]? I don't feel I require them at Countess.

Kilo   Would you send them to Parkhouse?

TO1   Roger. Will do.

Kilo   Thank you.

1857   BW1   We must know as soon as possible, please, where the vehicles, the heavy vehicles are, which are coming to us. We need this information urgently.

Kilo   Yes, appreciated. They have been despatched. There is no radio contact.

BW1   Where are they being despatched from?

Kilo   Amesbury.

Excerpts from the police radio log, June 1st 1985

A group of police officers prepares for the final assault on the travellers in the pasture field and the Beanfield at 7pm.

1858	BW1	Have ACC for...
	Kilo	Roger. Go ahead.
	WH3	[ACC Grundy] There are signs of movement on the field. We are preparing to go in. We have not got the heavy plants but we are going to go in nonetheless, in the form of three Wiltshire PSUs, three Hampshire PSUs, three Thames Valley PSUs, and take it from there. My conversation with them with a view to their coming out safely was of no value, although it's quite clear that a number of people in there do not want confrontation. But I will take it from here because I understand that there are a number of people moving up towards us. Understood?
	Kilo	Yes, all noted.

1900	C5P	This crowd [around Countess] is now contained at the side of the A303 on the westbound carriageway. Any instructions as to what is required of them? They are all peaceful at the moment.
	Kilo	Yes, at this stage just monitor them, keep them happy.
	C5P	Yes, thank you.

1901	C5P	They are now approaching, they are walking up the A303. As I say, we have the road blocked here. Do we let them through? Bearing in mind they are going towards Parkhouse, which is some distance yet away, but at the same time they are getting away from Amesbury.
	Kilo	Yes, C5P, if you are in a position to arrest them take them to Amesbury. If not, all we require is urgent messages. Received?
	C5P	Roger.

1902   Kilo   [Message to all mobiles] Only urgent messages to be passed.

1905   DA3   We have approximately 150 on foot Woodhenge towards Stonehenge Inn roundabout. We will try and disperse into even smaller groups.

        Kilo   Obliged.

1905   HC1   We are now airborne from this location [Parkhouse]. We are moving out of the way so as not to give any pre-warning of any operation. Would you call us when required by the ground units?

        Kilo   Roger. Received.

1907   MC4   Request from E1 [PSU] Commander. We have these persons now at the Bulford junction on the A303 western side. It is a non-pass situation. What are we to do with them?

        Kilo   Can you confirm they have been read the PDF?

        MC4   That I can't confirm, but they will be.

        Kilo   Roger. Received.

        MC4   The problem is, we are blocking the road east to them. If they say they wish to go home east, then we ought to let them go, I think.

        Kilo   Yes, as it says on the guide, if they are prepared to go home, ideal.

        MC4   Roger.

1910   SO2   [Message to Kilo] I understand the police are going in from the other side of the [pasture] field. Do you want us to take any action?

1911   HC1   All vehicles are being pushed away from the field in which they are sited and moving across the adjacent field [the Beanfield], north towards the small coppice.

        Kilo   Roger. HC1 received.

1912   BW1   What have you got from the chopper?

        Kilo   Yes, they are all moving north towards the A338, B3084 junction. Received?

        BW1   Yes, that's noted, thank you.

1914   C5P   The situation [around Countess] is contained at present. They are going off in small groups, some heading down towards Amesbury, but [we] are informed they intend to go down towards Salisbury and down south. A small group have gone up the A303. The others are slowly breaking up. Situation is contained at present. This mobile is going to Amesbury – two prisoners.

        Kilo   Roger.

1917   HC1   From Chief Inspector Denning: request more police officers are deployed

		in the rear field [the Beanfield], and to be instructed to take care on approach to vehicles. They appear to have no hesitation in driving at and towards police officers.
	Kilo	Roger. All noted.

1917	BW1	Make urgent arrangements please for Social Security personnel to be brought to the scene. We have a number of women and children destitute. They are going to cause us some problems. This is to be done urgently.
	Kilo	Received.

1918	Kilo	Can you make your way towards the rear of the field, taking care as they may have no hesitation in driving at you. Received?
	Hotel	No, broken. Repeat, please.
	Kilo	Will you go to the rear field? Go towards the vehicles but take care as they have no hesitation in ramming vehicles.
	Hotel	Thank you, 10/4.

1919	WH3	[ACC Grundy] Have you had a briefing yet?
	Kilo	Confirm what you mean a briefing.
	WH3	Has anybody told you what's happening?
	Kilo	Negative, Sir.
	WH3	The situation is that we went onto the field with about nine PSUs. We've taken a great number of... [message lost]... Peace Convoy made their way into the adjoining field during which time they were driving at our officers and they are now in the next field. Chief Superintendent Illman has deployed nine PSUs along the road leading along one side [and] we are talking to them through sky-shout telling them to stop their vehicles and leave. ACC Hampshire is here, he's deploying his PSUs across the field towards them. Understood?

1921	BW1	Information for ACC: what's burning?
	HC1	They have set fire to one of their vehicles, their old vehicles at the rear of the back field. There is no danger currently. Do not call Fire Service at this stage.
	BW1	Yes, noted. I'll pass this on.

1922	BW1	To date 70 prisoners arrested being processed.
	Kilo	Roger. Received.
	BW1	Where do you want these prisoners taken?
	Kilo	Amesbury.

1926	WH3	[ACC Grundy] Can you give me a report from the helicopter as to whether the vehicles are still moving and where we need to deploy further reserves?
	Kilo	Willco.

1926	Kilo	Would you go on talk-through with WH3? He requires to know if the vehicles are still moving and where you need to deploy more police officers. Received?
	HC1	Reference your last: we have approximately three vehicles still moving around the site. They are cream-coloured coaches and they are making every effort to drive through any attempt of police officers to stop. All other vehicles are stationary. We are left with three vehicles – one in the north field, two in the south. Got that?
	Kilo	Yes, noted.
1933	HC1	The situation is now well-contained. The last vehicles which attempted to ram a number of police officers have been blocked and the drivers arrested. All vehicles on the site are now stationary and contained by police officers.
	Kilo	Yes, well done.
1934	Kilo	[Message to all mobiles] From WH1, Chief Constable: well done.
1934	AM15	There's a gathering of motorcyclists and other such persons at the exit of the A303 at Folly Bottom. There are no PSUs in sight there.
	Kilo	Roger. Standby.
1936	MC6	Can you inform Hampshire we are en route on the A303, Andover to Basingstoke – three coach loads of prisoners.
	Kilo	Confirm Basingstoke police station. Estimate of prisoners?
	MC6	Three coach loads, so 30-plus at this stage.
	Kilo	Roger. Noted.
1936	BW1	For your information, a second vehicle has been fired by the occupants. There is no danger to any police personnel at this stage. It is in fact the vehicle that was leading the convoy throughout the operation. [This was Phil Shakesby's vehicle, and the police account differs considerably from Phil's own].
	Kilo	Yes. Roger. Success.
1940	HC1	There is little that we can do here now. It's all in hand. Request authority to go to Stonehenge, overfly that area, report there.
	Kilo	Yes, request granted. Happy flying.
1940	Kilo	Would you go to Folly Bottom? A gathering of motorcyclists – AM15 requires assistance.
	A2P	Yes. Roger. Do you require a complete unit to go?
	Kilo	The PSU that's with you to go.
	A2P	Roger.

Excerpts from the police radio log, June 1st 1985

With the last assault on the travellers in the Beanfield complete, an officer leaves carrying riot shields.

1941   WS75   We have approximately half a dozen dogs here at the rear of the site which need to be conveyed. There is a vehicle at AM for this purpose but also the empty Transits, because the prisoner problem is rather pressing.

      Kilo   This is in hand.

1945   BW1   Can you contact please Romeo Control? As soon as possible can the night dog handlers bring the Transit van to the scene? We are inundated with dogs.

      Kilo   Yes. Roger. Do you have the Dorset prison vans within your vicinity?

      BW1   No, we are completely out of prisoner handling units. I think they are now going to use our force coach. The prisoners are getting very restless. The sooner we get something here the better.

      Kilo   Yes, noted.

1950   Kilo   Can you go to Woodhenge hut? There are some hippies causing damage, graffiti to the hut.

      A2B   Yes, all received. En route.

      Kilo   Roger.

1951   HC1   Approximately 100 of the foot persons that left Stonehenge are now at the top of Beacon Hill making towards Parkhouse. They are being

While waiting for the 'heavy plant' to appear, to remove vehicles to the pound, various officers appear to be rifling through the contents of a caravan.

		accompanied by about a dozen police officers... Stonehenge area now completely clear, other than police personnel...
	Kilo	Roger. All noted.
1953	WH3	[ACC Grundy] For your information, we have at least – conservative estimate – 150 prisoners here. We must have transport from whatever source available. Every coach coming into Kiwi must be sent down and anything else you can get your hands on.
	Kilo	I can confirm they are en route to you.
	WH3	Yes. Can somebody at Kiwi Control find out how many coaches are coming to us, bearing in mind we have a potential with each coach of only 20 prisoners with escorts? Do a quick sum and see how many other coaches we need and make an attempt to find some.
	Kilo	Yes. Roger. We estimate seven coaches.
2000	Kilo	There are five coaches plus four vans en route to you...

	BW1	Yes, noted. Can you try and get fairly quickly to us, if possible before the coaches arrive even? Can you get some soft drinks for children, shall we say 50 children?
	Kilo	Roger. Willco.
2000	A2P	Reference Folly Bottom and the motorcyclists... [message lost]... We have also attended Woodhenge re: damage. Somebody with a flail being removed and then... [message lost].
	Kilo	Yes. Roger. Just confirm both locations all resolved.
	A2P	Confirmed.
	Kilo	Roger. Thank you.
2009	Kilo	All officers, including adjoining forces, who made an arrest today, to call at Amesbury police station, Prisoner Handling Unit, to identify prisoners and officers by photographs...
2010	BW1	These instructions are altered. The coaches, the first three coaches from here are being taken to Lyndhurst.
	Kilo	Roger. Received. Can you estimate how many prisoners? We will notify them.
	BW1	Yes, they will be taking something in the region of 60 prisoners between them.
	Kilo	Yes, obliged to you. We will contact them.
2015	BW1	Two things: please can we, at your earliest convenience, have the dog van? And the second thing is, can you please contact Chief Inspector Dunn of the RSPCA, Salisbury? He is urgently required here to deal with assorted livestock.
	Kilo	Roger. Noted. Willco.
2028	BW1	Will you contact Chief Inspector Sandall please, as a priority? He is to make arrangements to record BBC and ITN news this evening. Let me know when he has been contacted.
	Kilo	All noted.
2034	BW1	For your information, the first three coaches are going to Lyndhurst, the next one is going to Aldershot, the last two are going to Portsmouth. This is the latest information.
	Kilo	Roger. Thank you for that.
2036	DD76	I have just conferred with WS75. I am en route back to Kiwi to pick up the Transit and go back and sort these dogs out.
	Kilo	Well done. All noted.

| 2040 | A5B | We've had a report from passing member of public of hippy types cutting the wire on the track, on the south of the monument side [at Stonehenge]. We are going to make a move gently down that way to have a look. |
| | Kilo | Roger. Thank you. |

2054	BW1	Can you contact Hampshire Control, please? They have been organising the transfer of prisoners. We have got a coach load of prisoners here now. Can they please tell us where penultimate coach to go?
	Kilo	Roger. I understood the last but one was going to Portsmouth.
	BW1	Thank you.

2055	Kilo	Reference your last message: the message passed to me was that the last two coaches would go to Portsmouth. Is this correct?
	BW1	I think in fact we have tagged another coach on the end. Is this also going to Portsmouth?
	Kilo	Do you wish me to ring Hampshire Control to see?
	BW1	It's not going to hurt if we send them there. We'll despatch anything else we've got to Portsmouth and they can sort it out their end.
	Kilo	Yes, I am obliged.

2058	DQ27	We are just leaving DM back to Delta. For your information there have been... vehicles and personnel... Savernake Forest... look like... overnight [most of message lost]. For your information.
	Kilo	Confirm you are R2A. Last caller identify yourself.
	DQ27	DQ27.
	Kilo	Yes, and confirm those that went into the forest look as if they are going to spend the night.
	DQ27	Yes, somewhere in the region of 40 vehicles and a large amount of personnel.

9

Chapter Nine

Interview with Deputy Chief Constable Ian Readhead

Conducted by Richard Hester. Originally published as Appendix IV in *Mediaeval Brigands? Sedentarism and Postmodernity: The Social Control of 'New Age Travellers' 1985-1995*, a PhD thesis by Richard Hester, The University of Birmingham, 1998.

Can you say how it happened; what were the developments? What do you think were the things that came together to make the 'Beanfield' confrontation happen?

Well, I think firstly you have the Wiltshire Constabulary, which are saying, 'we're not going back to having that free festival anymore.' What should have been a week's festival has now aspired to a month's festival, which went into six weeks. There were significant difficulties in policing that event. We had some deaths in the tent that caught fire [at the last festival in 1984]. Drug use was open. [There were] young people in that environment, and if you take what the current legislation is saying about exposing children to moral danger that cannot be the consistent thing for us to live with. The sanitation, water, all of these things weren't consistent, and [the] Wiltshire [Constabulary] took the view that there was no mid-point we can get to on this: there will not be a festival. So in comes an exclusion zone around the Stones for the three weeks people want after the summer solstice.

What happened then is [that] around that exclusion zone, especially in the north of Hampshire, you have what I would call people living on the perimeter of that site, some in 'green lanes', some moving occasionally, some actually getting consent from landowner[s]: 'Yes, that's ok, you stay there.' You then get the landowner of Savernake Forest: 'Yes, you can come up here, you can stay on this forest land.' He is then put under pressure, because historically there is some kind of Forestry Commission right which says, 'You can now not give that consent; only we can give that consent', and indeed he is involved slightly, he is philosophically akin to the travelling ethic as it were.

At that time I was an Inspector in this force, and I was told I had to go to Bulford Camp at six o'clock in the morning (it's a military camp in Wiltshire). And in Hampshire, at that time, there were three highly trained Inspectors, of whom I was one, who were trained to deal with public disorders. So if you take shields – riot situations, if you like – we were the officers highly trained in our unit to deal with that kind of event. I was trained years in advance for that. Our training was not just focused on travellers, it came from... if you go back to riots which occurred in [the] inner cities, in the metropolitan areas of Liverpool in a number of years, that's why we were originally trained and that's how we were equipped. So we've got three Inspectors and I'd say about 80 police officers from Hampshire who were told to go to Bulford Camp, where you will meet with other Commanders, where you will get briefed in relation to this policing operation, because it was perceived [that] you've got

STONEHENGE

THE NATIONAL TRUST AND ENGLISH HERITAGE REGRET TO ANNOUNCE THAT THE FREE FESTIVAL WILL NOT BE ALLOWED ON THE LAND AT STONEHENGE CARED FOR BY THEM THIS YEAR OR IN FUTURE

The monument and the area around it form one of the most important archaeological sites in Europe, and for this reason must be given careful protection. The festival which has taken place in June in recent years has caused serious damage, particularly in 1984, to the National Trust land near the monument which contains many achaeological features associated with the stone circle itself. The Trust has consequently decided, that it should no longer make its land available for the festival. This decision is fully supported by English Heritage. Please do not make plans for a festival at Stonehenge in 1985 and help safeguard our heritage by supporting our efforts to protect Stonehenge and its setting.

Warren Davis
Information Office
National Trust,
36, Queen Anne's Gate
London SW1H 9AS
Tel. (01) 222 9251

Gillian Raikes,
Information Office,
National Trust,
Wessex.
Tel. (0747) 840560

Information Office
English Heritage.
Tel. (01) 734 6010

Help us to preserve the past for the future

The 1985 English Heritage/National Trust poster announcing that the Stonehenge Free Festival will no longer be taking place...

all these travellers in the Savernake Forest and you've got an exclusion zone and there is obviously going to be some kind of attempt to get to Stonehenge.

Now, with all the benefits of hindsight, the policing operation had not been thought through very well, because when we arrived we were told to get to Bulford for a six o'clock briefing in the morning. It became immediately apparent that the traveller community of Savernake had decided to up camp early and were going to get onto the road early, so we actually never had the briefing. What we were given were huge documents: 'Read these and go to the Parkhouse roundabout' (which is a roundabout underneath the A303, which actually is just slightly inside of Hampshire). So I quickly read this plan and the plan went something like this: 'We have got all these lorries full of gravel. If there is an attempt then we will tip this gravel. People will be unable to proceed. We will then try and prevent them going backwards. We [will] then – because it will be a clear contravention of the actual injunction – move amongst them and see what offence has been committed.'

...and the travellers' response. The text reads: '1985 will be the 12th consecutive year Britain's biggest anarchist picnic, Stonehenge Free Festival, has taken place on the same site; if it goes ahead, the festival will be eligible for a Queen's charter making it a legitimate fair forever. The powers that be have said the festival may be 'allowed' to happen again in 1986 (albeit under certain commercial guidelines) but not this year. Wonder why? The National Trust and the Heritage Commission say it won't happen this year but thousands of people say yes it will! For many of us, the midsummer centring on Stonehenge is a religious observance, and has as much to do with religious freedom as personal freedom. Stonehenge is an earth/sun temple which has been our midsummer solstice festival site for 4,000 years. Whose heritage do they think they are protecting? From whom? For whom? Who do they think they are kidding?'

That kind of plan logistically causes a lot of problems, if you think it through. What about their injuries? How do ambulance crews get to the scene? For example, there was one vehicle, which for reasons best known to the travellers, they set on fire. But if you've got 120 [vehicles] in a line [and] you've then got a fire situation, where do all the people go, the children, the adults, all of them? There were some things about it which hadn't been thought through. It had been more about... I would call it 'Fortress Stonehenge', rather than, 'Here is a travelling environment. What can we do?'

I went with the three units to the Parkhouse roundabout, and we were then told, 'This convoy is on the move and it's heading in your direction.' Now, there's a minor road which runs from the Parkhouse roundabout, so we deployed along this road, and ahead of us we had these great big lorries of gravel. I remember saying to the Superintendent for Wiltshire, who we were reporting to at the time, I said, 'You know, you really don't have to tip this gravel, because they're not going to get by these lorries anyway. If you tip this gravel then when we deploy we've got to get over these huge banks of gravel to get to the other side. Whatever we do will then detach us from our own vehicles and all the support and it becomes... it's not a sterile area, it's a very confusing area.' And he assured us, 'I won't tip. Don't worry, I won't tip.'

Well, the moment — this is a long straight road and you can see a mile along the road — the moment the first vehicle came round, he said, 'Tip the gravel, tip the gravel.' So up went 20 yards of gravel, and there was another junction, so the first vehicle saw all this gravel being tipped and turned left, as did everyone else. So if you can imagine: there was a big triangle, so they start going up across the hypotenuse, and we go back to the roundabout and start to come up in the other direction. They then turn right to come back up to the Parkhouse roundabout and are mixed up with members of the public — lots of people there, on what was the A303 — I mean, a major trunk road, [with] lots of other vehicles. Of course they come down and they're met by police vehicles then — not gravel, just police vehicles — and everything comes to a stop.

So the police officers get out and go to the people in that coach and immediately a violent confrontation starts. The next coach sees this, comes out of the traffic and goes straight through a very small fence into the Beanfield, and then in behind drive all the other coaches. So what you end up with is coaches, travellers in the Beanfield, members of the public on the A303... It was affected more by chance, not design, that it actually developed in that way, and I don't think there was... well, there couldn't have been any plan to put travellers into the Beanfield. I mean, I'd like to think we were that organised, but the reality is that we're not...

So in went the travellers. Now the travellers, when they were in the field, actually are not... there wasn't immediately confrontation, and this is what I mean about different people. Some parked down in the valley, and these were families with small children, and there was some confusion as to what was going to happen next. There was this harder element, which stayed very near to the fence, and I can remember this big wrecker that was very near to the fence, and of course we had all the members of the public that were all mixed up on the A303. And you've got this incident going on with the police officers and the one bus which hit each other. And of course people were getting arrested in that coach where the accident people were getting arrested and that was an Avon and Somerset unit. It was their bus that had been hit. We went on past there. We deployed our officers and started to get the members of the public out, seeing the confrontation around the coach. There are the hard element inside, who then get very angry [and] come to the fence [and] then we start getting things thrown. So we then deployed shields — long shields — and along where the public vehicles were... [we were] getting the public vehicles through and there was a stop on any other vehicles going along the A303.

Now, that confrontation between ourselves and those in the field took a number of different turns during the day. To start with it was mild. There then was a period of quite hard activity and at one stage, because we were having so much thrown at us, and it was a range of items — it included petrol, diesel, but with nothing to actually ignite it — so it was more, 'This is what... we could do more than this, this is what we're going to do.' We had things like hand-made spears, stones... because it was a recently ploughed field, so there were stones and the area up here lends itself to flints, and quite a barrage of abuse, and vehicles were beginning to get driven around and driven towards the fence, as if to

'Police officers in uniform are frightening': a female 'prisoner' is escorted off the pasture field. Copyright Tim Malyon.

say, 'we could cut through anytime we want to', and certainly, because we were the only three units there and nobody else was in this road...

What was, I think, the key problem was this: if there had been someone, at that moment, at that time, willing to say to the travellers, 'Let's stop this now, let's sit down and talk this through', I think it would have got sorted out. But when we got someone in authority there – and it was this Superintendent I'd seen at Bulford and, I think, at one stage an Assistant or Deputy Chief Constable – it was very much along the lines of, 'There have been acts of criminal damage caused at the Beanfield and to the fence, and we want to apprehend the people who did that' – well, that was a bit of an unrealistic prospect. A huge amount of coaches had gone in the field. They'd gone in the field not to cause criminal damage but because, in the main, they were confused, didn't know what to do and were, I suspect, frightened, because, you know, police officers in uniform are frightening, police officers in the kind of equipment we were wearing on the day are frightening, and so, I mean, there is that reality about it and that's not a debate about the rights or wrongs.

I actually think we got into that position more by coincidence and chance rather than by, 'This is a design, this is what we intend to do.' At that stage my unit in particular was coming under an awful lot of pressure and I took... I think two of our officers got injured and I knew that I couldn't sustain the position of standing here with people only by the wall, masked behind our shields – I knew that things had got really bad. So I decided to go into the field. Now actually that was a bad decision. On reflection, that was not the wisest thing to do, but I had in my mind, 'If I can just put some distance, if only to frighten people, to make them go back and stay by their coaches rather than let them go on throwing things at us', then I thought that I'd have resolved the situation. So I took the unit into the field and we did go into the field.

We'd only got in about 20 yards when the vehicles began to be driven. Now, the reality is that police officers stood up were no match for people driving coaches, but there was, at that stage, almost hand-to-hand combat taking place – I mean, an open field, and all the rest of it, and we got into the field. All the tactics you were actually taught about street deployment of officers go out the window, because when you actually... all of our training had been, 'this is how you would approach a street or riot situation', 'this is how you deploy people', 'these are the angles' – it's nothing, so you've got nothing other than a vast field, and immediately I actually lost control of my officers. They couldn't sensibly deploy. They were running around avoiding coaches and everything. So I said, 'Right, back', and back we went over the fence, much to the cheers of the travellers, as you can imagine, but that experience was sufficient for me to know that deploying police officers in a field was high risk. It wasn't going to be the best option.

Now, after about four hours – it was that long; they'd keep going up and down and they'd get fed up and have a cup of tea and then come back and do a bit more – there was a meeting of the Inspectors, the Chief Inspectors, the Superintendents and the Deputy Chief Constable, and it took place at the little hotel down the bottom of the hill near the Parkhouse roundabout. And when I got there I said to the Deputy, 'Look, I've been into the field [and] if you go into the field there is going to be a serious problem, because some of the travellers can drive. We won't be able to control it there, [because there is] no way in which [those of us] deployed on foot will be able to handle that situation.' And I said, 'It's very difficult to keep control of your unit if you can't deploy in the traditional sense', and his response was along the lines of, 'Well, that isn't what I'd do anyway. We won't do that. I can assure you we won't deploy, because we'd rather consult and resolve it, and it's probably going to be something we're going to do tomorrow.'

So I actually thought somebody was going to have a proper debate. I went back to my unit and we were then stood down. We'd got from a position of walking down a hill and just taking off fireproof overalls – now, we'd been in them all day, so you can imagine we were wet through – so we took them off and within an hour of that meeting we were told everyone was going through [into the Beanfield] and I think you've seen the pictures.

Interview with Deputy Chief Constable Ian Readhead

If you just look at what the travellers did at that time, because I think it's very important... The first part they went in wasn't the Beanfield. It was actually grass. They drove from the grass up into the Beanfield and up a hill and many of them... the vehicles got bogged down but there weren't any confrontations. They were trying to drive away. They were trying to get away from all these hundreds of officers going into the fields and I remember a helicopter being over top was in there saying, 'Get out of your vehicle, walk towards the police officers', and most of them did. I went into the Beanfield and people just walked and said, 'We've left our vehicle over there.'

Dogs, animals – suddenly all these people were walking back to what was the A303. In the field itself there was complete lack of control. You had some vehicles which were set on fire down in the corner, and I don't know how they were set on fire. I don't know if they were torched by their owners, I don't know how they were set on fire, that wasn't where I was. But as I went back down towards the field, because the Beanfield... you didn't have to go across the field to get into the Beanfield; we went through the hotel and then you're in the Beanfield, and the main activity of this driving around was on the grass area more than it was on the lower end of the Beanfield... but certainly you had these vehicles going round and round, and you've seen it as well as I did that you had the vehicles that eventually came to a halt, and you had officers going in with truncheons, and all in all at the end of the day we ended up with 500 people stood along the A303 being taken all over the place to various locations. And because of the methods used, because of the violence used – which was perceived rightly as being very much police-orientated – the public reaction to that [was that] on the whole the police will go out looking for extreme violence. Yes, they wanted to go to Stonehenge, but perhaps if they were dealt with in a different way they wouldn't have been persuaded to be put in that position.

Do you think there was any relationship between the tactics, or the development of the tactics, leading to the Beanfield and the previous inter-force cooperation around the Miners' Strike, because that's what people believe?

I said about the training. Many of the officers that had been with me had also been in the north, but the reality is that, on that day, we didn't often deploy shields. In the main we were deploying cordons and this sort of thing. With the miners I think the real issue was [that] we had not thought through, 'how do you actually deal with mobile situations with people?' – some people, who are prepared to drive coaches at police officers, how do you deal with that? We dealt with that on the day of the Beanfield in a tactically naïve way. We could have got people killed. You never deploy police officers in situations where they can get killed. It was only by the grace of god that no one was hurt – I mean, some people who were hurt, were hurt by police officers, who, you know, were giving them a bash with their truncheons, and that can't be right either. If you believe in a police force operating in a democracy, they must operate within the law, otherwise you do not have policing by consent; you have a different form of policing...

10 Chapter Ten
'Beanfield Battle Trial'

By Don Aitken and Alex Rosenberger. Originally published in 'Festival Eye', Summer '91

On June 1st 1985, Stonehenge became the alternative society's front line – in what became known as 'The Battle of the Beanfield.' A convoy of 550 men, women and children, on their way to begin the Stonehenge People's Free Festival, were ambushed by 1,400 riot police. All were arrested and locked up, many had their homes smashed, and some had their dogs killed. Last February, 24 of those people heard the verdicts in their four-month civil action against the police. So who won?

The result of the Beanfield trial confused everyone, especially the media. Anyone expecting a simple yes or no verdict was disappointed. In what was probably the longest-ever civil action against the police, the judge and jury had to decide more than 180 questions. It certainly confused the defendant, the Chief Constable of Wiltshire, who put out a press release claiming victory before all the verdicts had been reached.

One of the travellers being arrested during the first assault on the convoy, on the A303 near Parkhouse roundabout. Copyright Tim Malyon.

'Beanfield Battle Trial'

Press reports suggested that the plaintiffs (the people suing) would get damages totalling £28,665.22 – which is also what the jury thought. But the judge had a sting in his tail, which he reserved until most of the journalists had gone – none of the plaintiffs will ever see a penny of the money that the jury awarded.

The plaintiffs were suing for unlawful arrest and imprisonment, assault, and damage to property:
- Though 21 out of 24 plaintiffs won some of their claims, the judge – not the jury – decided the main issue. He ruled that the police decision to arrest everyone that day was lawful.
- Because the plaintiffs had lost the main issue, the judge decided to award them only half of their legal costs. This means that the police will still have to pay the damages but the money will go to the legal aid fund, not to the plaintiffs.
- The police also have to pay all of their own legal costs and half of the plaintiffs' costs – probably over a million pounds.

Those were the decisions of the judge. What about the jury?
- The jury awarded 'exemplary damages' to ten plaintiffs (Helen, Moz, Ribs, Karen, Paul, Steven, Michael, Phil, Keith and Lin). This means that the police were guilty of 'oppressive, arbitrary and unconstitutional conduct'. The largest award was £1,000 to Helen.
- Phil and Mick claimed that the conditions in which they were held (at Bournemouth police station) were so intolerable as to be illegal. The jury agreed and awarded them a total of £1,360.
- All of the serious assault cases succeeded. Eight plaintiffs (Helen, Ribs, Gwyn, Paul, Steven, Michael, Phil and Mick) were assaulted by police officers. Helen was awarded £1,000 for assault, and Mick £2,000. Four claims for minor assaults failed.
- Paul, Steven and Michael, whose dogs were killed on the orders of Superintendent Haste, lost their claims for compensation because the police proved that a local vet and the RSPCA had advised that this should be done. But the jury awarded them £500 exemplary damages each.
- Phil's claim for the loss of his home by fire failed. The judge ruled that there was no evidence that the police could have put the fire out. The jury were only allowed to consider whether the police started it deliberately.
- 11 plaintiffs (Helen, Tash, Mo, Moz, Krystof, Ribs, Gwyn, Karen, Paul, Alan and Lin) won claims for loss or damage to their property (vehicles and contents). One property claim failed. The largest amounts were £3,400 to Moz and £2,210 to Lin.
- The police denied that any plaintiffs had been strip-searched. 11 plaintiffs claimed they had but the jury accepted this in only two cases. Each was awarded £250.
- 22 plaintiffs said they had not been given any reason for their arrest. The jury accepted this in 13 cases and awarded amounts between £140 and £820, depending on how long people had been kept in custody before being told the reason.
- One plaintiff (Krystof) claimed damages for malicious prosecution, including £5,000 loss of earnings. The judge dismissed this claim.

Cover of the first issue of 'Festival Eye', 1986. The magazine was conceived to address the problems surrounding access to Stonehenge and the reInstatement of the free festival, and it remains a focus of the magazine to this day.

During the trial many reasons were put forward to justify the police actions. The police claimed that their operation had been set up to stop the Stonehenge Festival by turning people away. The police knew that a convoy of mostly New Age Travellers would be the first to arrive at Stonehenge to 'take the site.' When they planned their strategy for stopping the festival, the target set firmly in their sights was that convoy.

The minute-by-minute police radio log for that day, a crucial exhibit in the trial, makes it abundantly clear that they regarded the convoy as a military enemy. It contains messages like, 'Vehicles seven through to 15 appear to be the personnel carriers and the

'Festival Eye' was not the only magazine to take an interest in the Beanfield trial. This is the cover of 'The Trial of the Beanfield: Miscarriage of Justice UK', a Suburban Guerillas publication, affiliated to the Stonehenge Campaign.

ones to concentrate on.' One of the most chilling messages came moments before the convoy was stopped: 'Hotel Charlie One [helicopter] to Kilo [headquarters]: Confrontation is imminent. Have you got ambulances standing by?'

Another exhibit, the confidential 'Operation Stonehenge 1985', described the 'Peace Convoy' in the following terms: 'They resent all forms of authority and ownership of property, can be regarded as anarchists and rely on their weight of numbers to maintain, by violence if necessary, their way of life.'

The Battle of the Beanfield

In fact, the convoy stopped on June 1st consisted mainly of New Age Travellers who had only recently gone on the road and city-dwellers who'd come for the festival. Out of the 24 plaintiffs in the trial, only eight were travellers in 1985, only one for longer than a year.

In court the police claimed that all they had wanted to do was to stop the convoy and warn people to turn back. Not according to Inspector Martyn Meeks, a police support unit commander during the operation. Under cross-examination he said that the plan was to arrest everyone 'irrespective of whether they had done anything wrong, beyond being there at that time.'

It was obvious from the start that the judge disliked the plaintiffs – people with alternative philosophies, who had dared to challenge the establishment on its home ground, the High Court; people described by the police as 'lawless anarchists.' His attitude is best illustrated by an incident during the final day of evidence, when Lord Gifford QC, leader of a team of six barristers for the plaintiffs, was cross-examining Lionel Grundy, the police officer who master-minded the Beanfield Operation. The judge – as he had done so many times before, almost always in favour of the police – interrupted. Gifford snapped, 'If Your Lordship will stop batting for the defence...' The judge, taken aback, blustered, 'L-L-Lord Gifford...' Gifford was ready with his apology – after all, this was a serious breach of court etiquette. But the point had been made.

One of the plaintiffs made the point in stronger terms: 'While there's a hole in my arse there'll never be justice in this country.'

Though most of the plaintiffs felt that their main aim – to get the story told –had been achieved, they also felt a strong sense of injustice at the way the judge, Sir Gervase Sheldon, handled the trial. By taking the main decision into his own hands, he was able to deprive the plaintiffs of the damages the jury had awarded for the police atrocities. In the words of one of the plaintiffs' barristers, 'The system of justice has failed.'

Chapter Eleven

Interview with Lord Gifford QC

Conducted by Neil Goodwin and Gareth Morris

How did you become involved in the Beanfield trial, and why did you decide to take the case on?

Well, I became involved in some of the first cases after I defended Don Aitken and Helen Reynolds, when their cases came up before the magistrates' court. And those cases were cases which I accepted from the solicitors, like any barrister does, because, as you know, it's not the barrister who goes to the client or the client who goes to the barrister; the barrister is chosen essentially by the solicitor. And I and other members of my chambers were briefed to take these cases, because our chambers has a broadly 'civil liberties' reputation. Then, when it came to the main trial, there was a general agreement among the different barristers and solicitors who were representing all the different clients, that it was important to have one QC leading the case, and they decided on me, and I was very happy to take it on, because I felt that the issues involved were very serious, and I had no hesitation in accepting the case.

During your summing up, you categorised the principal events of the day in terms of an eight-part mini-series. Could you briefly describe the significance of each of these categories?

What I was trying to do was to make what was inevitably going to be a very long speech have meaning for the jury, so I tried to divide the episode up into chapters or parts, and then to bring together the different evidence that had come in from different places on each part. I knew that, when the judge came along, they were just going to have a long recital from witness 'A' through to witness 'Z', with not very much coherence, and I felt that our case needed to be put across with a kind of coherence. So I started with the previous festivals – Who were the Peace Convoy? Who were the people going to Stonehenge on that day? What were their motives? – pointing out that this whole tragic episode took place because people wanted to have a break, have a holiday, have a festival which they valued as a peaceful gathering. So, part one was the gathering of the festival-goers.

Then I switched the attention, as it were, to the police, and talked about the preparations of the police. And what I was trying to get across was that the police were preparing for a battle, and that, from what one could judge of their plans, it wasn't just a preventive action that they were planning; it was an aggressive action. And I started to go into this very important question, which had arisen during different officers' evidence, as to whether their approach was going to be to persuade people not to go to Stonehenge, or to physically arrest them, confront them and provoke a situation where they could prevent them by taking them into custody. And I gathered together various strands of evidence, which indicated that the real intention was all along to stage a confrontation, whatever the members of the convoy were going to do.

And then the third part was the confrontation of the two sides, as it were, and what actually happened when they met on the main road; and there, of course, I was trying to deal with the question of whether the members of the convoy were showing aggression and a desire to break through the police, or whether it was the police who, in effect, started it.

The fourth part was the lull – I think I called it the 'bogus negotiations' – where there was this period of time when it was quite clear that, whatever people's original intentions, having faced and seen the force which was up against them, the vast majority had decided to go home, to go back. But of course they were never allowed to do that, they were never given that choice, because any officers, including one Superintendent who was on the spot, who would have accepted that... those officers were countermanded by the Assistant Chief Constable, Mr Grundy. And so I was playing up how the agenda of the Chief Constable and his assistant was belligerent and was fixed from the start.

Then part five was the invasion of the Beanfield, and dealt with the actual events, which of course were captured, many of them, on video, and I tried to illustrate, from the way the police behaved – or many of them behaved – what in fact their orders were.

Part six was the nightmare weekend, which the arrested people, all four or five hundred of them, spent in various police stations, being subjected to strip-searches, miserable conditions, being herded around from place to place, and it was trying to capture for the jury the unpleasantness and trauma of that, which of course was what they were going to have to consider in compensating them and awarding damages. So that part of it was really geared towards the sort of damages that they should award.

Part seven was the trashing of the vehicles. I think I called it 'picking up the pieces', but what it really was about was the terrible damage that was suffered to people's vehicles and people's homes by an operation which was completely unrestrained, and people's belongings – which most of them were – were just turned topsy-turvy, and many of them were ruined.

And so that was an important part of the case to devote a chapter to, and then at the end I said that I'd come to the end and that they might wonder what part eight was, and part eight was the verdict of decent people. And that, I said, was the part that you have to write and you have to script, because the saga is not finished, and it can only be finished if decent people pronounce that the behaviour of the police was quite unacceptable in a decent society. So that, in a sense, was the preparation, but it was put in that form so that they felt that responsibility of being actors in the drama, as it were.

It was a very difficult trial for the jury, wasn't it, given the extensive issues involved?

Yes, it was difficult. The most difficult thing for them was that they weren't really deciding the crucial question: were the police entitled to arrest the people in the field? But they didn't realise that, I think, until the very end, where the question started being asked, and...

Trashed vehicles in the police pound: clear examples, to quote Lord Gifford, of 'the terrible damage that was suffered to people's vehicles and people's homes by an operation which was completely unrestrained.'

perhaps, in a moment, we ought to go into why that wasn't up to them to decide. But generally, it was difficult because of the great numbers of people involved. It's very hard for people even to keep a recollection of what the evidence was affecting plaintiff number 15, who may have given evidence three months ago; but a number of them took notes, and the way they considered the issues showed that they had been able to separate out the different issues, so they were a very, very attentive jury and they were a tribute to the seriousness with which people do consider cases when they're jurors. This is something I've always believed in, that the jury system is one of the most brilliant and remarkable parts of our law in that it places upon ordinary people the responsibility of deciding important questions. And they decide them basically on their own, even though the judges and the lawyers speak to them. When they're in that jury room, they're on their own. No one is there to tell them how to go about it, and they have to try to arrive at a view which they can all share, and in this case they came up with some extremely perceptive verdicts – as they do in many other cases.

What do you feel to be the risks involved in a jury trial, given the media's input in creating an atmosphere of hostility towards certain minorities?

I think, in general, the risks of that sort of prejudice are very small; I say, in general. There are times when public prejudice against certain minorities is overwhelming. I think there's a direct link between convictions like the Guildford Four and the Birmingham Six and the Broadwater Farm Three, all of whom were convicted at a time when there was deep, pervasive prejudice against Irish people and against black people. And they were, of course, very notorious cases, where there was a desire to find someone responsible. But in the average case, including this one, people attend to the evidence; they don't attend to the media.

Why did the police think that they were reasonable in their belief that members of the convoy had a common purpose to commit a breach of the peace by establishing a festival at Stonehenge, by force if necessary?

The case that the police put forward was that there were two forces which were bound to confront each other – there was an irresistible force of people wanting to go to Stonehenge, and there was an irresistible force of people trying to stop them. I think the way to put their case, which is really most creditable to them, is that they were faced with the fact that, whether or not they agreed, the festival wasn't going to take place on National Trust land, and, whether or not they agreed, a lot of people felt very outraged by that, and were very keen, if not determined, that a festival should take place. Even a neutral police force would have had some responsibility to ensure that some breach of the peace didn't take place when those two interests clashed. The problem in this case was that the police were not neutral and clearly approved of the decision of the National Trust, and disapproved of the people going to Stonehenge. Their case was that here was a large body of people, some of whom were quite tough, who would have used some force, whether it was by breaking down fences or pushing people aside, to carry through what undoubtedly they all wanted, which was to have a festival. I think this is what the jury also thought by their verdicts, that the police were entitled to take some action to prevent a confrontation, but were not entitled to go over the top as they did.

Behind this case was quite a separate issue, which in a sense the case could not go into, which was: why should the festival be banned in the first place? And that in a sense is the real social question: why shouldn't young people, who have nowhere else to go, who only want to enjoy themselves, without being molested or molesting other people, not have some piece of public land somewhere in this beautiful countryside, in which they can have a few weeks of gathering? And a society which refuses that is not a very humane or civilised society. Now that whole argument, of course, was at the back of the case, but, because of the state of the law, it couldn't really affect the jury's decision or even, I suppose, the police's actions; that's to say, if the law gave the power to the National Trust to say, 'No one will come on our land, and anyone who tries will be thrown out, and we'll take out injunctions against anybody that we know about', then that is the law of the land, and the jury can't really question it, and nor can the police. So once you get that far – however unreasonable that law is, or however unreasonable the action of the National Trust is – there isn't a legal argument to say that they are being unlawful in putting fences around their land.

So that helped the police to make the case that here was a law being enforced – the law of rights of possession of land by the National Trust – and here were a lot of people, who,

The violent underbelly of the 'Heritage' industry? A cartoon reproduced in 'Festival Eye', Summer '91.

frankly, for reasons which I can well sympathise with, thought the law was an ass, and therefore might have taken some steps to subvert that law. I mean, there is no doubt that people did not give much of a thought, or much respect, to the property rights of the National Trust. They felt that the National Trust was a public body – it wasn't like going into someone's back garden – and that the National Trust, as a public body, had no business to fence off its land against the festival. But because they thought that, and some of them thought that very strongly, the police were able to say, 'We think there is a risk of a forcible entry being made to the National Trust land', so it was quite difficult to defeat that case, especially the case, which was put in the first question, that the police did have a reasonable belief that the convoy were going to use force.

It seems to me that that whole question revolves around the use of the word 'force', and I've spoken to a few people who feel that if the word had been 'violence', perhaps there would have been a slightly different answer to that.

It's impossible to say. 'Violence' would not have satisfied the judge, because the legal criterion for a breach of the peace is quite a slippery one, it's quite a low threshold, so that the law would say, and the judge would have said, that a great mass of people marching towards a destination shouting slogans would probably amount to strong evidence that they were going to get to that destination by force if necessary. So we had to steer a course, between what the judge would have accepted as the proper legal touchstone and what the jury might have found, so that violence would not have fulfilled the legal requirement.

After the case for both sides had been presented, how was the verdict reached in the matter of wrongful arrests?

The question of how the verdict was reached on the main claim for false imprisonment, or wrongful arrest, is quite difficult to explain, because the law is a little bit confused. The law says that, in a false imprisonment case, the plaintiff has the right to a trial by jury, but the law doesn't give the jury the right to answer the basic question: has the plaintiff won or lost? Has the plaintiff proved his or her case? The law says that the jury should only be asked specific factual questions, and, on the basis of the factual questions, the judge decides whether the police had enough grounds to arrest the plaintiff. Now that works alright when someone has been the victim of a complete fit-up, where, let us say, the police accuse someone of possessing drugs, and the reality is that they've planted the drugs, because then the jury can decide the factual question, 'Did the police plant the drugs?' and if the answer is yes, the judge obviously has to give the verdict for the plaintiff. But this was a different case, because there was this whole sequence of events, and the facts against us were in some cases quite clear – some people did throw stones, some people did put about leaflets saying there was going to be violence, some people did have sticks, some people did shout angry slogans, so that we had to try to argue with the judge as to what questions to leave to the jury.

And in fact I think we did quite well. We had five questions agreed by the judge and by the police as being the right questions to ask to the jury. And in four of the five cases, the question was, 'At this stage of the day, did the police reasonably believe that the convoy was going to use force?' Right up to the last of the five questions, which was the really important one: 'At seven o'clock, when everyone was arrested, did the police reasonably believe that the members of the convoy had a common purpose to continue a breach of the peace?' Now when we asked that question, we thought, and I think the police lawyers thought, that that was the key question that governed whether the arrest of everyone was lawful, because we thought that the proper standard was that, before you can arrest a whole crowd, you've got to have some evidence on which you can say, reasonably, 'the whole crowd are in this together. They're either fighting or threatening, or they're tacitly supporting and encouraging the people who are fighting and threatening.' And when you, for instance, get a football crowd at one end of a ground who charge through the streets or who charge onto a pitch then the police are entitled to arrest the whole group without having to say, 'he did that or she did that.' And so we agreed that question on that basis.

Now the problem arose when the jury answered the first question, about the intentions of the convoy at the beginning of the day in favour of the police, and the last question, and some of the earlier ones, about the intentions of the convoy later in the day, in favour of the plaintiffs. And that's what caused the real schmozzle. The judge considered that question one was decisive, and that, once the police had reason to believe there was going to be a problem, they more or less had carte blanche to do what they thought right. We said no. Even if question one... we accepted the right of the jury to find question one in favour of the police, and we said any ordinary person listening to this case would say that what the jury think is, at the start of the day, the police were entitled to put up their road blocks, but, as the day wore on and the passive, non-threatening nature of the majority of the people in the field became clear, the police ought to have allowed them to go, which was what they wanted, and they shouldn't have arrested them. And that's obviously what the jury considered. But the judge wouldn't accept that verdict. And so eventually he said that he would pose another question to the jury, which was... well, when I first understood it from the judge, it was: 'At seven o'clock, when they arrested all the people in the field, did the police reasonably believe that the members of the convoy still had a common purpose, to establish a festival at Stonehenge by force if necessary?'

Well, when I heard that, although I thought it was the wrong question, because it directed attention to Stonehenge rather than to what was happening in the field, I wasn't too worried, because I thought the jury would probably give the same answer as they had to question five. But when the question got written out, it said this: 'At seven o'clock, when they arrested the people in the field, did the police reasonably believe that members of the convoy still had a common purpose, to establish a festival at Stonehenge by force?' So it was subtly but very importantly changed, from the police's perception of the convoy as a whole to the police's perception of what some people might do.

The Battle of the Beanfield

And so I immediately asked the judge to come back into court, and said, 'Look, you've made a mistake. There should be a 'v' [for 'various'] in front of 'members of the convoy', which is what there had been in all the previous questions, and he said, 'Oh no, it wasn't a mistake. It was quite intentional.' And I was quite upset, because he had never asked us to comment on that; he'd just thought of that himself. So we did start to comment on it – well, I started to comment on it – and I said that that's not the law. The law doesn't say that if you've got a crowd of 400 people, and you think that 20 or 30 of them might make trouble at some point, that you can arrest all 400. You've got to believe that 380 are supporting the 20; in other words, there's a common intention in the general assembly. And he said no, he didn't agree. He said that the police couldn't distinguish between who was peaceful and who was still wanting to make trouble, and the only way they could find out – or the only way they could prevent trouble – was to arrest everybody. Now, I think if that's the law it's a very serious state of affairs.

But nevertheless that's what the judge said, and he put the jury in a terrible quandary. And the jury showed that they were in the quandary by sending a message to the judge saying, 'We are puzzled by the words 'members of the convoy.' Does it mean all the members, or a few of the members, or a section of the convoy?' And the judge had them in and he said that it means 'any significant number', in a sense anything more than two or three. And so the jury, particularly the ones that were the most sympathetic to the plaintiffs, were in a real dilemma, because they couldn't honestly answer that question in favour of the plaintiffs, because they believed that there was a section of the convoy, however small, that would still have made trouble if it could. And that's why the judge forced the jury into a corner, and that explains why, in the final result, the jury answered the question that, yes, the police did reasonably believe that some members of the convoy still wanted to make trouble. And once they said that, the judge said, 'Well, automatically, they're entitled to arrest everybody, and therefore the plaintiffs' claims have failed, all of them.' So that was it, and I know full well that it leaves the most sour taste in the mouths of both the jury and the plaintiffs, because they feel that they secured the verdict of the jury on the questions as they were put with everyone's agreement, and then the judge changed the goalposts.

Most of the plaintiffs feel strongly that the judge was overtly biased against them. To what extent do you feel they are justified in this claim, and what explanation would you offer for this failure in our judicial system?

There is no doubt that the judge thought that the police had acted reasonably from first to last. That became clear at quite an early stage, and he didn't even try to disguise his view. On the whole, he allowed the evidence to be given and questioned without intervening, so that in his actual behaviour during the evidence, with some exceptions, he was perfectly polite, and he allowed the evidence to be tested and explored before the jury. But there was just one moment, when I was cross-examining Mr Grundy, that I felt so upset by the tone of his interventions that I accused him of batting for the police, and I withdrew it, because it was an unlawyerlike thing to say.

When he came to sum up, he also showed that bias. Now, how does that matter? Usually, in fact, it doesn't matter that much. Usually, a jury has to answer the question: is the defendant in a criminal case guilty or not guilty? They know that that is their decision, and a good barrister will warn them that the judge may be biased, and will emphasise that it's their decision. And sometimes, the more biased the judge is, the more the jury sees through it, and it's actually counter-productive from the judge's point of view. The trouble was, in this case the jury weren't making the final decision, so that the bias of the judge... it still didn't affect the jury, because the jury answered the questions as they thought right, which was not as the judge thought right, but the only problem is that, when the questions were answered, the judge didn't like the answers, which was a serious problem.

But I think what you're more asking me is: is it right that the judge should show bias in this way? My answer is no, it isn't. Particularly in a jury trial, the role of the judge should be to hold the scales evenly between the two parties, and then present the evidence to them dispassionately for the jury to decide. If the judge has to make the decision himself, then of course, in the end, if he thinks something is reasonable, he's got a duty to say so, but he should say so at the end of the case, after he's listened to everyone, after he's listened to all the arguments, and not show his feelings early on. So I do think that that judge did behave in an unjudicial way, and he's one of many who do, and I think that it is a serious flaw in our judicial system, because even if the jury don't listen to the judge – which often they don't – it does give a very bad impression to the plaintiffs, to the litigants, to the public, who sit there and listen and think, 'This judge is not impartial', and one of the things that a judge is meant to be – one of the supreme duties of a judge – is to be independent and impartial. And for a judge not even to give the appearance of impartiality is very serious, and that's so whether or not his own views – from his own social formation – might well be in favour of the police. I think there is a duty on a judge, or there ought to be a duty... it ought to be part of a code of conduct of judges that they conduct themselves in a strictly impartial way, until the time they come to a decision, when they have to decide, obviously, for one party or another, and that is the time that they give their views, but not before. And of course the time they make the decision comes at the end of all the evidence, at the end of all the arguments of the barristers, so they should be showing that they've got a completely open mind until that point. So I think that this case does show up a general weakness in our judiciary.

Following on from that, the plaintiffs have been advised not to appeal against the decisions. Why do you feel that it would be unwise to do so?

The trouble is that in cases involving the police and public order, the judges show a marked tendency to side with the police, particularly over questions of general disorder as they see it. They may be happy enough to uphold the rights of an individual 'X', but, when it comes to the general police deployment against a whole group, it is very difficult to get judges at any level, right up to the House of Lords, to accept what you might call a 'civil liberties' view of individual rights, and a restrictive view of the powers of the police to cause the sort of traumas in people's lives that they did. Now in this case, the appeal court judges will take the case from the judge's summing-up, and the judge's summing-up will underline various features of the evidence. First of all, there are the preliminary questions which led to the jury's answer on question one, that is to say the whole lead-up to this confrontation, and the finding of the jury that the police had reasonable grounds to fear a breach of the peace. Then they will look at all the things that happened – the missiles that were thrown, the pictures of cars and lorries driving at the police – and they will say that the police were justified in what they did, and they may lay down standards of reasonableness, in their terms, which go far beyond what the law has said in the past. So the risk is that, not only do you lose the appeal, but you make very bad law, and make things worse for others if you get an authoritative ruling that, for instance, if the police fear that some people may breach the peace, they can arrest them all. So that what I was saying is that you're not likely to win, and although there are arguments, very strong arguments, that can be put forward, if in fact they're not likely to win, then by losing the case you can make things worse, at any rate for civil liberties in general. So you have to think very carefully whether to try an appeal which may go in that way.

Our best hope was always that a jury could be asked the right questions and give the right answers, and that they would apply their standards, which would be much more in line with what a sensible balance should be between the police and the individual, than the standards of the judiciary. Because what the judiciary think is reasonable is not what you and I think is reasonable, and not, as it turns out, what the average juror in Hampshire thinks is reasonable. And when we got those questions asked, and got the answers to them, we thought that we had got that verdict, but of course the judge took it away, and it's going to be very, very difficult to persuade any other set of judges that that judge was wrong.

How much would you estimate that the police and the government spent on the Beanfield operation in total?

I have no idea, but it must be vast, because the legal fees for a four-month case are huge, there was enormous employment of police just in the preparation and presentation of the case, but it's quite clear from their attitude that they thought it all worthwhile. There was never any hint that they might take a sensible view and make a modest offer, which the plaintiffs might have been well-advised to accept, because their claim was a chancey one, and a fraction of the costs which were incurred could have settled the case at an early stage. But that was never offered at all, and I think it wasn't offered at all on some kind of point of principle that they wanted to establish. Off the record, it's a bit like the Gulf War. You know, you'd apply a vast array of legal and police forces in order to make the point that these people aren't justified in doing what they're doing. And so the costs were huge, but I think that the police had decided to bear them in order to prove a point.

Interview with Lord Gifford QC

How many charges did the police manage to sustain as a result of the arrests on June 1st 1985?

I think it was about 70 out of 500. There was a batch of people, I think, who pleaded guilty to various minor offences at a point. The people who pleaded not guilty were, with very minor exceptions, acquitted. I know of only one case where someone pleaded not guilty and was convicted. In all other cases, people who pleaded not guilty were either acquitted by the magistrates – or sometimes on appeal by the judge – or the charges were dropped against them. But there was a batch of people who pleaded guilty, which increased the conviction rate a bit more than it would have been if everybody had decided to fight.

How do you see the future for civil liberties in this country, in the light of this trial?

I think that the future for civil liberties in this country is very worrying. It's not just this trial. This trial was one of a number of events in the mid-80s, other examples being the miners' strike and the Wapping policing scandals, where a heavy use of police person power, police weaponry and police equipment was deployed, when people were arrested en masse and railroaded through the courts because they were taking a stand which was unpopular with the authorities. I don't want to pretend that that is something completely new, because it isn't. If you go back over history, the police have never sided with those who take a stand against the authorities, and there have been many strikes and many popular demonstrations which have been put down by the police, but in the old days, I think, the tactics were a bit more crude. They would make a baton charge and people would be dispersed, and some would be arrested, but now it seems to be very much more scientific, and likely to get more so.

As against that, the position is never static. One should never look only on the apparent victories of the police, because, for every victory of the police, there are hundreds and thousands of people who are shocked and who are appalled and who make their voices known, particularly when those who are attacked by the police stand up for their rights. And this is why I don't think that the 24 plaintiffs in this case should feel that it's all been in vain. They have focused the attention of a large number of people on the rights and wrongs of this exercise. They have called the police to account. They have forced the senior officers of Wiltshire to come out and justify what they did. They have shown up contradictions between the police in what happened. They have secured a number of verdicts in their favour. They have got a lot of media interested in the case. They have shown that people don't take these things lying down.

And all this is part of the restraining factors which stop and which affect police commanders when they decide what sort of operations to mount, so that you must always have a certain faith in the power of people, even in a very indirect way – of which this is one – to restrain the powers of authority. Now that doesn't mean to say that the

Lord Gifford: 'I think that the future for civil liberties in this country is very worrying.'

legal situation is good; it's not. When the police choose to deploy these large forces, they can usually get away with it, or get away with it certainly to the extent of getting people arrested and not having to pay for it. But even so, the fact is that they don't always act like that, and, when these things happen, there are a lot of people – including some people inside the police – who think to themselves, 'Maybe next time there's a different way of doing it. Maybe next time, we'll do it in a way which doesn't mean that we have to go through all this hassle, with Lord Gifford cross-examining us and thousands and thousands of pounds – if not millions – taken up.' So the case has achieved something, and because of the way in which people stood up for their rights, and, in fact, the way in which the jury responded to that, I still feel positive about the struggles to come.

We've tended to reflect on the gloomy side of the trial, but there were successes. Can you briefly categorise those successes in terms of the individual plaintiffs?

No, I'll categorise them in terms of types of successes. The successes were that the jury found, in about 14 or 15 cases, that people's belongings had been treated with gross disrespect, and that they had suffered serious damage at the hands of the police. They found that the police failed to take proper care, and in many cases thousands of pounds worth of damage resulted. Secondly, the jury found that, in the way that the operation was carried out, the arrests were illegal, because people weren't told why they were arrested, they were just scooped up off the field, and that is against the law, and that was something that they awarded damages for. Thirdly, in two cases they found that people had been held in intolerable conditions, which were quite outside the basic minimum of detention conditions. Fourthly, in two cases they found that people had been strip-searched in a police station for no reason at all. Fifthly, they found that, in about a dozen cases, people had either been assaulted when they were being arrested – in two cases very badly assaulted – or their vehicles had been smashed without any justification, so that again the manner of conducting the arrests was violent and brutal, and one only has to imagine the terror which is created, when police officers come and smash your windows, to know that, when the jury said that, they were saying something very important. And the significance of that was that, in the final success, in about a dozen cases, the jury awarded exemplary damages; that is to say, they said that the conduct of the police was oppressive, arbitrary and unconstitutional, and the police ought to suffer a punitive, extra penalty over and above what would otherwise be awarded for compensation, because of the way they conducted themselves that day. So all those findings amount to a very serious indictment of the way that the various police forces behaved.

Could you explain something about the way in which the judge arranged for the plaintiffs' damages to be nullified?

I think the issue of the judge in effect nullifying the damages, by only awarding the plaintiffs half the costs, is quite a complex one. When you think of it, if someone brought two claims against you, and one claim was unjustified and took up over half the time, and the other claim was justified, but you'd had to pay twice as much costs in defending the case because of the unjustified claim, you would say to the court that you shouldn't have to pay all the costs of the other side, which they've incurred in pursuing the unjustified claim. Why should you have to pay for their lawyers' costs in pursuing a claim which has failed? And if it was your individual money, and you were the defendant, I think you would see the reasonableness of that. It was that principle that was applied to the situation between the police and the plaintiffs. The plaintiffs had in fact lost the claim which took up at least half the time of the court. Now the police still have to pay their lawyers' costs for defending their claim, but what the judge was saying was that they shouldn't have to pay the plaintiffs' costs for the half of the case which was taken up on the false imprisonment claim.

There is a real logic in that, even though the effect of it is to take away the damages. The reason why it takes away the damages is that the legal aid fund is paying for everybody's legal costs. The legal aid fund is putting in a lot of money, and what the law says is that if, in fact, the plaintiffs get some damages then the first chunk of that should go to pay back the legal aid fund. Now normally that doesn't matter, because when you get damages you get costs as well, but here of course it means that the whole sum of damages goes to the legal aid fund. Now I can see how heart-rending it is, but the fact is that we did lose the main claim, and there are reasons therefore why the costs order was made in the way it was.

What about the interest?

The interest is added to the damages, but again it's swallowed up, so the effect is that the police have to pay all those damages and all that interest and half the costs and their own costs. So they have to pay out a lot of money, but because the plaintiffs haven't had to pay for the court case they don't see the results. If in fact the plaintiffs had had a fund and had brought the action privately, of course they wouldn't have recouped the whole of the fund, but they would have got the damages for themselves, but because it was a legal aid case those rules apply, and it wasn't therefore the worst decision that the judge made; it had a logical basis to it.

Given that you spent a considerable amount of time on this trial, how did the verdict affect you personally?

Well, it had different effects on me. I was very, very pleased with the first answers the jury gave, because it seemed to me that they had made a balanced judgment. They hadn't gone all the way down the line for us; on the other hand, it was almost impossible to expect that people would think that the police shouldn't have done anything, but at each point where people were arrested, they had said in effect that there was no reasonable belief that they were doing the things which would have justified the arrest. So I was very happy. I was really upset when the judge didn't accept that verdict, and even more when he changed the basis of the questions. I was upset both as a lawyer, because that was done without any proper argument until I forced it out into the open, and I was upset as a person – and as a civil liberties campaigner – because I thought that the legal principles being applied were far too much stacked towards power in the hands of the police, and far too little in the hands of ordinary people going along the road.

Overall, I'm very happy to have done the case. I'm happy that the issues were brought out into the open, I'm happy that the jury did see the justice of the case, and I'm happy that they did make the awards they did. I've learned a lot from the plaintiffs, and have enjoyed representing them and getting to know them, so I will have a very precious and happy recollection of the case. Obviously, it would be happier if I knew that people were actually getting some damages for what was done to them, but I don't feel, overall, negative about it, because I think it was well worth fighting, and frankly, before it started, I didn't think we had any hope of getting a Hampshire jury to make a favourable decision in favour of people who they would see as some kind of undesirable outsiders.

I think that we took an important stand on the second day, when the press started calling this 'the hippie trial', and that Lord Gifford was representing 24 'hippies', and I just put my foot down and said, 'This word is a racist word, it is a word which is derogatory, it is not accurate and I don't think it should be used in this case.' And I think the jury – and everyone else – then began to see these people as individuals, who had individual integrity and individual ideas about their lives and their children, and they began to see the justice of their case, and the injustice of the way they had been treated. So I think that a lot was achieved, but I wish we could have won.

Chapter Twelve

The Making of the 'Operation Solstice' film

By Neil Goodwin

In the autumn of 1990, during my second year of studying film-making at the London College of Printing (LCP), I teamed up with Gareth Morris to make a documentary about the free festival scene and the travelling lifestyle – two things I knew nothing about. What was originally intended to be a meagre two-week production slot – the briefest taster on the road to gaining my degree – turned into a full-blown 18-month odyssey into the murky world of brutal state repression, media manipulation and judicial farce. It would centre on one of the most sickening chapters in British police history, and join several other high profile revelations of police corruption – the Birmingham Six, the Guildford Four, the Broadwater Farm Three and the investigations into the West Midlands Serious Crime Squad – thereby nailing once and for all society's rose-tinted view that a policeman never lies.

That event – which we were also soon to discover was the tip of a very large iceberg of state trashings aimed at destroying the travelling lifestyle – became known as the Battle of the Beanfield, a massive police operation that was engineered to ambush, capture and decommission a convoy of travellers and festival-goers on their way to the 12th free festival at Stonehenge.

In 1985, I was completely unattached to the free festival scene. Like millions of other people, I had lived my life largely oblivious to the fact that free festivals posed a serious threat to state security. Throughout the early 1980s, the temporary inconvenience felt by holidaymakers and a few local residents rarely broke through a news agenda steeped in mutually assured destruction, famine and inner city turmoil. I had got used to seeing images of our increasingly paramilitary police force grappling with the miners during 1984, but the sudden and startling sun-drenched image of New Age Travellers apparently trying to run down hapless bobbies in a gently rolling pasture field was, in the words of an ITN voice-over at the time, 'difficult to put into context.' I remember thinking that there was something not quite right about the piece. It smelt of panic. As I was later to discover, it was the panic of men, women and children fleeing a marauding army of police thugs, and the panic of hastily erected news censorship to cover up the crime.

Gareth, on the other hand, had attended a number of Stonehenge festivals in the early 1980s, including the last one in 1984. When the time and resources presented themselves at the LCP, he jumped at the opportunity to make a film about the scene. He knew about the Beanfield, but had been in India in 1985. No one, it seems, except a handful of conspirators within the police, the County Council, English Heritage and their solicitors, had any inkling that 1984 would be the last gathering. The festival had gone on for a decade. To Gareth, missing one wouldn't matter. But I have subsequently met many for whom the choice of whether or not to go to Stonehenge in 1985 was inadvertently one of the biggest decisions of their lives.

During the summer of 1990, Gareth conducted an extensive interview with Phil Shakesby (also known as Phil the Beer), who had driven the lead vehicle on the day, and it was through that encounter that he had learnt about a forthcoming Beanfield trial where 24 people were due to sue the Wiltshire Police for assault, damage to property and false imprisonment. The trial was to take place at Winchester Crown Court, and was expected to last four months.

So we cobbled together what little grant money we could and hit the M3, first in Gareth's battered estate car, and later, when living on site became the only sensible option, in an equally battered camper van. Just how we intended to square the covering of a mammoth civil case with a pathetic two-week production slot at college, we had no idea, but from day one in Winchester we knew that here was a story that had to be told, that every person that we'd hoped to interview – journalists, witnesses, travellers – and every shred of evidence that we'd hope to incorporate – videos, reports, photographs, radio logs – would fall into our lap. And despite an initial local media blitz, and the occasional piece in *The Guardian*, no one was on hand to capture the inside story.

During the first week, the court screened two videos back to back – one taken by an ITN camera crew, the other by the police. The ITN material lasted about 50 minutes and mainly covered events from the point at which the convoy, having been attacked at a speedily erected roadblock near the Parkhouse roundabout, took flight into an adjacent pasture field. The quality was about second generation VHS, its once crisp image now rendered grainy with a heavily bled, almost lurid colour. It had the look and feel of something that had been hastily copied and smuggled out.

The bulk of the material concentrated on the ensuing standoff, beginning with the aftermath of the attack – general shots and interviews with injured people being cared for by ambulance crews on the outskirts of the field. One unconscious man is seen being stretchered off with head injuries. Then the camera crew ventured further into the field, capturing a number of interviews with frightened travellers, including a man and his heavily pregnant wife: 'I just want to go, so the baby can be born, like, and have a decent start in life, not surrounded by a thousand coppers with sticks and shields.'

Later on, the Assistant Chief Constable of Wiltshire, Lionel Grundy – who was also the custody sergeant at Guildford Police Station on the night when the Guildford Four were taken in for 'questioning' – is shown telling a crowd that those who give themselves up will be interviewed and dealt with, and that there will be no negotiations. In response, Phil Shakesby, who had had his home destroyed during a similar police operation at Nostell

**Flight in the Beanfield: watched by a cameraman, numerous vehicles attempt to escape the police.
Copyright Tim Malyon.**

Priory in Yorkshire the previous year, is shown pleading with ITN (and by extension the wider British public): 'We're genuine people like yourselves and we need help. Help us, please. Help us. Stand by us.'

Then the police move in – in lines of short shield units, with truncheons drawn – belting across the field towards the travellers' vehicles. Some start to move off. A policeman says, 'Pick a vehicle?' The ITN crew try to film three youths being searched on the ground. One of the officers punches the lens, snarling, 'Get out of it!' Several short shields then block the image. On one occasion, we see a clearly hyped-up officer maliciously smashing a coach window. A senior officer orders him to 'Just calm down!' before trying to coax some obviously terrified travellers from the vehicle. The camera follows the action round to the driver's door, where a man emerges with his hands up. 'On the deck! On the deck!' growls a policeman, before punching him in the face with the side of his truncheon, and dragging him to the ground. A pair of jackboots can be seen stepping on the hand of the now-weeping man. Some of the officers at this point can be seen wearing light blue scarves round their necks. It was pointed out during the trial that the more violent officers on the field wore these scarves across their faces to avoid identification. Many officers also didn't have their numbers showing.

In contrast to the clearly unfolding human tragedy in the ITN footage, the police video was shot at a fixed wide-angle at the edge of the field, and felt and looked like CCTV. It gave nothing away except for the logistical nuts and bolts of the operation. A rare close-up showing 'an array of weapons gathered up' – household implements and tools that can be found in any house in the country, let alone a traveller's bus – was later used by the BBC, presumably without question.

However, the police video does reveal an extraordinary chase. Towards the end of the operation, the police commandeered a coach and, in scenes reminiscent of a demolition derby, tried to run down the so-called Rasta Bus, the last vehicle to hold out. As officers on foot throw rocks and fire extinguishers at passing windows, the police coach can be seen swerving into and shunting the rear of the fleeing Rasta Bus, trying increasingly desperate measures to bring it to a halt.

The ITN footage only showed brief snippets of the chase, but it did capture what happened when the Rasta Bus was finally taken. At this stage, the police turned into a frenzied mob, and rushed towards the crippled vehicle. We can see the police jostling the ITN camera crew out of the way, followed by a few seconds of erratic camera movements. Somewhere a young voice pleads/screams, 'Someone help me! Someone help me!' and we suddenly see the sickening sight of a boy, perhaps 15 years of age, being frogmarched past, his terrified face covered in blood. The shot lasts for a fraction of a second, after which the camerawork becomes erratic again, and we hear more screams.

With that one bloody image – to me the most graphically violent on the tape – it's as if a heavy curtain of censorship has parted just for a moment to reveal a glimpse of pure wickedness, the true tone of the day's events. Most of the court flinched when shown this image, as has every audience to whom I have ever shown the film. A young woman is shown being removed from the field. 'See what they're doing to us!' she screams at the camera. And we start to wonder whether we have really seen what 'they' were doing to them.

Moments later, we see a clearly shaken Kim Sabido, ITN's reporter on the day, delivering his piece to camera. Standing in the middle of the field, with several officers walking past, some quite cheerful, he states, 'What we, the ITN camera crew and myself as a reporter, have seen in the last few minutes on this field, has been some of the most brutal police treatment of people that I have witnessed in my entire career as a journalist. There must be an inquiry. I don't know what the results of it will be. But at this stage, the number of people who have been hit by policemen, who have been clubbed whilst holding babies in their arms in coaches around this field, has yet to be counted. But there must surely be an inquiry after what has happened here today.'

On the evening of June 1st, the ITN broadcast, which I had seen at the time, chose to entirely ignore Sabido's piece to camera. Instead, the voice-over was delivered by the company's solicitor, and the piece focused on shots of coaches supposedly bearing down and attempting to run over officers in the field, coaches that we now know were desperately trying to flee from police brutality.

The Battle of the Beanfield

In the early 1980s, Kim Sabido was practically a household name. He had covered Northern Ireland and the Falklands War. He was a trusted member of staff, not given to exaggeration and hyperbole. He had been injured in a traffic accident, and the Beanfield was one of his first assignments upon recovery. During the trial, still appalled by what he had witnessed six years before, he appeared as a witness for the travellers, and later repeated his testimony to us on camera (as reproduced in Chapter Six). In the courtroom, however, the police tried to assert that his accident had left him a nervous wreck, prone to confusion.

We later paid a visit to ITN's offices in London to search through their archive, and were shocked to discover that only two or three minutes of Beanfield footage remained. We were told that, due to storage problems, only the transmitted news pieces were saved, that they simply didn't have the space to store tens of thousands of hours worth of rushes. Even so, the paltry material that they had hung onto contained only amputated scenes, where all the shots were cut before anything remotely controversial happened. For example, we saw a policeman running towards a bus, but we never saw him arrive, and this is probably to do with the fact that in the abandoned seconds after that cut, the policeman smashes the windscreen with his truncheon.

Soon after we'd trawled through ITN's archive in London, we visited the headquarters of HTV in Bristol to investigate whether or not they held any Beanfield footage in their library. We had heard that Kim Sabido's material had been sent back to London via a landline from HTV. Was it possible, we wondered, that a copy of the rushes had been made at the time and had been inadvertently stored away? If so, perhaps it contained additional material to the tape shown in court. As it turned out, we were shown a tape that matched entirely – right down to the tape glitches – our video. Exactly, that is, except for one significant addition.

At the beginning was a press conference with Donald Smith, the then Chief Constable of Wiltshire. This had been shot on the morning of June 1st, and in our final cut of 'Operation Solstice' it's the scene where Smith, seated in front of a huge aerial photograph of the 1984 festival site, says, 'We are prepared for any contingency which may arise.' However, on the HTV tape, there's this little pre-amble scene, presumably shot whilst all the other cameras and microphones were being set up, where Smith states, 'I hope that you are aware of the memo that was sent out to your senior editors.' He then seems to grasp the context within which he's saying this, and slips in a quick, 'Of course, this is completely off the record', whereupon the camera instantly cuts. With all the censorship that we now knew had taken place during the media's coverage of the Beanfield, we were left wondering just how cosy the relationship had been between the police and so-called independent news gatherers such as ITN.

After the screenings, the jury was clearly pensive. Since being called up for jury service they must have wondered what kind of a trial they would end up getting. Now they knew. They were about to spend the next four months in a foreign land, a mysterious and dangerous country, a land of arcane attitudes and rituals, where chief police officers run their counties like mini feudal kingdoms, a place where landless peasants get 'twatted' and 'fitted up', their animals destroyed, their homes burnt out. Somewhere more akin to Robin Hood's day than a modern democracy. Somewhere called England – perhaps a million miles away from where they'd been told they lived.

Many of the travellers involved in the trial had parked up on the outskirts of Winchester on a green lane site known as Kingsworthy. It was a strip of muddy track, surrounded by farmland, a place to walk dogs and ride ponies, and occasionally for local youths to burn out stolen cars. For four months, it became our home and production base, and during those freezing winter nights of 1990-91, on a strict diet of tuna and mayonnaise, it became a kind of university, where we'd huddle around wood stoves in candlelit 'Blim' caravans, 'proper' Routemaster buses, and coaches, taking in and recording a fascinating, sometimes hilarious, often terrifying, oral history and herstory. As I have said, the Beanfield was the tip of a very big iceberg, and for four months Gareth and I sunk deeper and deeper beneath the waves.

Ten years after Vietnam and ten years prior to the road protests of the 1990s, civil disobedience largely focused on preventing the deployment of Cruise missile bases around the country. In exchange for bailing us out during World War II, the US had managed to wrangle possession and legal jurisdiction over a number of British airbases. And during the 1980s, at what turned out to be the start of the final, and arguably the darkest, dirtiest and bloodiest chapter of the Cold War, people started to blockade these bases, drawing daily attention to the insanity of a foreign policy that amounted to little more than the promise of mutually assured destruction. This was Wild West diplomacy, a time of Afghanistan, CIA-backed death squads in Central America and 'Protect and Survive' public information leaflets on every high street. This was also a time of the Women's Peace Camp at Greenham Common, and the Peace Convoy at Molesworth.

Many of the travellers living at the Kingsworthy site had been part of the Peace Convoy – a highly mobile, self-sufficient and effective makeshift village of activists that could lay siege to the gates of Cruise missile bases and nuclear power stations. Part of their shared vision came from the Hopi peace prophesy of the Rainbow Warrior, which says, 'When the earth is sick and all the animals have disappeared, there will come a tribe of people; people of all races and all cultures, people who believe in deeds not in words. They will restore the earth to its former beauty. These will be known as the Warriors of the Rainbow.'

During the early 1980s, traveller numbers had swollen yearly with thousands of people now choosing a 'bedsit on wheels' as a viable alternative to just scraping by in a decaying inner city. An increasingly vibrant summer season of free festivals offered opportunities to make cash, which could then be squirreled away for home improvements and basic survival during the long winter months. At the time of the Beanfield, some 12,000 so-called New Age Travellers had sussed out that this alternative lifestyle offered an escape

Pre-Beanfield optimism: 'You have been misinformed (as usual). Stonehenge 1985 Free Festival shall happen.' Copyright Alan Lodge.

route out of long-term unemployment and recession. Clubbing together with a few mates to buy a VW van gave you freedom and placed you on a kind of alternative property ladder, from which you could save up for a horsebox or a coach. A double-decker bus could be converted into a three-bedroom home within which to raise a family. The lifestyle also gave you the freedom to lay siege to Cruise missile bases. (As a reversal of fortune, in the 1990s, and in the context of the emerging Criminal Justice Act, laying siege to road protest sites provided many travellers with the only means by which to have a lifestyle at all).

The highlight of this growing festival season, and the main engine room for a flourishing black economy, was the free festival at Stonehenge. By shutting down the festival, and destroying the homes that allowed the lifestyle to flourish, the state knew that it would not only kill the threat of a good example, but also undermine an increasingly expensive and troublesome protest movement. 'Stonehenge was just the excuse', said Mo Lodge, who was arrested at the Beanfield and later strip-searched and kept caged in a freezing cold garage for six hours. 'They knew how strongly we all felt about Stonehenge, and knew that was a good reason. But the real reason was the threat to the state. The numbers of people were doubling every year for four years. Well, that was a huge number of people that were suddenly flocking into buses or whatever and living on the road. And the festival itself, once it came to be a month long, it functioned perfectly well. It had its own economy. It had its own system for everything. And it was so successful in that sense that it must have been a huge threat to the state. It was anarchy in action, and it was working. And it was seen to be working by so many people that they wanted to be a part of it too.'

Living on site gave us a window into a secret history, one much maligned by the mainstream media, who viewed the Peace Convoy as an oppositional force or army, a marauding pack of revolting peasants terrorising the countryside. Consider the spin that the HTV journalist Brenda Rowe gave the convoy on the morning of the Beanfield as it wound its way down to Stonehenge. 'This is the front of the convoy', she said. 'The women and children have been left at Savernake Forest. They're all heading to Stonehenge, which is 18 miles away.' The media's spin required the notion of a hippie assault, and invasion forces tend to leave the women and children behind. The tone of the news matched the police's mindset. The police radio log contained lines such as 'vehicles seven through to 15 would appear to be the personnel carriers and the ones to concentrate on', and most journalists soaked it up. After the Beanfield, one of the tabloids actually carried a cartoon of 'hippies' invading Stonehenge in tanks marked 'Peace Convoy.'

Each morning during the trial, we'd prise ourselves out of the camper van, smoke several rollies, and head into town. We'd brief ourselves on the way in, reminding ourselves of the previous day's events. Don Aitken, who had helped to set up the Windsor Free Festival in the 1970s, and had been the traveller and festival scene's legal representative for over a decade, provided excellent insight into the legal shenanigans. Alex Rosenberger, editor of *Festival Eye* at the time, had taken exhaustive notes throughout the trial, and knew who'd said what to whom weeks down the line.

So much people-watching goes on in court: watching the judge, watching the witnesses, watching the jury, watching the judge watching the jury watching the witnesses. And all the time analysing body language – facial expressions, twitches, furtive or defiant glances; even, perhaps, the odd Masonic signal. When, during a difficult cross-examination, Lionel Grundy clamped his open palm to his forehead and peered up at the public gallery, looking for all the world like an admiral in an amateur dramatic production of Gilbert and Sullivan, was this in fact a Masonic distress signal, a cue for the judge to interject? On the level, that's exactly what happened.

In the court canteen, we'd sit across the room from huddles of police witnesses and jury members. Between the tea and biscuits we'd scan photographs or snippets from the police radio log. On most days we were finally given the chance to put faces to names:

You can't kill the spirit (1): Maggie Dixon and friend, who helped out with the operations of Festival Welfare Services, making cakes at Savernake after the Beanfield. 'Chocolate Crispies, still only 10p. Same price as last year', was their cry, according to Alan Lodge. Copyright Alan Lodge.

Kim Sabido, Nick Davies. And having witnessed their court appearances, Gareth and I would seize our moment to nail that all-important interview.

One unusual eyewitness to the Beanfield was the Earl of Cardigan, whose memories of 'unspeakable' police violence, including the sight of a heavily pregnant woman 'with a silhouette like a zeppelin' being 'clubbed with a truncheon', and riot police showering a woman and child with glass, are described in detail in Chapter Seven. During the Beanfield trial, the Earl made the poignant observation that 'I had just recently had a baby daughter myself, so that when I saw babies showered with glass by riot police smashing windows, I thought of my own baby lying in her cradle 25 miles away in Marlborough.' And it was his testimony – that he had witnessed a policeman attempting to drag one of the plaintiffs, Helen the Hat, by her hair through a window 'framed with broken glass' – which, together with photographs of the incident, eventually persuaded the Winchester jury to find in favour of Helen's assault claim.

After the Beanfield, some of the crippled vehicles had managed to crawl back to Savernake Forest. Bolstered by the green light that they had now been given by a complicit mass media, the Wiltshire Police approached the Earl of Cardigan to gain his consent for an immediate eviction. There was to be no sanctuary. 'They said they wanted to go into the

You can't kill the spirit (2): site meeting at Savernake, after the Beanfield. Copyright Alan Lodge.

campsite 'suitably equipped' and 'finish unfinished business.' Make of that phrase what you will', said Cardigan. 'I said to them that if it was my permission they were after, they did not have it. I did not want a repeat of the grotesque events that I'd seen the day before.' Instead, the site was evicted using court possession proceedings, allowing the travellers a few weeks' recuperative grace.

As a prominent local aristocrat and Tory, Cardigan's testimony held unusual sway both at the time of the Beanfield and at the Winchester trial. For over five years, he had become an unforeseen thorn in the side of those seeking to cover up and re-interpret the events on the day. In 1985, in an effort to dampen down the impact of his testimony, several national newspapers began painting him as a 'loony lord', questioning his suitability as an eyewitness, and drawing farcical conclusions from the fact that his great-great-grandfather had led the disastrous Charge of the Light Brigade. An editorial in *The Times* on June 3rd claimed that being 'barking mad was probably hereditary.'

As a consequence, the Earl of Cardigan successfully sued *The Times*, *The Daily Telegraph*, *The Daily Mail*, *The Daily Express* and *The Daily Mirror* for claiming that his allegations against the police were false and for suggesting that he was making a home for hippies. He received what he described as 'a pleasing cheque and a written apology' from all of them. His treatment by the press was ample evidence of the united front held between the prevailing political clampdown and the media's backup, with Cardigan's eyewitness account as a serious spanner in the plotted works: 'I hadn't realised that anybody that appeared to be supporting elements that stood against the establishment would be savaged by establishment newspapers. Now one thinks about it, nothing could be more natural. I hadn't realised that I would be considered a class traitor. If I see a policeman truncheoning a woman, I feel I'm entitled to say that it is not a good thing you should be doing. I went along, saw an episode in British history and reported what I saw.'

For four months during the trial, every detail of the operation was examined in minute detail. Dozens of photographs taken before, during and after the Beanfield were shown to the jury, the police radio log and report were picked apart sentence by sentence, and there were more than a hundred police witnesses. According to Don Aitken, 'Inconsistencies were two a penny. Whenever more than one policeman saw the same event the descriptions were completely different. And to some extent you expect that. The things that surprised me were not so much the inconsistencies as the omissions – and how critical some of them turned out to be. For instance, on the police video, which turned out to be quite important, there is a piece missing. Nobody knows how large a piece. Estimates vary from a few seconds to more than a minute, where the tape, we are told, accidentally broke. But that is at the crucial moment where the convoy is stopped.' In addition, the police radio log contained breaks of a couple of minutes, where the tape had supposedly been changed. As each inconsistency came to light, and cracks in the police's version of events seemed to lengthen and widen, we studied the faces of the jury. Had they got it?

As it turned out, the question of whether or not the jury 'got it' didn't seem to matter. On the central issue of whether or not the police were entitled to mass arrest everyone on June 1st 1985, as was discussed in Chapters Ten and Eleven, it was the judge who determined the verdict by ensuring that the question put to the jury hinged on whether 'members of the convoy' (anyone on the Beanfield), as opposed to 'the members of the convoy' (specifically the 24 plaintiffs), 'still wished to force their way to Stonehenge' at the time that the police moved in. As Nick Davies mentioned in his interview, there was a point, during the stand-off on the day, when someone had argued with Grundy when he refused to distinguish between those he alleged had actually committed offences, and the rest, by saying, 'That's crazy. If you had a couple of football hooligans in a football stadium, you wouldn't arrest everybody in the stadium just to get at the hooligans.' But that was the police's position on June 1st 1985, and the outcome of their operation. And that was the verdict that the judge managed to swing in Winchester five years later by dropping the word 'the' from the key question. As Lord Gifford said in his interview, and in an excerpt that was used in the film, 'It leaves a very sour taste in the mouths of both the jury and the plaintiffs' – so sour in fact that some of the jury, once they realised the coup, left the court in tears.

After the verdict, everyone headed back to the site to discuss the options. This included Lord Gifford and his team of barristers. There was talk of lodging an appeal, but the likelihood of another stitch-up might have created a dangerous legal precedent, increasing police powers of mass arrest. Plus, having waited five frustrating years for justice, and enduring the legal and emotional mangle of a four-month trial, everyone was burnt out. Gareth and I kept out of the meeting, deciding instead to rattle off a few cutaways. I remember thinking that it would be good to get a shot of Gifford on site when he emerged from the meeting, perhaps even a vox pop. Throughout the trial we'd largely steered clear of him, but he knew about the film, and a future full-blown interview with him was definitely at the top of our wish list.

As we removed the camera from the boot, a police car appeared from nowhere and came careering along the track, its wheels slipping and sliding in the mud. Its two occupants stared straight ahead, fixed and determined, as their left wing ploughed into the back of a truck, sending a loud crunching sound across the valley. Gareth and I were amazed, as was the owner of the truck who came steaming out of his caravan. 'What the fuck are you doing?' he shouted, to which one of the policemen cockily replied, 'Well, you shouldn't have parked it there!' This had to be provocation. For the past four months the trial had afforded the site immunity from police harassment, but on the very day of the verdict, with everything now done and dusted, the police were obviously trying to pick a fight, the classic fast-track approach to eviction. It was a typically heavy-handed way of saying, 'OK, party's over. It's time to leave.'

With feelings already running high, they were expecting an 'incident', something requiring 'back-up', something that could be flashed across the front page of the local paper. But those hapless coppers got a lot more than they bargained for, because, within seconds of the crash, not only did a team of top barristers suddenly appear from Phil's bus, but also a camera crew. Embarrassment is not the word. They had, 'How the hell are we going to explain this one to the Sarge?' written all over their sheepish faces. And while Gareth focused on a deliciously uncomfortable close-up, I remember twisting the knife by saying, 'I bet you must be wondering what else we managed to film?'

All that time spent on location in Winchester was playing havoc with our studies. We were initially only given a two-week production slot, and we eventually spent over 30 days on site. Trying to convince the head of the course about the urgency of covering the trial was proving hard. We were completely on a mission, and perfecting the very skills that we'd gone to film school in the first place to master, but 40 percent of the course was theory and we'd missed dozens of tutorials.

To make matters worse, our personal tutor, an expert in Cuban cinema, whose main claim to fame appeared to be an interview with Fidel Castro, had taken a dislike to us. He was so intent on bringing us to heel that he tried to enforce a compulsory tutorial on the day of the trial verdict, knowing full well that we wouldn't turn up. Consequently, the college banned us from continuing with the film and withdrew all facilities – although the course leader, who was apparently an ex-Israeli tank commander, secretly admitted to us that he admired 'impossible' students. The ban meant that we had to find other means of production, and this came in the shape of the Video History Trust, which had been set up to archive contemporary history. Editing was provided by Faction Films in Clerkenwell, who let us use generous amounts of down-time on their VHS off-line suite.

Throughout the production, we travelled over 7,000 miles in order to capture some 50 hours of testimony. The Gulf War had just kicked off, and we knew that, without our film, the trial would be buried, and precious few people in the wider society would appreciate the gravity of the Beanfield. Our plan was to use the trial as a window into the events of 1985, and expand the public gallery at Winchester Crown Court to the size of thousands of living rooms across the country. As luck would have it, this became 1.3 million living rooms, or enough people to fill 16 Wembley Stadiums.

There's a saying in the world of TV: it's not what you know, but who you know. And so it was with landing a commission from Channel 4. In this case, the 'who you know' turned out to be a friend of a neighbour of a friend: Gareth had an old friend whose neighbour just happened to be a TV producer, and he had a friend who just happened to be an Assistant Commissioning Editor at Channel 4. The TV producer was Rebecca Dobbs, who ran a production company called Maya Vision, and we managed to set up a screening of our rough cut round her North London flat. 'Operation Solstice' wasn't quite Maya Vision's thing. They were more into travel, ancient history and adventure. However, Rebecca's old pal at Channel 4, Caroline Spry, was on the lookout for hard-hitting documentaries for her 'Critical Eye' series. During the previous run, 'Critical Eye' had taken on Despite TV's 'Battle for Trafalgar', a condemnation of the heavy-handed policing methods used during the 1990 Poll Tax Riot in London. Spry and her boss, Alan Fountain, liked to nurture up-and-coming talent: it was one of the original and fundamental values of the channel. And like us, Despite TV (later to become Spectacle Films) were anarchist film-makers, coming from the sharp end of Thatcher's Britain, and championing the cause of marginalised people.

We were eventually called in to Channel 4, where it was decided to give us 25 minutes, or half the slot. The other half would go to another production about the Battle of Orgreave. At the time of the Beanfield trial, the police had coughed up substantial compensation to miners injured and falsely imprisoned during demonstrations at the Orgreave coking plant in Yorkshire in 1984. There were many similarities between Orgreave and the Beanfield. Both the travellers and the striking miners were considered to be 'an enemy within', a threat to democracy and the economy. Both were depicted in the right-wing press as an invasion force – the 'other' – a marauding army intent on occupying private land, abusing local people, and openly flouting the law. Both provided the Thatcher government with the ideal public order situations with which to manufacture and sell increasingly draconian police powers to an increasingly gullible British public – in both cases, laws preventing movement and congregation. Both Orgreave and the Beanfield involved a pre-ordained police operation, the cooperation of several neighbouring county forces, and an increasingly para-militarised style of policing, which was pro-active rather than responsive. Finally, both the Battle of Orgreave and the Battle of the Beanfield involved a media cover-up — ITN's cover-up at the Beanfield, and the BBC swapping the order of events during their coverage of Orgreave, where a police baton charge provoked a stone-throwing incident, and not the other way around as reported on the BBC news — although at least the BBC later apologised.

So that was the deal: half a slot, with over four months of court evidence, hundreds of photos, nearly 50 hours of testimony, and over 50 minutes of previously censored ITN footage needed to somehow fit into a 25-minute film. We vowed to make it as concise and as hardcore as we could. The transmission date was set for November 7th 1991.

Two days before transmission the police made their move. A series of trailers containing snippets of previously unbroadcast ITN footage had alerted Wiltshire police to the potentially explosive nature of the film. What they hoped had been buried during the depths of winter in a Winchester courtroom was now about to reach hundreds of thousands of people. But what, exactly, did the film contain?

The police demanded to see it, warning that Channel 4 could be in contempt of court due to a dozen outstanding civil court cases. At the time there were still a number of outstanding civil cases involving people suing the police for damages for unlawful arrest and false imprisonment arising from events closer to Stonehenge on June 1st 1985. Like the Beanfield trial, the system had kept these civil actions in a seemingly permanent state of pending for several years. But now that 'Operation Solstice' had snuck up on the Wiltshire Old Bill completely unawares, they had been panicked into furiously attempting to get a court date set for these civil cases in order to persuade the Attorney General that the documentary was somehow sub judice. Of course, to pull the film then — it was the second to last slot in the series — would have meant that it would probably have never got shown. And if it had, the police would have no doubt worked it so that valuable air-time would have been soaked up with their chapter and verse.

One of the daily obsessions of the state at the time was with 'balance' and 'impartiality.' Television had to somehow work in a social vacuum, and audiences had to be allowed to 'make their own minds up', as if their daily lives weren't bombarded in a million other different ways by corporations and politicians. As far as the Beanfield was concerned, the police had completely sewn up the media's interpretation of the events on that day (as well as countless other events since, involving New Age Travellers and their right to live an alternative lifestyle). If anything, 'Operation Solstice' was merely a drop in the ocean in terms of countering a decade of black propaganda and state-sponsored terrorism against this minority group. To give the police their so-called right to reply would have meant losing two or three sound-bites from people who had been deprived of their voice for too long. As far as we were concerned, the police made their position perfectly clear on June 1st 1985, with smashed windows and broken limbs. 'Operation Solstice' in its entirety was the travellers' right to reply (and a meagre 25 minutes, at that). So Channel 4 refused to cave in to the police's demands, and just two hours before transmission the Attorney

General agreed. Nothing could now prevent the truth from escaping out into the collective consciousness, frame by frame, at 25 frames per second.

On the evening that the film was aired, there were over 80 calls to Channel 4's duty officer – 76 in favour, 12 against. Comments ranged from 'blood ran cold' and 'courageous and frightening, to 'biased rubbish' and 'brainwash the public.' Some were made by both serving and ex-coppers. All were anonymous. One, who was involved in the Brixton and Southall riots, said that he was 'not at all shocked by what he saw, because he left the Metropolitan Police because of just this sort of thing.' Another call came from the wife of a serving policeman. She was clearly in a quandary. She didn't dispute the facts, but felt that 'such programmes are not doing the police any good.' She felt frightened for her husband: 'He is not sure how long he can continue with the job, when the police receive so little respect from society.' Even though she thought that Channel Four was 'brilliant', she blamed the media for their portrayal of the police, which 'makes the policeman's job very hard.'

Some of the callers couldn't believe that Channel Four had actually had the nerve to show it, which was a feeling that I shared. During the 1980s, it had largely stayed true to its remit to cater for minority groups and unorthodox attitudes. Free-thinking radicals and liberals had made it their home, a place where injustices were exposed and government policies challenged. Even 'Brookside', its resident soap opera, was relatively gritty and 'on it'. By the early 1990s, standards were starting to slip. Minority interests could now be construed as wine-making or military history. Apparently the ABC1s, the consumer spending bracket most likely to attract advertising – the channel's life blood – weren't interested in human rights and social justice any more. We weren't aware of it at the time, but documentary strands like 'Critical Eye' were on the way out. Even so, many of the callers to Channel Four that night seemed to be welcoming a return to form.

A few months after the broadcast, we got a surprise phone call from our producer. 'Operation Solstice' had been nominated for a British Film Institute (BFI) Archive Achievements Award, and Gareth and I had been invited to an awards ceremony to be held at the National Film Theatre in the presence of HRH Diana, the Princess of Wales. What a trip that turned out to be. There I was, completely burnt out, broke and living in a squat in Peckham, and I had to somehow track down the funds for a tuxedo and start hob-nobbing with the rich and famous. Thanks to my folks, who bailed me out on so many occasions, I hired a 50-pound penguin suit from Moss Bros.

On the night, the hundred or so paparazzi that were waiting for Diana to make an appearance gave me my first real glimpse of the rising cult of the celebrity, a trend that would eclipse so much real news throughout the last decade of the 20th century. Needless to say, Diana looked wonderful. Needless to say, we didn't win. And needless to say, we were the last to leave the dinner that followed the awards ceremony. They were literally taking the marquee down around us as we stuffed as much booze, fruit and nibbles into our pockets as we could and began the journey back to Kennington.

Chapter Thirteen

A conclusion of sorts

By Andy Worthington

While the full details of what took place at the Battle of the Beanfield – and in the fields and roads around Stonehenge – on June 1st 1985 may never be known comprehensively, I hope that this book has gone some way to creating a fuller picture than has been documented before.

Of particular interest to me, as I have compiled this book, has been the viewpoint of the police and the details of their operations, as revealed in particular through the extensive excerpts from the police radio log reproduced in Chapter Eight. As it stands, this document is not the 'smoking gun' that some readers may have anticipated, containing no evidence of direct incitement on the part of the commanders to encourage their men to commit the acts of brutality which undoubtedly took place – and which are reported, with such shocking candour, by the various witnesses interviewed in the preceding chapters. The investigation of this theme is not something I propose to abandon, however – and it's something I will return to and examine in further detail towards the end of the chapter. First of all, though, I'm going to analyse two specific areas in which the police radio log explicitly reveals significant failings on the part of the police, from the top of the command chain downwards, for which the travellers paid a heavy price on the day – the failures of intelligence gathered in advance, and the dreadful significance of errors that were made during the day.

Failures of intelligence

The intelligence gathered by the police in advance was inadequate in a number of alarming ways, relying on a mistaken interpretation of the convoy as an armed and hostile force, an inability to determine the travellers' motives, and an inability even to understand that what was referred to as one entity – 'the convoy' – was in fact made up of many varied components. These misconceptions are evident, in the police radio log, in the oft-quoted suggestion, from Chief Superintendent Denning in the helicopter, that 'The vehicles seven through to 15 would appear to be the personnel carriers and the ones to concentrate on.' Assistant Chief Constable Grundy's description of Phil Shakesby as the convoy's 'leader' is equally mistaken, as is his comment, which I have not seen reproduced before, that 'there is a red coach, which is next to last of the convoy, containing 20 hardcore members.'

At the trial in 1991, it became apparent that many of these misconceptions were based on a confidential 'Operation Solstice' report, prepared by Wiltshire police in the build-up to the operation, which was revealed to the plaintiffs during the case. One of these passages was quoted by Don Aitken and Alex Rosenberger in Chapter Ten: 'They resent all forms of authority and ownership of property, can be regarded as anarchists and rely on their weight of numbers to maintain, by violence if necessary, their way of life.' Another was quoted by Jim Carey in 'A Criminal Culture?', his authoritative article for *Squall* magazine in 1997: 'There is known to be a hierarchy within the convoy; a small nucleus of leaders making the final decisions on all matters of importance relating to the convoy's activities. A second group who are known as the 'lieutenants' or 'warriors' carry out the wishes of the convoy leader, intimidating other groups on site.'

A succinct overview of these failures was presented by Nick Davies, who stated, in his interview with Neil Goodwin and Gareth Morris in Chapter Five, his conviction that the police were 'ignorant' about the travellers, that 'they had virtually no solid, reliable information' and were 'relying on rumour and really very dishonest newspaper reports.' A good example of the latter is 'Sex-mad junkie outlaws make Hells Angels look like Little Noddy', a *News of the World* headline quoted by Davies in 'Inquest on a rural riot', his compelling article about the Beanfield that was published in *The Observer* on June 9th 1985. In this same article Davies also pointed out that Robert Key, the Conservative MP for Salisbury, had spoken about the Stonehenge festival in the House of Commons, when he had mentioned 'hand grenades, shotguns and armed law-breakers', and 'had called for the army to be brought in', but that he had later 'conceded that he had no direct evidence to support his allegations.' For both the police and the majority of the media, however, this seemed not to matter. In 'The Battle of Stonehenge', published in *The Sunday Telegraph* on June 2nd 1985, Paul Williams stated, 'It was believed that some armed police were standing by because of unconfirmed reports of firearms being seen at last year's Stonehenge festival', which perhaps vindicates the suggestion by Phil Shakesby, who had come across armed police during 'Operation Amethyst' in autumn 1984, that the police 'had been considering whether to use... high-powered single-shot rifles to put a single shot into each engine lock to stop it.'

Given this level of paranoia, it's unsurprising that the police reacted with such alarm to a rumour that members of the convoy at Savernake were preparing petrol bombs, a rumour which was probably generated by the Earl of Cardigan in his interview with Devizes police on the morning of June 1st, when, as he explained in his interview in Chapter Seven, 'I may well indeed have said that some of them had been putting petrol into milk bottles, but I don't think I actually saw it. It was just a reported threat.' It was, nevertheless, taken seriously enough that at 1359 hours, before the first roadblock had been raised, when Grundy was instructing his officers to stop all the vehicles and to tell their occupants that the festival was cancelled, he specifically mentioned 'information that they... possibly have inflammable material on board', and that he wanted 'every one of those vehicles searched with a view to finding out if there are any dangerous weapons or such material on board.' It's also worth noting that, by the time this was reported to the media, after two unlit bottles containing petrol had indeed been hurled at the police lines, a number of newspapers failed to mention this crucial distinction.

Potentially more disturbing than all of the above is Nick Davies' exposure of the dubious arrangement whereby a known fascist, Les Vaughan, was entrusted with collating the names of the travellers to be used in the injunction that was delivered to the convoy at Sharnbrook lay-by in April. The suspicion is that this was more than just an ill-advised choice, and was, in fact, an attempt to 'frame' convoy members by providing them with weapons (as Davies was told by various convoy members, who 'made signed statements to the effect.') This is reinforced by Vaughan's response to Davies' subsequent article on his activities, in which, after threatening to sue, he singularly failed to do so.

It also adds a certain poignant edge to Nick Davies' final description, in his interview, of the police's failure to gather worthwhile evidence: 'There may have been points where they really believed they were up against some kind of army that had hand grenades and machine guns, but if that's so then it's a very bad failure, because the police are supposed to be able to gather intelligence. But they did fail. They really didn't understand the people they were dealing with.'

The front cover of Bruce Garrard's pamphlet about Rainbow Fields on the Road, published by Unique Publications in 1986.
Image copyright Bruce Garrard.

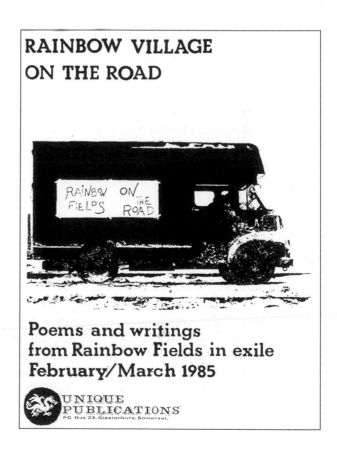

RAINBOW VILLAGE ON THE ROAD

Poems and writings from Rainbow Fields in exile February/March 1985

UNIQUE PUBLICATIONS
PO Box 23, Glastonbury, Somerset.

As for 'the convoy' itself, the police seemed unable to distinguish between the 'Peace Convoy', the convoy that had come from Molesworth, and other groups of travellers who had come together in Savernake Forest on May 31st. Bruce Garrard offered a succinct appraisal of the fate of the 'Peace Convoy' in 1986, when he wrote that, 'As an identifiable group, the [Peace] Convoy had been broken up by very heavy-handed police action [at Nostell Priory] near Wakefield, South Yorkshire, nearly a year before.' Afterwards, some of them – amongst them Phil Shakesby – had made their way to Molesworth, while others were part of the convoy that arrived at Savernake Forest on May 31st from Wick, accompanied by Nick Davies.

Even more telling was the police's ignorance surrounding the convoy that had originated at Molesworth, particularly as they had been scrutinising it for four months. David Taylor, the Green Party activist who organised the initial Green Gathering at Molesworth in August 1984, which developed into the Green Village, and then the Rainbow Fields Village, and then, after the eviction, into Rainbow Fields on the Road, pointed out to me that 'One thing to note about the 'Rainbow Fields on the Road' convoy was that it was different in many respects to the earlier convoys. It was essentially the evicted residents of Molesworth; and as such comprised an interesting and different range of people (many of whom were not regular Stonehenge types) – a group of travellers who'd been evicted violently from Nostell Priory, green activists (including members of the Green Party), CNDers and local peace campaigners and peace camp folk, hippie travellers who hadn't been in convoy before and others who'd never been on the road before.'

David Taylor's description of the make-up of the convoy that set off from Savernake Forest is corroborated by Don Aitken and Alex Rosenberger, in their analysis of those involved in the 1991 trial: 'In fact, the convoy stopped on June 1st consisted mainly of New Age Travellers who had only recently gone on the road and city-dwellers who'd come for the festival. Out of 24 plaintiffs in the trial, only eight were travellers in 1985, only one for longer than a year.'

The significance of errors

The most grievous tactical error, which had a knock-on effect on the rest of the operation, was the botched roadblock on the A338, which was supposed to stop the convoy so that, with other police vehicles blocking the rear, the whole convoy could be contained and dealt with. The failure is highlighted in the police log, in the exchanges between the various commanders at 1425 hours, just one minute after the gravel had been tipped, which begins with Denning (in the helicopter) advising Grundy, 'We have a motorcycle outrider now approaching Shipton Bellinger. If he gets anywhere near our ground unit they suggest they may attempt to take him out, because [he is] obviously intending to return and report.'

It's worth noting, however, that Ian Readhead expressed doubts about the plan to tip the gravel, saying that it would make it difficult to deploy officers safely, and that he

A conclusion of sorts

Arrests – in the bushes – during the first assault on the travellers, at the roadblock on the A303 near the Parkhouse roundabout.

complained to Richard Hester that his advice was ignored. Even more significantly, he also expressed doubts about the practicality of the whole of the original plan – stopping the convoy in a long line and then moving along them to 'see what offence has been committed.' As he put it, 'the policing operation had not been thought through very well... That kind of plan logistically causes a lot of problems, if you think it through. What about their injuries? How do ambulance crews get to the scene?' His overall opinion of the operation at this point, that it had been conceived from a 'Fortress Stonehenge' mentality, rather than by looking at the specific question of how to deal with 'a travelling environment', was to prove more prescient as the day went on.

Having failed to stop the convoy according to the original plan, the police were then compelled, at short notice, to set up a second roadblock on a far more significant 'A' road – the A303, with all the disruption to 'ordinary' traffic which that entailed – as Ian Readhead also noted. What happened next is not entirely clear. The most reliable source would appear to be the Earl of Cardigan, who witnessed a vehicle coming up on the verge of the road from further down the convoy, which then 'did a right turn and went smartly headfirst through the hedgerow at the side of the road and ended up in the field, leaving something of a hole in the hedge right in front of the police roadblock.' This was followed shortly after by the accidental collision between a traveller's coach and a police Transit van, which, in his opinion, precipitated the first wave of police violence against the travellers (at the front of the convoy at least).

The Battle of the Beanfield

On the other hand, George Firsoff, in his review of the day's events in the 'Robin's Greenwood Gang Yearbook 1985', suggested that, when confronted by the roadblock on the A303, 'The first convoy van tried to go round the block but was rammed. Other vehicles smashed into the roadblock writing off three police vans.' George's source seems to have been an article in *The Guardian* on June 5th 1985 ('Irresistible force faces summer solstice'), in which the journalist Stephen Cook quoted the opinion of Dr Peter Waddington of Reading University, who had 'just completed a study of police order policing', that the police decided to make the ultimatum that 'everyone there should be arrested and processed', only 'after three police vans in the roadblock had been written off by the convoy.' As Waddington was mistaken about the ultimatum (which was conceived later in the afternoon), it may be that his opinion about the collision is just as unreliable.

Following this incident, as the Earl of Cardigan described it, a wave of police officers began to make their way down the sides of the vehicles, battering them with their truncheons, demanding that the owners get out and hand over the ignition keys, and smashing windows. As Cardigan witnessed these events personally, it also seems fair to accept, as he suggested, that in some of these cases 'the smashing up of the vehicles, and the instructions to 'Get out! Get out! Get out!' and hand over your keys, were given absolutely simultaneously, and therefore there was no possible chance to understand what was being shouted at you, and to respond and comply, before your vehicle started disintegrating around you, with your windscreen broken in, and your side panels beaten by truncheons, and so on.'

Whatever the exact sequence of events, the convoy's flight into the pasture field – which increased in intensity after the first wave of police began trashing the vehicles at the front – provided the next major shock for the police commanders. As Ian Readhead described it, 'there couldn't have been any plan to put travellers into the Beanfield. I mean, I'd like to think we were that organised, but the reality is that we're not...' Once this had happened, and the police's original plan was finally scuppered for good, the radio log clearly reveals the commanders scrabbling to establish a new basis on which to proceed.

This began at 1450 hours with the 'breach of the peace' message to Grundy from Denning: 'It is stressed that we allow them to enter the field, and, should the owner at our request then assist or request them to leave, we have a suitable breach of the peace situation, which we could contain in the field and deal with.' At this stage, it was also stressed that no officers on foot were to enter the field.

Half an hour later, at 1522 hours, the situation changed – rather drastically, from the police's point of view – when Superintendent Burden made the following call to Grundy: 'We have an impasse situation here where if we are not careful they are going to start to win. The signs are they are starting to make petrol bombs inside [and] my men on the road are being stoned from within the field.' This in turn led directly to discussions between Burden and Grundy about the difficulties of combating moving vehicles, Burden's wish that he had vehicles 'which we can ram them with', and the abortive attempt to invade the field on foot, the failure of which was covered in detail by Ian Readhead.

By 1600 hours, when this attempted invasion had been repulsed, and when 12 vehicles had driven from the pasture field into the Beanfield, the police discussion turned to fears that all the available exits from the field were not securely covered, and something close to panic seems to have set in, so that by 1610 hours, when Burden requested permission to talk to the travellers with a view to allowing them to leave, if 'as a group they would be willing to come out peaceably from the field [and] on a condition that no festival will take place and they are not to go near Stonehenge', Grundy made the fateful decision that there were now no options available: 'No, the position now is that, from the information you have given us, they have committed a series of offences, and as far as I am concerned they are to be arrested as soon as you or Chief Superintendent Illman tells me that you have adequate resources to go in there and deal with them as efficiently and with as little trouble as possible.'

Once this decision had been made, very little changed for almost the next three hours. The first indication that the commanders were once more intending to invade the field on foot, but with better back-up than was evident in the previous abortive attempt, came with an urgent request from Burden, at 1755 hours, for the heavy plant to be delivered to Parkhouse: 'There cannot be any delay. We must have vehicles, we must have heavy vehicles, we must have them urgently.'

What the police radio log also reveals, in great detail, is that an additional reason for the delay in finally dealing with the travellers contained in the pasture field and the Beanfield was that much of the police's resources were taken up in trying to contain the situation around Stonehenge. This is a part of the story that was unreported at the time, and that has gained little coverage in the years since, but it clearly deserves its place in the account. It's apparent from the radio log that people were trying to get to the monument throughout the day, but that the situation was particularly fraught for a crucial two and a half hour period, from 1650 hours until the final assault on those in the pasture field and the Beanfield began at 1910 hours. During this time, up to 350 people on foot attempted to approach Stonehenge from various directions, and there was also the more problematic irritant of groups of bikers, whose activities were described by George Firsoff as 'the kamikaze action by 300 Hell's Angels who some time during the afternoon succeeded in breaking through the police lines and reaching the Stones.'

George suggested that most of them 'were subsequently arrested', but this was not in fact the case. Arthur Pendragon – whose role in the struggle for access to Stonehenge is described in the final chapter – was, at the time of the Beanfield, a biker leader known as John the Hat. He told me that, although the various biker groups that converged on Stonehenge were arrested, they were almost immediately 'unarrested.' Probably because the police were struggling to cope with the numbers of people already in custody – but perhaps because the bikers were more difficult to 'decommission' than either pedestrians or unarmed travellers trapped in a field with their homes – they were actually given the option of leaving the area under police escort, which they accepted. The police escorted them – via a warren of minor roads away from the A303 – to Westbury hill-fort, 12 miles from Stonehenge but still in Wiltshire, where they set up the advance camp of the Stonehenge festival-in-exile that the Savernake travellers joined on June 16th when they were finally evicted from the Earl of Cardigan's forest.

It was sometime after 1800 hours, at the gathering of commanders in the hotel near the Parkhouse roundabout, that Ian Readhead once more expressed misgivings about the operation, telling Grundy that if they entered the field on foot, they would be up against vehicles and would be 'unable to control' the situation. Although Grundy reassured him that 'We won't do that. I can assure you we won't deploy, because we'd rather consult and resolve it, and it's probably going to be something we're going to do tomorrow', the urgent call for the heavy plant that Burden had put out just before the meeting suggests that the commanders were not being entirely straight with Readhead, and that they were only waiting for the heavy vehicles to arrive before ordering the final assault.

In the end, their continuing fears about the travellers breaking out of the field provoked Grundy into taking action before the back-up vehicles even arrived, after one of the officers stationed around the field reported, at 1856 hours, that 'There are now ten-plus coaches and about 20 other vehicles moving in the field. They are forming up in a circle, going round and round. I am virtually certain they are going to rush a gate in a minute' – an opinion which, ironically, contrasts with the viewpoint of the travellers themselves. In Sheila Craig's account in Chapter Four, George stated, 'Just before we were charged by the police, we heard on the radio that they were about to charge, so we started our bus', and Maureen Stone recalled that 'When they came in at seven o'clock, we had just got into the vehicle moments before. We didn't actually know they were coming in at that moment, but it was almost like intuitively we got in the vehicles, we knew they would be coming in soon.'

Given the various decisions made during the day, after the police's original plan crumbled and the travellers introduced a new and unexpected problem by occupying the pasture field, odd discrepancies remain between the various accounts, of which the most prominent is the extent to which the arrest of all those travelling from Savernake Forest was predetermined. This is not mentioned in the police radio log, but it was stated explicitly to the Earl of Cardigan during his conversation with a police officer at Devizes police station on the morning of June 1st, when he was told that, 'regardless of what happened that day, every single one of the people – all 500-strong or whatever – was going to be arrested before the end of the day.' It's also something that was admitted during the 1991 trial by Martyn Meeks, a police support unit commander, who, as Don Aitken and Alex Rosenberger reported, admitted under cross-examination that the plan was to arrest everyone, 'irrespective of whether they had done anything wrong, beyond being there at that time.'

But whilst this 'total arrest' scenario was certainly the police's intention as part of their original plan (the roadblock on the A338), their hurriedly revised second plan (the roadblock on the A303), and Grundy's insistence, after 1610 hours, that everyone in the field was to be 'arrested and processed' in the search for those who had committed 'a series of offences', there were, curiously, two moments during the day when other options appear to have been available. The first of these was at 1359 hours, before the first roadblock, when Grundy was instructing his officers to check all vehicles for inflammable material, when he also told them, 'What I want you to do is stop each one of them and be very specific in the advice that you give them. You are to tell them that the Stonehenge Festival is cancelled, as we have previously discussed in the terms of the Order, and tell them to go away.' The second was Superintendent Burden's assumption, at 1610 hours, just before Grundy informed him that there were to be no further negotiations, that the travellers would be allowed to leave if they came out peaceably as a group and promised not to try and hold a festival or approach Stonehenge.

The bigger picture (1): the build-up to the Beanfield

Apart from these two occasions, when – for the briefest of moments – other options appeared to be available, it would, I think, be fair to say that the objectives of the operation were not only to prevent the convoy from reaching Stonehenge, but also, as the Earl of Cardigan and Martyn Meeks indicated, to ensure that everyone was arrested. It's also apparent that, in the act of doing so, the police were committing themselves not only to the threat of violence but the near-certainty of its taking place, as is indicated by Ian Readhead's assumption of 'injuries' in his criticism of the operation, described above, and, more subtly, in Lord Gifford's assertion, in his interview in Chapter Eleven, that 'the real intention was all along to stage a confrontation.' Perceptively, Gifford also added that, despite Grundy's brief flash of apparent tolerance at 1359 hours, his countermanding of Burden's attempts at conciliation at 1610 hours demonstrated that 'the agenda of the Chief Constable... was belligerent and was fixed from the start.'

What I'd like to do now is to look at the background to the Beanfield, to peer beyond the evidence for the day's operation that is contained in the police radio log, in the hope of glimpsing the overarching rationale and justification for the event, which can only be gleaned by reading between the lines.

Clearly, this was an operation that had been planned for several months in advance, and, in the case of Phil Shakesby's descriptions of the manpower invested in the mass arrest at Nostell Priory and the events of 'Operation Amethyst', even longer. What we can state with confidence, however, is that the operation began to be planned in detail in February

1985, when a meeting of the Association of Chief Police Officers took place in Trowbridge, as mentioned by Neil Goodwin and Gareth Morris in their interview with Nick Davies, and also in Alan Lodge's account of the Beanfield, which is featured on his website. It was also around this time that, as Nick Davies put it, 'the whole of the Wiltshire establishment had sat down to decide what to do about the convoy, and this involved various landowners and the County Council and the police and their solicitors', who then came up with the civil injunctions 'to justify all that then happened.'

It's also clear that one particular strand of the operation began with the eviction of Molesworth, which also took place in February 1985, after which the 'Rainbow Village on the Road' convoy, which was part of the larger convoy that left Savernake Forest on June 1st, was regularly monitored and/or harassed. The significance of the Molesworth contingent is not only clear from Maureen Stone's description of her arresting officer at the Beanfield – who revealed that he had been assigned to her specifically, when he said, 'You're the people that built the chapel at Molesworth, aren't you? I'm a Cambridgeshire Ministry of Defence policeman' – but also from other sources.

David Taylor, who described Molesworth as 'the biggest land squat since the Diggers in 1649', wrote to me recently to offer the following opinion, which, I believe, helps to explain the influence that Molesworth had on the subsequent Beanfield operation: 'The Beanfield was more violent but Molesworth was, I reckon, more significant politically... In the end we forced Heseltine's hand, provoked an absurd over-reaction (a classic non-violent direct action strategy) and set Heseltine's reputation on a downward trend from which it never recovered... We knew when we were evicted that Thatcher was after us, and looking for an opportunity to trash 'the convoy.' At Molesworth they were made to look stupid. We knew the mood and were expecting them. The trashing nearly happened at Grafham Water (a reservoir near Molesworth) where we parked up [shortly after the eviction]. There were helicopters, and some heavy and physical policing, but we moved on... So the Beanfield was brewing for months (if not years) before it happened.'

The significance of the Molesworth convoy – as well as further insights into the intelligence-gathering that took place before the Beanfield – were also described in a contemporary report from the 'Molesworth Bulletin' by Brig Oubridge, which was reproduced in Bruce Garrard's 'Rainbow Village on the Road' pamphlet, published in January 1986: 'When we got to Desborough airfield [in late February], we had at first a quiet week, with only one car on the gate and daily helicopters overhead.' In early March, however, 'as the miners went back to work, a special squad of 35 'national' police took over Corby police station to deal with us. We call them the 'A' team. They are from outside of Northants and are accountable to a central office – possibly the National Reporting Centre used for the miners' strike. They include at least one representative each from the Serious Crimes Squad and the Metropolitan Police drug squad, but exactly who all the others are we don't know – Special Branch, MI5, SPG, even the SAS; any or all of these are good possibilities.'

Preparing for battle: the use of the police as a paramilitary force.

While Brig may well have been correct in his suspicions that representatives of numerous 'special forces' were part of the surveillance operation, it seems likely that the scrutiny of the travellers was primarily focused on one of two newly-created National Intelligence Units, which was based in Devizes. These, according to an officer who responded to a questionnaire distributed to the police during Richard Hester's research into his 1998 PhD thesis, were set up in 1985 for 'the collation, evaluation and dissemination of intelligence in relation to the movement of potential illegal travellers', though specific details remain elusive. As Hester acknowledged, in 'Policing New Age Travellers: Conflict and Control in the Countryside?', a chapter he contributed to *Crime and Conflict in the*

Countryside, published in 1999: 'There is obviously some difficulty in discussing in detail methods of surveillance as they are, by their nature, secret.'

Brig Oubridge's mention of the miners' strike introduces another element into the build-up to the Beanfield operation, which has been noted by a number of commentators. In his article for *Squall*, Jim Carey wrote, 'The berserk nature of the police violence drew obvious comparisons with the coercive police tactics employed on the miners' strike the year before. Many observers claimed the two events provided strong evidence that government directives were para-militarising police responses to crowd control.' He then quoted from Wiltshire police's 'Operation Solstice' report, in which it was stated, 'Counsel's opinion regarding the police tactics used in the miners' strike to prevent a breach of the peace was considered relevant', and the news section of *Police Review*, published a week after the Beanfield: 'The police operation had been planned for several months and lessons in rapid deployment learned from the miners' strike were implemented.'

Further evidence of the widespread use of specific officers who had previous experience of politically-charged 'public order' disturbances was provided by Nick Davies, who noted in his article for *The Observer* on June 9th that 'The Wiltshire officers in charge, like those from the five rural forces who helped them, have all been on duty at Greenham Common and throughout the miners' strike.' It is reinforced in the following passage from an article entitled 'Last summer: how the public was lied to', by Alex Rosenberger, which appeared in the first issue of *Festival Eye* in 1986: 'Tash asked one of the officers in riot gear, 'When was the last time you wore that get-up?' The officer replied, 'Orgreave'.' George Firsoff also made the following observation about the 'legal contortion' that was required to arrest the travellers in and around the Beanfield, when they were clearly outside the specific remit of the injunction: 'This depended on the same kind of legal contortion by which Kentish miners were stopped at the Dartford Tunnel because they were thought to be going to picket in Yorkshire where it was thought a breach of the peace would take place.'

So who, in the end, authorised the operation that resulted in the Battle of the Beanfield? Surely Wiltshire Constabulary alone was not responsible for planning an operation that involved five other forces, the MoD, English Heritage, the National Trust, County Councils, the Forestry Commission and countless landowners? Again, no 'smoking gun' has been revealed. The Freedom of Information Act may yet reveal something nasty lurking in the records of the Home Office (if it hasn't already been destroyed), but in the absence of any firm evidence I can only reiterate the opinion that I expressed in *Stonehenge: Celebration and Subversion*: 'What Nick Davies omitted from his analysis of the establishment closing ranks to authorise and justify the events of the Beanfield was the presiding figure of Margaret Thatcher. At Orgreave, Stonehenge and Wapping, it was Thatcher's new army, a faceless, paramilitary police force, bussed in from outside the area, that broke dissent with extreme violence. At Stonehenge, as at Orgreave and Wapping, people were left physically and emotionally scarred, livelihoods were destroyed and communities torn apart.'

Alan Dearling comments: 'Under the Conservative government of Margaret Thatcher, travellers were branded as 'subversives', defined by Home Secretary Leon Brittan as even including those 'who, for tactical reasons or other reasons, choose to keep within the letter of the law.' Through agencies such as MI5's F2 Branch, Thatcher collated and sifted through an increasing amount of information on all kinds of 'subversives' – trade union leaders, members of CND, miners and travellers. It was, however, the Association of Chief Police Officers who issued the *Public Order and Tactical Operation Manual*, which Tony Benn, MP, described to the House of Commons (*Hansard*, July 22nd 1985) as follows: 'The manual provides for the training of police in para-military operations, including instruction in methods of incapacitating demonstrators by the infliction of actual bodily harm... through the manual, police were given instructions, descriptions of tactics and manoeuvres on the use of long and short shields, which laid them open to charges of assault by the rules as they stood.'

I leave the final word on this part of the Stonehenge operation to George Firsoff, who provided a wide-ranging review of the context in which the Beanfield took place, in his article for the 'Robin's Greenwood Gang Yearbook 1985: 'Some of us believe that the battle at Stonehenge was part of a wider plan. We do not think it a coincidence that long-established communities such as Tipi Valley, Llwynpiod Co-operative in Wales and Resurgence in Cornwall were threatened with eviction in 1985. We think that it is interesting that when the Ministry of Transport evicted Peter the Potter and his friends from the Green Lantern Café in Bath they did not need the site; yet the building was demolished on the same day. It was intended to smash up the Stonehenge convoy and destroy their possessions. Similar actions against the Peace Convoy at Nostell Priory in August 1984 and Fargo Plantation in April 1985 [when an advance convoy attempting to occupy the festival site had also been dealt with severely] had led to relatively little outcry. That it is wholly and totally illegal and contrary to law as old as Magna Carta is merely a detail from the authorities' point of view.'

The bigger picture (2):
violence on the day and various other acts of dubious legality

It remains only for me to look at a few of the outstanding issues surrounding the events on the day – the nature of the violence that took place, the police's attempted justification of it, and various other acts that seem to have been illegal.

I'll begin, briefly, with the police's attempts to justify their actions as preventing a breach of the peace, which, as previously noted, was stated explicitly by Superintendent Burden at 1450 hours, after vehicles had broken into the pasture field, and which was supposed to underpin the entire operation in its various guises. This whole argument was countered by George Firsoff in another extract from his analysis of the Beanfield in the 'Robin's Greenwood Gang Yearbook 1985', in which he argued persuasively that the opposite was true: 'But of course the argument that police acted to prevent a breach of the peace is absurd – they acted deliberately to cause a breach of the peace by a policy of escalation. Because the road was blocked the leading vehicle tried to go round. So it was rammed. Then police vehicles were rammed. So police started breaking windows. Because windows were smashed the convoy escaped into the field. Because they were in the field the riot police were brought forward. Because the police did not act so as to prevent a breach of the peace their action was illegal, not only in detail, but from its inception.'

Turning now to the violence that took place, I'd like, in the first instance, to revisit those portions of the police radio log in which there is no comment from the commanders while certain assaults were taking place. It may be, as some of those involved in the trial alleged at the time, that parts of the log, transcribed by the police and used in court, were deliberately excised. This is not an interpretation that I can either confirm or deny from my own reading of it, although I am aware that, despite providing detailed descriptions of the build-up to the final assault in the Beanfield, the log contains no instructions from any of the police commanders regarding two crucial incidents that took place early in the day – which is curious, to say the least. These are: the very first assault – on six vehicles at the back of the convoy, which had become separated from the rest – and the second assault on the vehicles at the front near the roadblock on the A303.

The assault on the front of the convoy could, conceivably, be seen as an immediate response to the collision – or collisions – that took place between traveller and police vehicles, as described above. Ian Readhead, for example, talked of driving past an Avon and Somerset unit, whose vehicle had been hit, who were arresting people in the coach that had collided with them – and seemed to be referring to it almost as a private matter between the two parties. On the other hand, the Earl of Cardigan had the distinct impression that 'the police who had been in ordinary police uniforms seemed to all stand to one side, and out from behind the barricade – where we previously hadn't been able to see – came quite a number of police in a very different manner', who then began to work their way down the line of vehicles, smashing windows and arresting people. Cardigan's interpretation suggests that the more heavily armed police who emerged to attack the vehicles were waiting for an excuse – a trigger, almost – and if this is the case then it's odd that there is no evidence of any instructions from the commanders.

More difficult to explain is the radio silence during the attack on the back of convoy, which was described by Nick Davies, who was actually travelling in one of the vehicles, and which clearly took place before any other incident had happened. Davies was not the only witness to this attack. George Firsoff noted that journalist Nigel Kerton and photographer Eric Hansen, of *The Gazette and Herald*, were also 'travelling at the rear and saw the stragglers mopped up. Handcuffed hippies were led away, crying children separated from their parents, lost dogs and vehicles abandoned by the roadside.' Davies, however, reported one particular incident, in his article for *The Observer* on June 9th, which hints that the police radio log may indeed have been tampered with. The police didn't know it, but some of the travellers had been listening in to the police radio. In

Davies' words, 'A young punk sprinted down the road, yelling: 'They're going to try and take the back vehicles. We heard it on the police radio", even though there is no mention of it in the transcript. More damningly, Bruce Garrard even reported the exact words used by the 'Police radio control', as described in Chapter Four: extra riot vans were ordered to 'cut across MoD land to 'deal with' the back of the convoy. 'You know what to do', they were told.' Neither of these phrases appears in the transcript.

While this would seem to prove that parts of the police radio log were indeed removed from the transcript – and, by inference, that sections relating to the final assault on the travellers in the pasture field and the Beanfield may also have been removed – it remains shockingly apparent that at least some of the violence that took place after 7 pm can be attributed directly to senior officers in the field encouraging their men to collective and individual acts of brutality. This is revealed in Kim Sabido's comment that 'to me they acted like a paramilitary force, and from talking to a few policemen, listening to what they were saying to one another, they intended to act that way. There seemed to be a preconceived idea of how they were going to act towards the convoy', and in particular in Nick Davies' report of a senior officer saying to him, 'My lads have been putting up with this lot for 11 years. They've had enough of it, and there's going to be some heads cracked in there today.' It's also worth noting that the most blatant incitement to violence, reported by Nick Davies in his article for *The Observer* on June 9th, came from the helicopter containing Chief Superintendent Denning: 'You're doing a great job. This is how they like it.'

Just as worrying as the above is the realisation that, if the violence was not attributable to either the commanding officers or the senior officers in the field, then it was the result, as the Earl of Cardigan put it, of officers 'running amok.' This is an aspect of the day's events that was described by Nick Davies, in his interview with Neil Goodwin and Gareth Morris, as 'the most undisciplined police operation I've ever seen – and I have quite often been in riots, and I have occasionally seen individual police officers blow it, but I have never seen an entire police operation run riot like that.' It's also a theme that he dealt with in detail in his article for *The Observer* on June 9th, in which he commented that it was 'a police operation that apparently slipped out of control', and described how, 'whatever their plans and tactics, the police operation became a chaotic whirl of violence', adding, 'The command structure of the officers appeared to have disintegrated.' Both he and the Earl of Cardigan observed the police hurling objects – including stones, hammers, fire extinguishers, truncheons and shields – at the travellers' vehicles in an attempt to stop them, and Cardigan in particular was nonplussed by the actions of a policeman who stepped aside from the action just to smash up the dashboard of an empty coach with a mallet that he found abandoned in the field.

Moving on to specific complaints, Davies noted that 'The guidance on the use of truncheons – to be used only as a last resort and only on [the] arms and legs of a target – was abandoned', that after the event 'witnesses saw the police gather the convoy's vehicles in the field and move through them, smashing windows and breaking possessions'– which the Earl of Cardigan also noted, in his description of the police's 'unorthodox' methods of searching vehicles – and that, overall, 'It was difficult to discern... the doctrine of minimum force that is enshrined in section three of the 1967 Criminal Law Act', which states that 'A person may use such force as is reasonable in the circumstances in the prevention of crime, or in the effecting of, or assisting in, the lawful arrest of offenders...'

Jay, one of the travellers quoted at length by Richard Lowe and William Shaw in their 1993 book *Travellers: Voices of the New Age Nomads*, indicated that the police had been 'hyped-up': 'It came out later that they'd been told there were loads of big blokes with big sticks on the vehicles when in fact it was all sorts – men, women, kids, and not violent people at all. They [the police] were mad, going round trying to ram vehicles... When we eventually stopped there was this copper who was really doing his nut in. It seemed like he wanted to kill me. He was out of control.'

There were other aspects of the operation that caused Nick Davies particular concern, which were also noted by other observers. One of these took place before the first roadblock, when the police stopped the convoy and went through the vehicles asking names. Davies commented, 'Some people pointed out that they had no legal right to do this. The police agreed, and carried on asking.' The unidentified author of an article entitled 'Miscarriage of Justice UK', which appeared in 'The Trial of the Beanfield', a pamphlet published by Suburban Guerillas in 1991, noted that these were "Personal Identification' forms, which described [the travellers] and their vehicles in detail, a practice opposed by the National Council for Civil Liberties (NCCL).' The author also noted that, after the Beanfield, 'All those arrested were photographed and questioned from a pre-typed sheet, described by the plaintiffs as headed 'Anarchist Convoy Exercise' (but never produced in court).'

Another worrying aspect of the operation, noted by most of the observers, was that the majority of the police had their identifying numbers hidden, which, as Nick Davies again pointed out, was 'surprising, in that during the miners' strike a year earlier there'd been a lot of complaints about the police in those big public disorder situations not being identifiable, and the Chief Constables and the Home Office had given all kinds of reassurances, on the record and officially, that that would never happen again. And yet here we were, with five different police forces involved, and I would say that 80% of the officers were not identifiable.'

And finally, a number of commentators were concerned about the role of the MoD. George Firsoff noted that, in the final assault on the Beanfield, the police were accompanied by 'some members of the Military Police, and it [was] shown in court that, being more than 15 miles from their base, they [were] out of jurisdiction.' The author of 'Miscarriage of Justice UK' was also concerned that 'The role of the MoD police was ambiguous and points to semi-military manoeuvres rather than a sudden breach of the peace' – which would seem to be an accurate assessment.

'Decommissioned': wrecked vehicles in the police pound.

Certainly, any claims that the operation was not planned well in advance are undermined by two final observations. The first of these came from George Firsoff, who pointed out that 'a canvas camp was set up at Holt for the children, an intensive care ward set aside at Salisbury, and Eversleigh tip secured for wrecked and impounded vehicles.' He also stressed that 'The co-operation of six police forces with full riot gear, and armed police in reserve, also indicate that a battle was intended and had been planned for a long time.'

The second observation – which had potentially disturbing ramifications for the freedom of speech of observers, but particularly of journalists – occurred during Chief Constable Donald Smith's press conference before the Beanfield, which was mentioned by Neil Goodwin in the preceding chapter, in which Smith stated, 'I hope that you are aware of the memo that was sent out to your senior editors', before adding, 'Of course, this is completely off the record.' Allied to this – and seemingly indicating that strings were being pulled in high places – is the replacement of Kim Sabido's voice-over on the ITN News, the disappearance of the rushes from the ITN offices, as predicted by his cameraman, and even the loss of Ben Gibson's negatives when *The Observer* moved offices.

The aftermath

For the travellers, some limited recompense was gained during the trial in 1991 – despite the intervention of the judge – when, as Lord Gifford described it, 'the jury awarded exemplary damages; that is to say, they said that the conduct of the police was oppressive, arbitrary and unconstitutional, and the police ought to suffer a punitive, extra penalty over and above what would otherwise be awarded for compensation, because of the way they conducted themselves that day.' It's noticeable, however, that no official inquiry into the Beanfield has ever been held (despite Kim Sabido's emotional plea on the day), and that no official apology has ever been forthcoming.

In 1995, Inspector Hunt, who had been a member of the Wiltshire Constabulary for 20 years, told an audience at the Big Green Gathering, 'You have to realise that the events at Stonehenge polluted the reputation of festival-goers in the eyes of Wiltshire police.' Afterwards, Jim Carey of *Squall* approached the Inspector and asked, 'Is there any acknowledgement in your Constabulary that the events of the Beanfield seriously polluted the reputation of Wiltshire police in the eyes of festival-goers?' As Carey described it, 'Persistence finally drew a reluctant answer: 'Look, Stonehenge Festival grew too large and out of control. The Battle of the Beanfield was just the beginning of the process of dealing with it. The laws that came after were even more effective'.'

On its website (www.wiltshire.police.uk/airsupport/history.asp, accessed May 2005), the Wiltshire Constabulary Air Support Unit congratulates itself on the part it played in 'Operation Solstice', which it describes as 'a very successful operation.' The full quote is enlightening: 'Having secured an aviation budget of £10,000, Dollar Helicopter contracted for six weeks to supply air support by way of a Command and Control platform and intelligence gathering in respect of the biggest operation ever mounted in Wiltshire in preventing the illegal Stonehenge Festival – an event of anarchy – involving serious crime, drugs, deaths and a mountain of peripheral crime. 530 were arrested in a very successful operation. The part played by the ASU was acknowledged – applause by officers on leaving site at the end of the day.'

A conclusion of sorts

Also unrepentant is the former Assistant Chief Constable, Lionel Grundy, who broke 17 years of silence on the matter to speak to Roisin McAuley for her Radio 4 programme on the Beanfield in 2002. Grundy began by reiterating familiar complaints about 'the convoy': 'The manner in which they travelled around the country was threatening... There was evidence of illegal drugs, there was also various forms of extortion', which apparently involved members of the 'Peace Convoy' 'demanding money' from stallholders to allow them to stay on site.

Asked about the smashing of windows during the first assault on the convoy, Grundy insisted that it happened because people had refused to come out of their vehicles when requested to do so, and that they had to be removed, because they were 'a continuing source of criminality or danger, or they [were] likely to overcome what we were trying to prevent, and that is this illegal incursion into those areas covered by the writs.' He also added, refuting the jury's verdict in favour of Helen Reynolds (Helen the Hat) and others at the 1991 trial, 'My understanding is that nobody was injured at that point.'

Explaining the 'serious offences' that justified his insistence that everybody in the field would have to be 'arrested and processed', Grundy said that, at a petrol station earlier in the day, 'some of the vehicles – not all of them – made off without paying for the petrol, so that was an offence of theft', and that 'They also took various items from the store, which they didn't pay for – some of them didn't pay for' – hardly, it must be said, sufficient crimes to warrant arresting everyone on the field, as was noted at the time by the traveller who observed, 'If you had a couple of football hooligans in a football stadium, you wouldn't arrest everybody in the stadium just to get at the hooligans.'

Grundy also reiterated that it was the fear that those in the field were 'lining their vehicles up... to make a run at Stonehenge' that finally prompted him to order his men into the field to arrest everyone, but when he was shown footage of the ensuing violence, with, as McAuley described it, 'people being pulled out by force' and 'policemen deliberately smashing windows in a coach', he still refused to acknowledge that anything was amiss. In his last exchange with McAuley, after she had asked him how he could defend what he had just seen, his only reply was that he was 'relying on the short clip you've just shown me. I don't know what preceded that.' To this day, the only moment that Grundy has ever shown any sympathy towards any of the travellers was at 1858 hours on the day of the Beanfield, as he was mobilising his forces for the final assault, when he commented, 'My conversation with them with a view to their coming out safely was of no value, although it's quite clear that a number of people in there do not want confrontation.'

Not every aspect of this story is so gloomy, however. An example of what Lord Gifford referred to as 'the restraining factors which stop and which affect police commanders when they decide what sort of operations to mount', which he described as people within the police force thinking, 'Maybe next time there's a different way of doing it', can be seen in the work of Mike Brown. A senior police officer, Brown wrote a thesis in 1995 – *Do Police Officers base their assumptions of 'New Age' Travellers on stereotypical images rather than empirical evidence?* – in which, as the title suggests, he focused a critical eye on the police's attitude to travellers.

Using 159 questionnaires completed by officers, Brown compared their perception of travellers with their actual experience of problems with them. The perceptions ranged from 'dropouts' (40.9%), 'benefit claimants/spongers' (38.4%), 'dirty smelly people' (25.8%) to 'drug users' (11.9%) and there were some particularly unpleasant individual comments, including 'it would be nice if they shot themselves', 'they are scum of the earth', and 'scrounging dirty thieving anarchists.' In their actual experience of travellers, however, the response was far less severe. The largest respondent group (31%) had had no problems whatsoever with travellers, and the four most common problems were 'drugs' (14%), 'traffic' (13%) and both 'trespass' and being 'uncooperative or abusive' (11%). Brown's conclusion, as described by Richard Hester, was that 'the response to the actual offences attributable to offenders is out of proportion to the response they have attracted from the police', and for this to come from a high-ranking 'insider' suggests that lessons would be learnt from it.

Noticeably, Brown also spent seven months visiting travellers' sites, where he investigated their reasons for being on the road, realised the importance they attached to festivals for trade and networking, and received what Richard Hester described as 'an extremely useful insight into the discrimination and victimisation experienced by travellers', which included being barred from shops and pubs, trouble from vigilantes involving petrol bombs, shotguns and physical violence, and police harassment through stop and search policies, damage to vehicles and assault.

Mike Brown is not the only senior police officer to make an attempt to improve relations between the police and travellers. As was seen in Richard Hester's interview with Ian Readhead in Chapter Nine, the former Inspector, who is now the Deputy Chief Constable of Hampshire, was aware of serious problems in the response of the police to the travellers at the time of the Beanfield. In his interview, he not only criticised the police operation, but also extended sympathy to the travellers, who, as he described it, fled into the pasture field from the A303 'not to cause criminal damage but because, in the main, they were confused, didn't know what to do and were, I suspect, frightened, because, you know, police officers in uniform are frightening, police officers in the kind of equipment we were wearing on the day are frightening.' His conclusion remains particularly relevant: 'If you believe in a police force operating in a democracy, they must operate within the law, otherwise you do not have policing by consent; you have a different form of policing...' In Roisin McAuley's Radio 4 programme, Helen Reynolds spelled out the meaning of this 'different form of policing': the police, she said, were there to 'ethnically cleanse us out of it... we became a mobile refugee camp.'

A conclusion of sorts

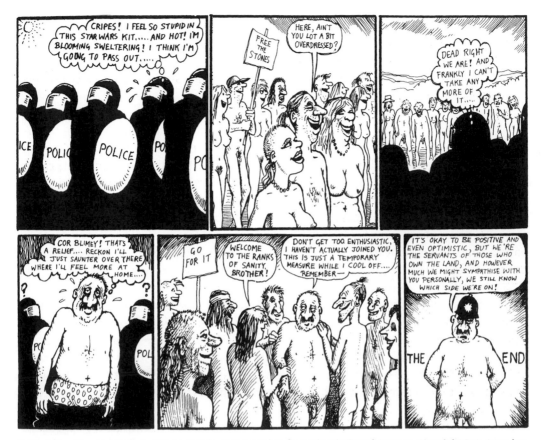

Extract from 'Law 'n' Order' cartoon strip by Pete Loveday, from Big Trip Travel Agency. Copyright Pete Loveday.

Despite these developments, the closest that the Wiltshire Constabulary has come to apologising for what took place on June 1st 1985 has occurred through actions rather than words – in the help offered to the Big Green Gathering by Chief Superintendent Fred Pritchard and the supportive role undertaken by Chief Inspector Andy Hollingshead (both of which are described in the next chapter) and in the comments that Superintendent Jerry Wickham, who is currently in charge of the police operations around Stonehenge every solstice, made to Roisin McAuley in 2002. After acknowledging that 'there have been actual requests for the Wiltshire Constabulary to apologise', Superintendent Wickham excused himself on the grounds that 'I find it quite difficult to apologise in respect of matters that weren't in my control at that particular time', but added, 'I think the extent of the apology... has come about through the very fact that we are now sat there, working alongside everyone [at the meetings to discuss the current access arrangements], and so I would like to think that our actions are the apology, if an apology is the appropriate thing.'

14

Chapter Fourteen
The legacy of the Beanfield
By Andy Worthington

In the immediate aftermath of the Beanfield, as was described at the end of Sheila Craig's account in Chapter Four, a number of the victims gained a brief reprieve in Savernake Forest before moving on to Westbury hill-fort for the solstice. Afterwards, as George Firsoff noted in the 'Robin's Greenwood Gang Yearbook 1985', some travellers went to Devon to attend The Festival of Performing Arts, a former free festival known as the Hood Fayre, while others went to a bikers' gathering in Wantage, and a few even attempted to revisit Molesworth.

Later that summer, a Peace Event at Brambles Farm in Hampshire took place, despite the raising of injunctions and obstruction from the local council, when a group of travellers shifted a pile of gravel to gain access to an alternative site. George Firsoff wrote that 'up to a thousand people gathered successfully', a friendly neighbour provided water supplies, and 'Hampshire police, earlier busy at the Cholderton battle, had changed their tune, regarding this injunction as purely a civil matter', and that as a result they 'kept a low profile.'

There were further mixed messages in the West Country. Goddon Free Festival took place on land near Tiverton provided by a farmer, and George commented that 'a lot of travellers were at this event.' Many then headed north to Rugeley, where they stayed for a fortnight until the council 'gave them diesel and spare parts to move on', and they almost secured the use of some land at Bromsgrove for a year, which was to have been provided by a friendly landowner, until the council prevented it. From here they moved to Cleeve Cloud Common near Cheltenham, where there was 'plenty of wood and water', before moving on to the long-running Cantlin Stone festival in Clun Forest in Wales. In late August, a small Meigan Fayre also took place in Wales, and in September a bold crew of new festival organisers set up the first Torpedo Town festival on the south coast.

Another group of travellers – including many of the 'Rainbow Village' convoy from Molesworth – found refuge in the orchard of Greenlands Farm in Glastonbury, which was owned by a woman called Alison Collyer, who had established it as a Christian community. In the words of Bruce Garrard, taken from his 1986 pamphlet describing the time the travellers spent at Greenfields, 'her principles and her nature both prevented her from turning away people in need.' Despite Alison's charity, the local press launched a campaign against the 'hippy invasion', which was so vitriolic and so sustained that Bruce wondered 'if the authorities, directed perhaps from within the Ministry of Defence and

The frontispiece of Bruce Garrard's 1986 pamphlet describing the vitriol and prejudice endured by Alison Collyer and the travellers at Greenlands Farm, Glastonbury. Copyright Bruce Garrard.

The Children of the Rainbow gathered in the Free State of Avalonia at the Christian Community of

GREENLANDS FARM

Greenlands: hippy problem

The other side of the story, July '85 to January '86

Bruce Garrard

1

utilising the national police force that had emerged (unofficially) during the miners' strike [and, it should be noted, in the period from the eviction of Molesworth to the Battle of the Beanfield], were fighting an unofficial war against them – unarmed and penniless though they were.'

Of all the venom directed towards the travellers, Bruce picked out, as 'probably the worst example', a piece of black propaganda published on the front page of *The Central Somerset Gazette* on September 12th. Under the headline, 'No Gipsy Site Wanted Here', Councillor Andrew Willis suggested that the police would 'perhaps... have to use riot shields' to disperse the travellers, as they did at the Beanfield, a suggestion that Bruce aptly described as 'surely the most insensitive, unhelpful, provocative and ignorant comment of the whole affair.'

As well as attacking the travellers through the local media, their opponents also launched a legal challenge. On August 24th, Mendip County Council served notice on Alison Collyer that 'she must clear the site within 28 days or face proceedings in the High Court.' As Bruce commented, 'Ultimately this could mean sending a 62-year old woman to prison for doing nothing worse than sheltering the homeless.' Nevertheless, the proceedings continued. On September 15th, Alison 'was hauled into the High Court in London and ordered to clear her 'unlicensed caravan site' within 28 days', and when that deadline passed, and some travellers were still on site, she was once more summoned to the Crown Court, to be given a six-month prison sentence suspended for one more month on November 1st.

Faced with the prospect of their guardian soon ending up in prison, the Greenlands travellers reluctantly moved on (although some settled in Glastonbury, where, as Bruce noted pointedly, they 'are indeed contributing to the life of the community.') Most spent the winter in the Quantock Hills, before relocating, in the spring, to Watchet, a small town on the Bridgwater Bay, and at both locations they 'established friendly relations with local people; it was only on their brief return to Glastonbury in the early summer of '86 that they encountered more hostility.' Another group was less successful. Having moved to Shippam Quarry near Cheddar over the Christmas period, Maureen Stone described how they were 'petrol-bombed by vigilantes', and in May they joined one of the ill-fated convoys whose attempts to reach Stonehenge are described below.

Looking back over the whole of 1985, from Molesworth to the Beanfield and the conflicts of the following months, Bruce Garrard reached a harsh but apt conclusion: 'Historians will look back on the 1980s as a time when the government of this country came dangerously close to fascism; when the moral and political climate was something quite different from that of the 'free country' we've all been brought up to believe in; a time when individuals seeking answers to the enormous problems landed on them – through institutional inertia or deliberate mismanagement – were treated with distrust, hostility, and even brutality.'

While all of the above was taking place, other travellers and festival-goers, along with green activists, festival welfare representatives, local people, sympathetic Christians, Druids and other pagans were attempting to resolve the problems at Stonehenge. Shortly after the Beanfield, a meeting was held to discuss a proposal put forward by English Heritage to hold 'a one-day Solstice festival at the stones, allowing the Druids and other groups to ritualise there,' as John Michell described it in a pamphlet about Stonehenge that he published at the time. Talks stalled over the provision of an official campsite, to divert 'the thousands who would otherwise have swamped the Solstice festival', and 'The National Trust and other local landowners closed ranks, refusing any festival camp on their properties.' In October, English Heritage invited representatives of all the interested parties to their headquarters in London, where Richie Cotterill, in a Green Collective mailing, described how 'It seemed fairly clear that there was ultimately no reason (apart from ignorance and fear) why the National Trust could not provide an alternative site on archaeologically inert land within walking distance of the Stones, and that the reasons that were their concern could all be resolved through communication and co-operation.' Even so, no solution was forthcoming, and on March 21st 1986 – the

Stonehenge 1986: a promotional poster that was, ironically, drawn before the Battle of the Beanfield.

vernal equinox of the pagan solar year – a Church of England forum in Salisbury Town Hall, organised by the Reverend David Penney, was similarly inconclusive. Although the meeting was 'good-humoured and tolerant', according to John Michell, and 'the majority of the Festival groups would doubtless have been appeased by even the slightest official concession', the main thrust of the meeting – that the National Trust should make land available for a free festival – was again thwarted when the Trust refused.

In fact, it transpires that, even before David Penney's intervention, the authorities had already decided that on the summer solstice in 1986 Stonehenge was once to be imprisoned and alone, that its defence was once more to become a quasi-military operation, and that, moreover, the travellers – through a policy which I can only regard as abusing the abused – were to become the target of an even larger war on their way of life.

The Battle of the Beanfield

The build-up began in December 1985, when the National Trust and English Heritage announced that no festival would be tolerated the following year. In February 1986, Wiltshire County Council recorded its own formal opposition to the festival, and in April the Wiltshire police, the National Trust and English Heritage applied to Wiltshire County Council for permission to close part of the A344 between May 9th and June 30th. In May, razor wire fencing was erected around Stonehenge, the Forestry Commission blocked all but one entrance to Savernake Forest with felled trees, and English Heritage, the MoD and 23 landowners applied to the High Court for another 'precautionary injunction', this time to prevent 49 named individuals from approaching within a four and a half mile radius of Stonehenge.

The injunction was granted on May 20th, although in the meantime, on May 17th, a convoy of 200 travellers in 70 vehicles scored a brief but symbolic victory, when they occupied the old festival site opposite the stones for half a day, before being evicted. Supervised by police officers, the convoy then made its way westwards from Stonehenge to Somerset, where they camped up 40 miles from Stonehenge at Camel Hill near Sparkford. Evicted after five days, the expanding collective, which now numbered 300 people and a hundred vehicles, proceeded to the nearby village of Lytes Cary, occupying private land belonging to a farmer named Attwell, who promptly collapsed with a heart attack. Although he recovered, the incident was an unexpected boon for the reactionaries of the establishment. Over the next few weeks, as anti-traveller hysteria was whipped up in the House of Commons, Margaret Thatcher declared that she was 'only too delighted to do anything we can to make life difficult for such things as hippy convoys', adding, ominously, that 'if the present law is inadequate, we will have to introduce fresh law' to deal with them, and Douglas Hurd, the Home Secretary, called the travellers 'nothing more than a band of medieval brigands who have no respect for the law or the rights of others.'

From Somerset, the convoy was shunted into Dorset, where Phil Shakesby, in a continuation of his interview in Chapter Two, takes up the story:

'We were stopped just inside one county, and we were left sticking out into another county. We weren't allowed to go back or forward. And then we had this few days of being under siege by the police and the media, and Paddy Ashdown coming out to help mediate and stop this stalemate. He got it so that we could carry on in small groups and we wouldn't be nicked for driving offences.'

'There was these strange types in overalls and peak caps on the roundabouts, like the SAS. They really put the woolies up you. You had the impression that these boys had the business on them to sort you out like, no messing. And that did make my arse tweet. These boys were directing you like they knew where they were sending you. You didn't have any choice. They actually blocked the road off and filed us onto Stoney Cross, [a disused airfield in the New Forest], because John Duke, the Chief Constable of

Evicted from Stoney Cross and deprived of their vehicles, 70 travellers set off on the long walk to Glastonbury, June 1986.

Hampshire, he wanted to deal with us. So he had us all filed onto his bit of turf so he could decommission us, as it were. So we were all put on Stoney Cross for the night. There was no going out. They'd actually sealed the gate. The days went on, and it became increasingly obvious that they were going to come in.'

'In fact, Mick and I had laid awake all night waiting for them. And sure enough, as daylight came, this 'Operation Daybreak' went down. 500 bobbies steamed on. And of course, because of the media circus it were all softly softly, like. They even laid on cups of tea and pie and chips, although through it all they impounded all but four of our homes.'

'We walked away with all the tat we could carry. That first day we covered 25 miles – and there was wodges of Old Bill still with us marching down the road. There was a high-ranking policeman there, and I asked him, 'You feel you've decommissioned us, do you?' I said, 'Just look at all these Old Bill you've got here, all these bobbies marching us down the road. You're still policing the true spirit of the convoy. It's marching down the road now on its way to another festival – Glastonbury.' Which he was quite upset about, because the penny had just dropped. They hadn't decommissioned us at all. They just took our homes off us, but it hadn't stopped the will.'

'We walked 70 or 80 miles in a matter of three or four days. That was a good number, that Stoney Cross, despite it all. It brought a lot of us together, because we were left with very little or nothing, and we became quite close, you know. When you haven't got anything, you get to know one another quite well. And of course, loads of Joe Public turned out to help us en route, like bringing food and bedding and all the things they thought we'd need.'

While the Stoney Cross convoy endured these ordeals, several hundred other people were making their way towards Stonehenge on a number of peace pilgrimages known as the Stonehenge Walks. These evolved from meetings of the Stonehenge Campaign, an alliance of festival-goers dedicated to 'the reinstatement of the Stonehenge People's Free Festival and religious access to Stonehenge itself, in which 'theatre groups, community

The Stonehenge Walk approaches Salisbury, June 1986. Copyright Alan Lodge.

groups, housing groups, all the alternative things that went on at Stonehenge were represented', in the words of Hilary Jones, one of its most prominent activists.

On May 1st, when the London group had set off, they had declared their intention – in true prankster fashion – to hold a nude protest in Salisbury on the Saturday before the solstice, and the council had promptly banned them from the centre of town. On the day, however, the walkers were met by several hundred supporters in vehicles, and this new convoy, escorted out of Salisbury by the police, then made its way north to the village of Hanging Langford in the Wylye Valley, where, in George Firsoff's words, 'the villagers were found to be communicative and helpful.'

Here they settled in for a fortnight, to the delight of the local landlord. Three days before the solstice, however, in the first of many attempts to establish an organised solstice event – with access restricted to limited numbers of ticket holders – English Heritage offered 300 tickets for the solstice, on the condition that the travellers left their vehicles behind and were conveyed to the monument in coaches allocated by the police. Committed to free access for all, and understandably wary of leaving their vehicles and trusting the police, the travellers refused. An eviction order was swiftly passed, and, on the day before the solstice, when the convoy moved off as requested, heading away from Stonehenge, they were immediately stopped by the police, who arrested 300 people for obstructing the highway and obstructing officers in the course of the duty. The charges were groundless, of course, and both sides knew it. The travellers offered no resistance to the police, and when the processing was over, and they had been dispersed to prisons as far away as Portsmouth, one of those arrested, Steve Hieronymous, noted that 'even the constables guarding us slowly admitted they found the whole thing farcical (except for the overtime they were all getting paid.')

The next day, the prisoners were taken by coach to Salisbury, where they spent the afternoon behind the courts, 'sexes segregated, one coachload handcuffed all day.' When they finally left the coaches, hundreds of supporters were there to greet them, but in the end the authorities triumphed once more. Observers from the NCCL (the National Council for Civil Liberties, now known as Liberty), who had been scrutinising the police's treatment of the travellers throughout the build-up to the solstice, noted that 'the effect of the arrests was to ensure that 230 travellers were off the roads and in custody over the period of the solstice.'

In the end, only a few hundred people made it through to Stonehenge for the solstice, where they held a defiant ceremony on the roadside, and there was little improvement in the years that followed, when further futile attempts were made to offer limited numbers of free tickets to would-be celebrants. In 1987, as Jim Carey later described it in *Squall*, 'people stood on the tarmac beside Stonehenge, having walked the eight miles distance from an impromptu site at Cholderton [Woods]. As clouds smothered the solstice sunrise, those who had walked the distance were kept on the road, separated from the Stones by rows of riot police and bales of razor wire. The anger mounted and scuffles broke out.' The anger was barely offset by the brief burst of tolerance that occurred at 6.30 am, after the Druids – who had privately regained their own access – had finished performing their ceremony. 300 people were allowed into the Stones for a few hours, which they celebrated by joining hands in a circle around the henge and spiralling into the temple, chanting 'The earth is our mother, we shall take good care of her.'

Two views of the exclusion zone: a photo from 1989 and a postcard by Gubby produced by Enabler Publications. Copyright Adrian Arbib (top) and Gubby's World, exclusive to Enabler Publications (bottom).

HAPPY SOLSTICE

The legacy of the Beanfield

This in turn was followed by another violent clampdown in 1988. In the week before the solstice, several thousand travellers and festival-goers had again gathered in Cholderton Woods, but this time, after making their way to the monument, they were set upon by riot police in a largely unprovoked outbreak of violence, in which the spectre of the Beanfield was all too apparent. The following year, having by now decided that any kind of access was unnecessary, the authorities came up with a new plan, which was so successful that it rolled on down the years. The four and a half mile exclusion zone, first introduced in 1985 to prevent the 83 people named in the injunction from approaching Stonehenge, was now imposed as a barrier to all, which was, moreover, enforced so tightly that almost everyone who tried to make it to the stones was either stopped or arrested.

Throughout this period, the aftershock of the violence at the Beanfield – and the continuing assaults on travellers' park-ups and on the free festival circuit that had sustained the movement – contributed to breakdowns in the travelling community that brought widespread misery. One of the most vivid descriptions of the true cost of the Beanfield came from Alan Lodge, who told Jim Carey, 'There was one guy who I trusted my children with in the early '80s – he was a potter. After the Beanfield I wouldn't let him anywhere near them. I saw him, a man of substance at the end of all that nonsense wobbled to the point of illness and evil. It turned all of us and I'm sure that applies to the whole of the travelling community. There were plenty of people who had got something very positive together who came out of the Beanfield with a world view of 'fuck everyone'.'

Alan also explained how, with the free festival circuit under constant attack, the autonomous economy that went with it collapsed: 'As soon as they scared away the punters, it destroyed the means of exchange. Norman Tebbit went on about getting on your bike and finding employment whilst at the same time being part of the political force that kicked the bike from under us.' By 1987, the festival circuit was a skeleton. A few established events survived – Cantlin Stone in Wales and the Avon Free Festival, for example – and a new festival at Ribblehead, in West Yorkshire, began that year, but it was not enough to support a living.

While some of the travellers bowed to the pressure and retreated from the road, and others abandoned Britain altogether, relocating to other countries in Europe where they hoped to encounter less hostility, many of those who remained found that their existing problems were exacerbated by the arrival on the scene of the Brew Crew. Mostly young men – some from within the movement, others arriving in droves from the inner cities – they developed what Jim Carey referred to as 'a penchant for nihilism, blagging and neighbourly disrespect', which spiralled into violence at some of the surviving free festivals of the time. In 2002, Lin Lorien explained to Roisin McAuley, for Radio 4's 'In Living Memory' programme on the Beanfield, that 'One of the things that followed on from the Beanfield – a lot of people, who'd been on the road for years, left. They just didn't want to be part of this violence, and because there was no elders, if you like, hundreds and hundreds and hundreds of people poured onto the roads in ratty old vans and buses, and they brought a lot of 'inner city values' and things with them, including drugs – the nasty hard drugs that people like myself just didn't want to know about –but there was so few of us that we couldn't stop it. There was gangsters moving in, you know, and all this sort of thing. It was just not nice.'

1987 was also the year that the Beanfield's legal successor, the 1986 Public Order Act, came into effect, with its notorious 'anti-hippy' clause 39, which edged closer to the criminalisation of trespass. Under the new clause, which applied to scheduled monuments (including Stonehenge), 'land forming part of a highway', and agricultural buildings, the police were enabled to arrest two or more people for trespass, provided that 'reasonable steps have been taken by or on behalf of the occupier to ask them to leave.' In addition, the previous requirement for arrest under these circumstances – damage to property – was amended to include the use of 'threatening, abusive or insulting words or behaviour' and/or the presence of 12 or more vehicles.

In its report on Stonehenge – based on its observers' reports during the build-up to the solstice in 1986, and published well before the Act was passed – the NCCL had been particularly wary of giving the police increased public order powers, when the ones that they already had, 'ranging from powers to prevent breach of the peace, to enforcement of road closure orders, to the use of the Road Traffic Act, were stretched to their limits to exclude, contain and, in the words of the Chief Constable of Hampshire, to 'neutralise' the travellers.' In almost every case monitored by the NCCL in 1986, grave misgivings had been expressed – about the legality of confiscating vehicles, the charges of obstruction and the extent of information gathering, as well as the road blocks and closures.

Doubts were also expressed about the legality of various procedures undertaken by the institutions that sustained the police: Salisbury District Council's order banning the planned demonstration on the Saturday before the solstice; the bail conditions imposed by magistrates, which required travellers to leave Wiltshire immediately; and the insistence of the police and courts in Salisbury that the defendants on June 21st were handcuffed in court. Subtly underlining the disproportionate hysteria that surrounded the travellers, the NCCL noted that the handcuffs were only removed when the defence lawyers pointed out that 'even those accused of terrorist bombing offences in the Old Bailey the previous week... had not been handcuffed in court.'

In the closing comments of its report, the NCCL accused the government, as well as all the institutions above, of a general failure to implement the terms of the Caravan Sites Act of 1968, which required local authorities to provide sites for Gypsies – defined, crucially, as 'persons of nomadic habit of life, whatever their race or origin' – and which empowered the Secretary of State for the Environment to force them to do so. Noting that in January 1986 less than 40% of 'official' Gypsies had been housed, that the Secretary of State had failed to enforce a single omission and that the new travellers

Spiral Tribe, one of the most influential sound systems – who also maintained a mystical focus on Stonehenge and the land – had a distinctive approach to design and presentation, as shown in the photo and flyer above. Images provided by Chris Riley.

YOU ARE NOW ENTERING THE NO GO ZONE

AFTER CARNIVAL

MASTERS OF DISGUISE

TECHNO MASSIVE

were not catered for, despite fulfilling the criteria outlined in the 1968 Act, the NCCL proposed immediate action to quell the traditional conflict between travelling people and settled people and to bring to an end the current situation whereby 'both central and local government sat back and waited for the police to use their public order powers to deal with the inevitable conflict.'

Predictably, the government ignored the advice of the NCCL. When the Public Order Act was passed, some of the worst fears of both the travellers and the NCCL were confirmed. By the time the solstice came around, many travellers were too preoccupied with the problems caused by clause 39 to worry about clause 13 of the Act, in which 'two people proceeding in a given direction can constitute a procession and can be arrested as a threat to civil order.' Clause 13 was aimed at Stonehenge. It was the prop that was to hold up the exclusion zone and keep the majority of travellers away from their temple at the solstice for over a decade.

Confounding all expectations, however, and demonstrating that counter-cultural youth movements have an uncanny ability to mutate in entirely unforeseen ways, the free festival and travellers' scenes were unexpectedly revitalised by the emergence of the Acid House movement at the end of the '80s, in which warehouse parties and outdoor raves brought the free party scene back with a vengeance. Although some of Thatcher's new entrepreneurs immediately began to exploit the new scene's boundless commercial possibilities, the many underground sound systems were directly inspired by the free festival movement, relocating themselves, as Nottingham's DiY sound system put it, 'in the free festivals of the hippies and travellers, in the ancient fields of England, so long denied to the landless.'

In May 1992, up to 50,000 people came together on Castlemorton Common in Gloucestershire to create the largest free gathering since the last Stonehenge Free Festival in 1984. As I observed in Stonehenge: Celebration and Subversion, 'This eight-day collision of 24-hour sound systems was the most exhilarating clash of bewildering alternatives to be seen for nearly a decade, an epic event of myth-making proportions, in which Castlemorton and the Bank Holiday weekend – neither sacred place nor holy time of year – to some people became both, the forbidden solstice at Stonehenge mutating into a vibrant contemporary alternative.'

A complementary view is provided by Alan Dearling, who was living in a narrow-boat just a few miles from Castlemorton. He remembers the event as follows: 'This was a full-on culture clash. The new travellers had parked up on Castlemorton Common after the event they were heading to – the Avon Free Festival – was prevented by the Avon and Somerset Constabulary. I was due to meet friends and they let me know that they had ended up on the Common below the Malvern Hills surrounded by the Spiral Tribe and Bedlam rigs. My traveller friends were not happy bunnies – they hated rave music, especially 24 hours a day. It was a magnet for the mobile-phone-rave-culture – but hardly a traveller event, at least not in the style of the '80s traveller scene.'

Other people were swept up in another new development – the road protest movement – which erupted spontaneously in 1992, but which clearly owed much of its impetus to the 'anarcho-spiritual' focus of the political protests conceived by the travelling community and the women of Greenham Common in the 1980s. From the beginning the road protestors demonstrated a raw, untutored form of grass-roots eco-paganism that went further than any previous protest movement in embracing the land as sacred.

The story began in February 1992 on Twyford Down near Winchester, an expanse of rolling chalk downland that was both a haven for wildlife and a repository of thousands of years of human history, including ancient tracks and Celtic field systems. When a local

'On the Freedom Trail 1995': the Dongas reclaim the green lanes of Albion. Copyright Graeme Strike.

rambler told Sam and Steph, two young travellers who had pitched camp there, that an extension to the M3 was shortly to be driven through the down, despite 20 years of protests by local people, they resolved to take matters into their own hands, and set up a protest camp that immediately began to draw numerous supporters.

In December 1992, the protestors were violently evicted from their camp by Group 4 Security. The naturalist David Bellamy, who had come to Twyford Down as a high profile political campaigner, witnessed the brutal events of that day, and his description echoed the shock experienced by outside observers like Nick Davies, Kim Sabido and the Earl of Cardigan at the Beanfield eight years before: 'I have been in many protests around the world... and have never seen such unreasonable force used, especially on women. These boys were putting the boot and fist in and they didn't care if they were men or women. There were ministry people there but no one tried to call them off. The security men went completely over the top.' All that had changed in eight years, it seemed, was that a quasi-military police force had been replaced by a private security firm that was, if anything, even less accountable for its actions than its predecessors.

Undeterred, the protestors – nicknamed the Dongas after an African name for the ancient tracks that crossed the down – reformed their protest camp in February 1993, and direct action took place on a daily basis throughout the spring and summer. Inspired by the Dongas, numerous other protest camps sprang up across the country in a matter of months, and it's noticeable that those who formed the core of the movement shared a profound spiritual response to the agenda of the road builders,

Protest vigil in January 1997 at the celebrated Fairmile camp in Devon, where protestors dug – and lived in – elaborate underground tunnels which were designed to collapse on the occupants if heavy machinery was deployed. Copyright Graeme Strike.

opposing the government's road expansion plans as 'the carving up of the 'Great Mother'.' For some, this concept had undoubtedly filtered through from the anti-nuclear protests of the 1980s, but for others it was simply an immediate response to what they perceived as the rape of the land. One of the Dongas, Gary, described his response to the bulldozers stripping the turf on Twyford Down as 'like seeing a person having the skin pulled off alive.'

The protestors also adopted a 'ritual year' of eight festivals, on the solstices and equinoxes, and on the quarter days at the start of February, May, August and November, which had become known by their Celtic names – Imbolc, Beltane, Lughnasa and Samhain. These had become widespread in modern paganism and had initially been developed in the 1950s by two influential refugees from the Ancient

Druid Order, the revivalists who had been celebrating the solstice at Stonehenge throughout the century – Ross Nichols, who founded the Order of Bards, Ovates and Druids in 1964, and Gerald Gardner, the founder of Wicca. It's also worth noting, however, that although the free festival circuit began, pragmatically, with events that ran on Bank Holiday weekends, the pagan festivals had also been adopted by the travellers, as the summer solstice at Stonehenge grew more and more significant, and as their relationship to the land intensified.

Donga Gary described 'following the old pagan calendar of pre-Christian England, which is very dear to me now, as with anyone who is close to Nature', and for this new wave of protestors Stonehenge once more assumed a central symbolic position, partly through the post-Beanfield mythology of the martyred festival, but primarily because of the enduring attraction of the monument and its solstice alignment. Gary called Stonehenge 'one big, stone calendar – one of the most historic places in the world', and added that 'travellers meet there because of the celebration of summer.'

What Gary meant, of course, was that travellers would have met there had it not been for the exclusion zone. Another of the Dongas – Alex Plows – recalled how she and others were effectively forced to abandon Stonehenge, as they were unwilling to spend the solstice 'having a ruck with the police.' She added, 'It was hardly like we were depoliticised – most of us were having a break from protest camps for a couple of weeks... We needed down time, to recharge in a sacred landscape.' The alternative sacred landscape chosen by the Dongas was Avebury, where, unlike Stonehenge, people were 'having lovely times in a more amenable landscape every summer', and the Dongas in particular were 'hanging out in this semi-permanent state of magic reality in West Woods [near Avebury], a whole bunch of us living in benders deep in the woods, wandering all over the landscape on moonlit nights.'

The adoption of other sacred sites – and Avebury in particular – was one of the many side-effects of the suppression of the Stonehenge Free Festival, but in the wake of all these movements came yet another onslaught on civil liberties. The first of these was Luton MP Graham Bright's Pay Parties (Increased Penalties) Bill, which advocated fines of up to £20,000 and/or six months' imprisonment for the organisers of parties on unlicensed premises and outside legal licensing hours. Although 15,000 people took to the streets of London to protest against the Bill in February 1990, it was passed by Parliament in July. The new Act was designed to curb the free party scene, 'pushing event organisation into the hands of large commercial promoters with the necessary sums required to pay for licences and policing', as Jim Carey described it. It was also immediately used to justify the only mass arrest in British civil history that exceeded in numbers – if not in the violence that was applied – the arrests at the Beanfield and around Stonehenge on June 1st 1985. At a party in Leeds, 836 people were arrested, although almost all were released within a few hours, and an official complaint was made against the police, who were subsequently sued for assault and unlawful arrest.

The Battle of the Beanfield

Despite Graham Bright's intentions, the free party scene refused to be cowed. Over the next two years its momentum was relentless, and for the most part, the anonymity of the organisers and the sheer numbers of people attending the events kept the legislation at bay. Jane Bussman caught the mood in her book *Once in a Lifetime*: 'there were raves bigger than towns... self-ruling mini-cities that appeared on Saturday afternoon and were gone by Sunday, leaving no trace apart from a mountain of Evian bottles and a man no one knows in a poncho asleep in a hedge.' The final breaking point for the authorities was Castlemorton, which many commentators believe was deliberately engineered by the police to create the outrage required to enable a new and even more draconian piece of legislation – the Criminal Justice Bill – to sail through a quiescent parliament with full public support.

Certainly, all the required ingredients were present, as they had been at the Beanfield seven years before. Firstly, tens of thousands of party-goers were somehow 'allowed' to gather on Castlemorton Common, as the travellers of 1985 had been 'allowed' to gather in Savernake Forest. Leaked documents revealed that Avon and Somerset police had been involved in an intelligence-gathering operation called 'Operation Nomad', and Jim Carey noted that the claim made by West Mercia police – in whose patch Castlemorton took place – that 'they had no idea that an event might happen in their district' relied on 'the unlikely situation that Avon and Somerset police did not inform their neighbouring constabulary of 'Operation Nomad'.' Then came the manufactured outrage: 'Hippies fire flares at Police' was a headline in *The Daily Telegraph*, which was followed by an editorial

A member of Spiral Tribe celebrates their trial victory in 1994.
Image provided by Chris Riley.

An excellent, satirical anti-CJB postcard produced by Kate Evans for Gathered Images in Brighton.

demanding 'New Age, New Laws', and then came the launch of the pre-planned legislation, accompanied by the expansion of 'Operation Nomad' into 'Operation Snapshot', the creation of a massive database of names, licence numbers, traveller sites and the movements of individuals. This was as legally dubious as the intelligence-gathering that had been taking place for years as a result of operations at Molesworth, the Beanfield and Stoney Cross, but now it was even more pervasive.

In a similar vein, when the Criminal Justice Bill soon appeared, it too was designed to add further draconian muscle to the already overheated 1986 Public Order Act, although it's worth noting that, ironically, the attempts to prosecute those deemed responsible for the Castlemorton Gathering – principally members of Spiral Tribe – collapsed ignominiously after a £4 million trial, and, according to an article in *SchNEWS* in 2003, even the police apologised for the court case: 'Later, on the steps of the committal proceedings, Superintendent Clift (the chap whose jurisdiction the Common was under) came up to the accused and said, 'I just want you to know that I don't agree with what is happening to you here. This is a political stitch-up'.'

Despite Superintendent Clift's misgivings, the government was undeterred. One of the most notorious aspects of the Criminal Justice Bill was that it specifically targeted the 'repetitive beats' of the sound systems, and was aimed at further limiting gatherings of travellers and the free party scene by reducing the numbers of vehicles which could come together in one place from 12 to six. In many ways, however, these were amongst the Bill's milder repressive measures. Also included were criminal sanctions against assembly – specifically through 'trespassory assembly', an amendment of the Public Order Act

The Battle of the Beanfield

After a huge, sunny, hassle-free protest against the CJB in London in the summer of 1994, the police pursued a deliberate policy of entrapment and provocation at the last great protest against the Bill, which took place in Hyde Park in the autumn. Copyright Graeme Strike.

whereby the police were enabled to ban groups of 20 or more meeting in a particular area if they feared 'serious disruption to the life of the community', even if the meeting was non-obstructive and non-violent – and 'aggravated trespass', which fulfilled the right-wing dream of transforming trespass from a civil to a criminal concern. Both had disturbing ramifications for almost all kinds of protests and alternative gatherings, and clearly had their origins in the problems encountered by the authorities both before and during the Beanfield, when there remained a quaint assumption in British law of a right of assembly without prior state permission, against which the ancient charge of 'unlawful assembly', attempted at the Beanfield, had been a spectacular failure. Most savagely of all, the Act repealed the 1968 Caravans Sites Act, which, by removing the obligation on local authorities to provide sites for Gypsies – 'persons of nomadic habit of life, whatever their race or origin', lest we forget – finally criminalised the entire way of life of Gypsies and travellers, with baleful effects that are still being felt to this day.

By the time the Bill became law in November 1994, its assault on civil liberties had been expanded to include the road protestors, who had not even been glimpsed on the horizon when the fallout from Castlemorton began. But what neither Home Secretary Michael Howard nor any other members of John Major's Cabinet had foreseen was the extent to which their proposals would create extraordinary new coalitions of protestors. The campaigning journalist George Monbiot, who described the legislation as 'crude, ill-drafted and repressive', observed that it had succeeded in creating 'the broadest, and oddest, counter-cultural coalition Britain has ever known', uniting 'Hunt saboteurs, peace protestors, football supporters, squatters, radical lawyers, gypsies, pensioners, ravers, disabled rights activists, even an assistant chief constable and a Tory ex-minister.'

The government also failed to predict how inventive and determined the protestors would become in their opposition. Just six months after the Act was passed, the anonymous street theatre of Reclaim the Streets announced itself in London, when activists shut Camden High Street for the day by crashing two old cars into each other to create a road block, filled up the street with carpets, armchairs, sofas, and a kids' playground, and held a huge party from noon until 7pm, when it was all cleared up again. The energy and ingenuity of the movement clearly owed much to the road protestors – and in fact the two movements came together the following year in an occupation of the M41 in west London. In the late '90s the art of protest conceived by these groups spread around the world, sowing the seeds for much of the anti-globalisation movement, which has become a creative force for campaigning on both human rights and green issues.

Significantly, as I've touched on above, the road protestors themselves were also undeterred by the varied threats contained in Criminal Justice Act, and in fact the largest road protest to date, the campaign against the A34 Newbury bypass, began two years after the Act was passed, and was – triumphantly – the multi-million pound irritant that eventually forced the government of the time to abandon its £19 billion programme of road expansion. It's also worth noting that the passion for land reform that the Dongas inspired was sustained through the subsequent activities of a number of campaigning groups and proponents of alternative lifestyles. Of particular note was The Land Is Ours (TLIO), a coalition of activists seeking sustainable small-scale developments, who organised a number of public campaigns, including two separate occupations of land near St George's Hill in Surrey, where Gerrard Winstanley's Diggers had begun their short-lived but influential land rights campaign in 1649. They also established a well-publicised eco-village on 13 acres of derelict land in Wandsworth. Some of those involved in TLIO are also part of Tinker's Bubble in Somerset, a visionary low-impact community whose members have, as at Tipi Valley in Wales (which was established by a number of Stonehenge regulars in the 1970s), been forced to engage in the most extraordinary struggles with short-sighted local officials to ensure their survival. The residents of Tinker's Bubble are also involved in an ongoing campaign to amend the existing planning legislation – which is often inept, outdated and/or geared solely to the requirements of the well-off – to enable similar experiments to take place.

Just as those involved in land reform have adapted to the post-CJA world, so too have those most affected by the legislation – the travellers and Gypsies. Though the repeal of the 1968 Caravans Act has, in many cases, imperilled their way of life, many have risen to the challenge by becoming much more organised and indeed politicised. Alan Dearling explains: 'Even amidst some distrust and suspicion, there was a growing awareness that nomadic people of all types needed to work alongside one another if there was to be any chance of survival in the UK. So, out of adversity, there were positive examples of both self-help initiatives and campaigning and advocacy work on traveller issues. A particular emphasis was placed on two fronts: education strategies for travelling children and work on legal reforms to protect nomadic people from persecution. Initiatives included films,

One of the Newbury pages from 'Copse: The Cartoon Book of Tree Protesting', Kate Evans' incomparable account of the road protest movement. Copyright Kate Evans.

reports, training events and lobbying taken by non-governmental agencies such as Save the Children, the Travellers' School Charity, Friends, Families and Travellers, the National Playbus Association, the Children's Society, the Commission for Racial Equality, Groundswell, the Traveller Law Research unit at Cardiff Law School, the Legal Action Group, the Advisory Council for Romany and other Travellers (ACERT), The Land is Ours, the National Council for Voluntary Organisations, Groundswell and the Gypsy Council for Education, Culture, Welfare and Civil Rights. Charlie Smith, the chair of the Gypsy Council, recently stated, 'There are 300,000 Gypsies and Travellers in this country and we have to stand together or they will pick us off one by one'.'

Alan continues: 'Another dimension of the evolving traveller and Gypsy scene in the last decade or so has been the presence of a number of regular magazines and publications that have allowed for networking within and between the travelling communities. These have included the newsletters from the Travellers' School Charity, Friends, Families and Travellers, *Travellers' Times, Groundswell News* and pro-traveller pieces in *Squall, Frontline, SchNews* and *Undercurrents* video diaries alongside old faithfuls such as *Festival Eye* and the Stonehenge Campaign newsletter. These have been complemented by the books about Gypsy and travelling lifestyles from publishers such as the University of Hertfordshire Press and Enabler Publications, authors such as C.J. Stone, George McKay and Jake Bowers, and an increasing number of websites. Collectively, they have helped to keep the travelling community informed on a variety of issues including planning laws, availability of legal advice, potential sources for funding and opportunities afforded by travelling outside of the UK.'

Alan suggests that 'Travellers and Gypsies have also benefited from the hard graft of some powerful allies and spokespeople, including Lord Avebury, Ann Bagehot, Margaret Greenfields, Andrew Ryder, Arthur Ivatts, Donald Kenrick, Colin Clark, Alan Lodge, Luke Clements, Jenny Smith, Zoe James, Susan Alexander, Richie Cotterill, Fiona Earle, Zoe Matthews, Rachel Morris, Peter Mercer, Thomas Acton – and even myself – to name but a few (and apologies to those I've missed out!) There have also been some interesting developments on the police side of the fence. Many forces have gradually moved towards seeking a dialogue with travellers. For example, Sergeant Nick Williams of the Metropolitan Police regularly invites Gypsies and travellers, who he calls 'Our critical friends', to meetings of the Met's Advisory Group, 'to look at anything that is going on within the police' (*Travellers' Times*, issue 21, Autumn 2004). So, in a rather strange way, although the repeal of the Caravans Act and the hostility both of local communities and of politicians – from the national to the local level – has made life much harder for Britain's nomadic people, there is evidence that the police and state attempts to 'decommission' the travelling lifestyle in the UK at sites such as the Beanfield, Molesworth and Stoney Cross may actually have partially backfired insofar as it brought about greater unity in the diverse travelling community.'

Also forced to mutate and survive from the mid-90s onwards were the different facets of the free festival and free party scene. The Criminal Justice Act certainly succeeded in suppressing large-scale 'free' gatherings to the extent that it's difficult to foresee how anything on the scale of Castlemorton or the last few Stonehenge Free Festivals could take place again. It's noticeable that the few attempts that have been made – the Mother Festival in 1995, and Steart Beach in 2002 – have ended ignominiously (the first was closed down almost before it began, and for the second 20,000 party-goers inadvertently occupied a Nature Reserve, provoking predictably widespread outrage in the media.) Nevertheless, the free party scene continues, in small gatherings, often held on private land with the permission of the landowner, and anyone with an eye for the history of youth movements will be aware that current media portraits of a generation of teenagers who are either blind drunk or deeply conservative may not be giving the complete picture.

More visible are the developments of the free festival scene, in particular those aspects of this long-running story which came out of the free festival spirit of the 1970s and the protest/convoy movement of the early '80s, and which were not absorbed into the E-fuelled euphoria – and subsequent crash – of the late '80s/early '90s dance scene. These include the various offshoots of the Ecology Party's original Green Gatherings at Worthy Farm in the early '80s – small camps which range from the anarchist principles and 'pass-the-hat' funding of the Rainbow Circle gatherings to the small-scale commercial enterprises run by Oak Dragon, Rainbow 2000 and a host of other (eco)-pagan groups. Then there are larger events like the Big Green Gathering, which has solar-, wind- and pedal-powered stages instead of generators, and which has successfully juggled the commercial and bureaucratic demands of running a contemporary alternative gathering without compromising its idealism. Also worth mentioning is Andy Hope's Green Roadshow, which has transformed the ecological leanings of the free festival circuit into a solar-powered roadshow providing education and entertainment, and which, with a rather delicious irony, is now paid to do so by the same councils who treated them with hostility and violence when they were part of the free festival scene in the 1980s. Likewise, the Rinky Dink pedal-powered stage and mobile sound system has become an emblem of the new, more green travelling movement. The brainchild of Dan Smythies, Rinky Dink has travelled throughout Europe at street events and festivals, and has even helped to dissipate violence and tension along the way.

Steve Muggeridge, who was at the Beanfield, and who is now a director of the Big Green Gathering, recently wrote to me, explaining his take on the developments of the last 20 years, and the progress that has been made: 'I sometimes think that the Big Green Gathering and similar events are partially a result of the changes to festivals and travelling, set in motion by the policy behind the Beanfield. The transition from free festival to limited company is an interesting one. Perhaps the disciplines learnt, in order to meet ever more stringent legal conditions, in order to happen at all, have given a more constructive focus and purpose to both the Green and festival/travelling movement. Although I have many varied memories of the ad hoc style of free festival management, events like the Big Green Gathering (although few!) have become far more constructive as

The Big Green Gathering 1996: this looks like traditional free festival fun and frolics, but it was actually part of a protest against police strip-searches. Copyright Alan Dearling.

agents of counter-cultural and environmental awareness and education, although there are, of course, ever more restrictions with regard to health and safety etc.'

The particular ways in which these gatherings developed is a topic that Brig Oubridge, a director and one of the founders of the Big Green Gathering, was also keen to point out when he wrote to me recently. As Brig described it, 'A story which has not yet been publicly told is that of the evolution of the festival scene since 1985 – the impossibility of finding festival sites after the Beanfield; the evolution in the later 1980s into many smaller mini-festival type camps (Oak Dragon, Rainbow Circle etc.); the co-option of the early 1980s Green Gatherings into the Glastonbury Festival Green Fields; and their re-emergence in 1993-4 in the setting up of the Big Green Gathering Co. Ltd. and the first Big Green Gathering in 1994 on the site of the 1975 Watchfield People's Free Festival.'

Brig continued by describing the ways in which Stonehenge had been re-absorbed into the narrative, a development that provides one of the more conciliatory gestures on the part of the police towards the disenfranchised festival/traveller community. This began with 'the move in 1995 of the Big Green Gathering to a site in Wiltshire, and the part played by the then Chief Superintendent of Wiltshire Police in charge of Salisbury division, Fred Pritchard (who had been the Inspector in charge of Amesbury police station in 1985, and previous to that a drugs squad officer who had worked undercover on 'Operation Julie' in the 1970s) in brokering the deal between the Big Green Gathering and Wiltshire police which allowed the Big Green Gathering to happen.' Brig then emphasised 'the part played by the Big Green Gatherings in Wiltshire from 1995 to 2000 in building confidence with Wiltshire police.' This was a factor in 'the reversal of the 'Fortress Wiltshire' anti-festival policy which had existed since 1985', and contributed to the re-opening of Stonehenge for the summer solstice in 2000.

While this bridge-building was taking place, three other developments also fed into the existing campaigns to regain access to Stonehenge. The first of these was the emergence, in the late 1980s, of a number of new Druid groups, drawn from the festival years, who held a similar eco-pagan perspective to that which was embraced by the road protest movement. These were the Secular Order of Druids, founded by Tim Sebastian, who had attempted to liaise between the festival-goers and the Ancient Druid Order during the Stonehenge Free Festivals, Rollo Maughfling's Glastonbury Order, and the Loyal Arthurian Warband, led by Arthur Pendragon, a former soldier and biker leader, who changed his name by deed poll in 1986 when it occurred to him that he was this generation's King Arthur, come to rescue Albion from the legacy of Thatcher.

Of these, it was Arthur whose commitment to free access for all bordered on the obsessive – and who was, in addition, media-savvy in a way that recalled the great prankster tradition of the free festival activists. His mission began in the winter of 1990, when he staged a one-man sit-in outside the temple for four months to protest against the entrance fee, and on the solstice in 1991 he embarked on the first of a series of voluntary – and high-profile – arrests for breaking through the exclusion zone, which persisted throughout the decade. The mid-1990s saw an extraordinary increase in his activities, both against the exclusion zone and as part of the road protest movement, which he had first become involved in when the Dongas had invited him to conduct a ceremony on Twyford Down in 1993. In 1996, he embraced the struggle on a full-time basis, joining the largest action to date, the campaign against the A34 Newbury bypass, and on the summer solstice he led the most concerted of all his assaults on the exclusion zone, in which 27 people, including 13 Druids, were arrested.

A second major development took place on May 8th 1995, the 50th anniversary of VE Day, when a well-planned dawn invasion by 400 people resulted in the first large gathering in the Stones since those on the equinoxes and the winter solstice – which had somehow been allowed to continue after 1985 – were finally halted in 1990. The occupation was conceived as a symbolically laden response to the Criminal Justice Act, with the organisers stressing their belief that 'the freedoms that our nation fought for during the war' were being eroded by the Act. It was planned the summer before as a direct result of the mingling of the older campaigners with the new wave of protestors at the road protest camps, and on the day the established campaigners for access to

'Lest we forget': VE Day 1995. Copyright Adrian Arbib.

Stonehenge were joined by members of the Dongas, including Theo, who sang his 'Motorway Song', which had become an anthem of the new movement at Twyford Down. The surprise on the day was that Clews Everard, English Heritage's Stonehenge Manager, allowed the celebrants to stay, but it was clearly a wise move, avoiding – for once – unnecessary conflict, and enabling the authorities to begin to put aside the prevalent 'folk-devil' image of the travellers.

The third significant contribution came from long-term campaigner George Firsoff, who established the Truth and Reconciliation Commission (as part of his Stonehenge Peace Process), along with Thomas Daffern, Director of the International Institute of Peace Studies and Global Philosophy. Based on 'the experience and vision that guided the builders of the new South Africa', the TRC was open to all, and its meetings duly attracted a number of travellers, festival-goers and pagans, as well as receiving regular visits from Clews Everard, English Heritage's Stonehenge Manager, and Chief Inspector Andy Hollingshead of the Wiltshire police. Along with another group that was established at this time, the Round Table, in which representatives of all the major bodies – English Heritage, the National Trust, the Wiltshire police and local and district councils, along with local landowners and farmers – sat down with the Druids and other pagans, these groups embarked upon the crucial discussions that would eventually lead to the new arrangements for access to Stonehenge from 2000 onwards.

The Battle of the Beanfield

By the mid- to late-'90s, the roll-call of those pressing for access to Stonehenge was astonishing. As well as those discussed above – the Stonehenge Campaign, activists from the road protest movement (and Reclaim the Streets), travellers, a generation of festival-goers, King Arthur and the festival Druids, the TRC, the Round Table, the Big Green Gathering and its police liaison, and the Christians and locals who had been involved in meetings in the aftermath of the Beanfield – there were also a number of archaeologists who had steadily come on board in the years since the Beanfield, other Druids from the more mainstream Order of Bards, Ovates and Druids and the British Druid Order, who sought, in particular, special access arrangements for small gatherings, and a host of other pagan groups and individuals. Despite their best efforts, however, it wasn't until 1998 that English Heritage finally came up with anything other than the blanket exclusion zone that had created a war zone around the temple on the summer solstice for a decade.

Even so, the proposals were almost exactly the same as those that had last been attempted with disastrous results ten years before. 500 free tickets – for dates on and around the solstice – were offered in advance, but although around 250 people took up the offer, those who were committed to open access for all had no option but to turn it down yet again. At the solstice, the gulf between those with and without tickets was as pronounced as it had been ten years before. While around a hundred people, including representatives of six different Druid groups, other pagans, local people, archaeologists and 40 press reporters and photographers, took advantage of the special access arrangements, everyone else who approached the exclusion zone was subject to the same indignities as ever.

The last stage in this long-running conflict between the authorities and those who viewed Stonehenge as a social, political and/or spiritual beacon took place in 1999, shortly after an Appeal Court of the House of Lords, which included Lord Hutton and the Lord Chancellor Derry Irvine, had finally ruled that the exclusion zone was illegal. This tortuous – but ultimately crucial – stage in the arguments for access began on June 1st 1995, on the tenth anniversary of the Beanfield, when two people, Margaret Jones and Richard Lloyd – a lecturer and a student – were arrested on the verge of the road outside Stonehenge during a demonstration against the Criminal Justice Act. Significantly, they were charged with 'trespassory assembly' under the first use of Section 70 of the Act, which amended Section 14 of the 1986 Public Order Act, prohibiting gatherings of 20 or more people, as described above.

Convicted by magistrates in Salisbury in October, the 'Stonehenge Two' had their sentences dismissed on appeal in January 1996. Salisbury Crown Court held that the protestors 'were not obstructing the freedom of movement of others on the verge nor were they causing a public nuisance' and concluded that, as they were not 'being destructive, violent, disorderly, threatening a breach of the peace or, on the evidence, doing anything other than reasonably using the highway', there was no case to answer. This time the police appealed, and the retrial, which concluded in January 1997, went their way. The implications were alarming. In *The Guardian*, Alex Bellos warned that

The legacy of the Beanfield

'People attending a wide range of peaceful gatherings, including environmental protestors and ramblers' groups, can be arrested for doing nothing more than walking down the road, following a High Court judgement yesterday.' As I noted in *Stonehenge: Celebration and Subversion*, '12 years before, there had been no effective legislation to stop a festival of 40,000 people occupying the fields across the road from Stonehenge; now, just two people on the verge of a road could be arrested for doing nothing.'

On March 4th 1999, the House of Lords finally overturned the police conviction of January 1997 against the 'Stonehenge Two', by a majority of three to two, demolishing the legality of the exclusion zone in the process. Lord Hutton in particular put forward a considered and far-reaching defence of civil liberties, taking in the right of free speech, the right to demonstrate, the right to protest on matters of public concern and the right of assembly. He quoted Lord Denning: 'These are rights which it is in the public interest that individuals should possess; and indeed, that they should exercise without impediment so long as no wrongful act is done. It is often the only means by which grievances can be brought to the knowledge of those in authority – at any rate with such impact as to gain a remedy.' For his part, the Lord Chancellor was concerned to establish, as 'an issue of fundamental constitutional importance', that 'the public highway is a public place which the public may enjoy for any reasonable purpose, provided the activity in question does not amount to a public or private nuisance and does not obstruct the highway by unreasonably impeding the primary right of the public to pass and repass: within these qualifications there is a public right of peaceful assembly on the highway.'

Despite these developments, English Heritage appeared not to have fully understood the potential threat posed by several thousand people being allowed to congregate outside the perimeter fence instead of being turned back or arrested on the edge of the exclusion zone. They offered a thousand free tickets over the solstice period, and those who were committed to open access were again obliged to refuse. On the night of the solstice, several thousand people duly turned up, and around 2 am a few hundred celebrants broke down the perimeter fence and proceeded to occupy the Stones. The night ended in clashes with the police and 23 arrests, and there was much lamenting from various commentators, who tried to blame the occupation on Class War activists. In reality, given that the exclusion zone had been lifted, but that the access restrictions on congregating at the monument had not, it's more reasonable to conclude that the invasion was simply a spontaneous demonstration of frustration by those with a long history of exclusion from the Stones.

Under these circumstances, few could have suspected how swiftly and decisively both English Heritage and the police would respond to the full ramifications of the Lords' decision, but in the months that followed the solstice in 1999 both parties reached the inevitable conclusion that the prohibition on access to the Stones at the solstice was now effectively unworkable. On the morning of June 21st 2000, over 6,000 people duly turned up to take advantage of the new arrangements – 11 hours of 'Managed Open Access', in

which those who gathered were allowed to roam freely amongst the Stones but were prohibited from bringing in amplified music, dogs or bottles. It was, and remains, an iffy kind of compromise for the old guard of festival-goers and travellers, but compared to the wilderness years of 1985 to 1999, it surely stands as some form of progress – compromised certainly; a tribal gathering in which, ironically, many of those taking part are oblivious to the suffering that was endured to achieve it – but progress nonetheless, with the option of amending it in future at least a possibility.

Indeed, by the solstice in 2002, Clews Everard commented, 'It's good to see so many people of all different ages, classes and creeds enjoying themselves.' Alan Dearling suggests, 'There have also been positive messages about the solstice negotiations as a 'healing process' from all concerned – police, travellers, Druids and assorted festival-goers. However, it remains a sanitised and restricted form of solstice celebration, and there is still substantial resistance from the police and English Heritage towards any return to an actual festival at the Stones', although he notes that, 'Interestingly, the National Trust has been seen as tentatively encouraging more access near the Stones area as part of a 'more relaxed' and positive approach to people using the land in their stewardship.'

So while what happened 20 years ago to a few hundred people in a field in Wiltshire may seem like ancient history, I suggest that it remains relevant in a number of ways, beyond the revulsion that is the only civilised response to the exercise of such brutal force on unarmed members of the public by officers of the law. It's true that those in charge have moved on – Thatcher, Hurd, Heseltine, Grundy, and all those in responsible positions in the other organisations involved, including English Heritage and the National Trust – but

The legacy of the Beanfield

The Kings Drummers by the Heel Stone, Stonehenge, summer solstice 2004. Copyright Andy Worthington.

the legacy they left has not. Without the events of the Beanfield – and in particular the distasteful influence wielded by politicians and the media to ensure that a day of terrifying violence inflicted on an unarmed minority of society can be spun to suggest that the very opposite is true – the steady erosion of civil liberties that has taken place over the last 20 years would not have been so easily achieved.

The development is clear: first came the Beanfield, then the Public Order Act, then the Criminal Justice Act, and lately – and most brazenly of all – the Blair government has enacted further draconian measures, under the guise of protecting us from terrorism, from various forms of political protest and from anti-social behaviour, that have stripped our rights still further. No attempt has been made to repeal the most vilified parts of the previous legislation. The way of life of Britain's new travellers and Gypsies – the resident ethnic minority towards whom it is still acceptable to express racist hatred – remains effectively criminalised, with no relief in sight, while communities close ranks against them, and politicians and the media use them as ammunition to prove how tough they are on 'law and order.'

Nor, it seems, is this process complete. At the time of writing the government is still committed to introducing ID cards, is seriously considering how to further effect a clampdown on legitimate protest to prevent people protesting outside the premises of arms manufacturers, and is preparing a 'ring of steel' around the summit of G8 leaders in Gleneagles in July 2005 that will dwarf all that has come before. I may be naturally suspicious of governments that lean towards authoritarianism, but it strikes me as somewhat ominous that the last occasions when such paranoia – and such wanton expenditure on civil matters – were in evidence was from 1992 to 1994, during the build-up to the passing of the Criminal Justice Act, and in particular from 1984 to 1986, those dark years for civil liberties that have been described, in sometimes harrowing detail, throughout this book.

This chapter is partly adapted from chapters in Andy's book Stonehenge: Celebration and Subversion.

And finally, just to prove that subversive humour is not dead, this cunningly disguised flyer for the 20th anniversary of the Beanfield has been circulating in cyberspace.

About the contributors

Don Aitken helped to establish welfare services at free festivals from 1972 onwards. He was a trustee of Festival Welfare Services, and one of the founding trustees of the Travellers Aid Trust. He was also involved in writing and producing the early issues of *Festival Eye*.

Adrian Arbib is a professional photographer specialising in human rights and the environment. He has documented the struggles of marginalised peoples around the world, and in the UK has covered many of the major political protests and alternative gatherings from the 1980s to the present day.
Website: www.arbib.org
Email: photo@arbib.org

Sheila Craig has written and broadcast extensively about community and family issues. Like many others she still bears scars from the traumatic events of 20 years ago. The scars serve to keep alive her commitment to personal, social, global and environmental change.

Alan Dearling is a full-time writer, researcher and book editor. In addition to his work in youth social work and housing fields, he has been involved in various ways with the festival, alternative lifestyles and environmental scene since the late 1960s. He has written and edited over 30 books and assisted in the production of hundreds of others. His own publications include: *Another kind of space: creating ecological environments and dwellings*; *No Boundaries – new Travellers outside of England* and *Alternative Australia – celebrating cultural diversity*. Much of his other work is undertaken with, and for, universities and agencies such as the Joseph Rowntree Foundation and the Chartered Institute of Housing.
Email: adearling@aol.com

Kate Evans has been marrying words and images for political effect for the last 10 years. Artistically adventurous, she has evolved a style of succinct comic reportage. She is an active environmental campaigner, and the author and publisher of Copse, a cartoon history of the road protest movement in the UK.
Website: www.cartoonkate.co.uk
Email: kartoonkate@fastmail.fm

Neil Goodwin has been making documentaries for 18 years. These have been mostly about environmental and human rights issues, and include *Operation Solstice* (with Gareth and Russell Morris), as well as campaign videos for Greenpeace UK, and a promo for Coldcut. In 1993 he was part of the No M11 Link Road Campaign and lived on Claremont Road for nine months until the eviction. He is also a writer, and contributed various pieces to *The Guardian*, *The New Statesman* and *Squall* magazine during the Third Battle of Newbury in 1996. In the late 1990s he helped to set up the 'Forever Green' campaign in Wanstead, and prevented the Metropolitan Police from selling off a beautiful chunk of greenbelt to an unscrupulous developer. He was involved in setting up and running the 491 Gallery in Leytonstone (the only squat ever to feature on *The Richard and Judy Show*) and went on to create the Vertigo Film Club (which was burnt down by a careless candle-wielding hippy in 2004). He is currently teaching English in Taiwan.
Email: neilgoodwinuk@hotmail.com

Richard Hester has written and published on the subject of 'Newer Travellers' over the last few years. He is an honourary lecturer at the University of Birmingham and is currently a freelance trainer in the field of 'Youth Justice' and crime prevention. He recently returned to the UK after an attempt to circumnavigate the globe in a small boat where he shipwrecked in Tahiti. Before going freelance, he briefly worked for Warwickshire Police.

Roger Hutchinson works as a multi-media public artist. Signed copies of his original Stonehenge Free Festival poster, reproduced on A2 acid-free paper from the original artwork, can be ordered by sending a cheque for £8 (£5 plus £3 p+p) – or £12 for two posters – made out to 'Intelligent Arts', to 39 Hazel Street, Leicester, LE2 7JN.
Email: rogerhutchinson@ntlworld.com

Alan Lodge is a professional photographer. Samples of his unparalleled archive of over 70,000 photos from the late 1970s to the present day, as well as numerous articles on free festivals, travellers, free parties and political protest, can be found on his website, 'One Eye on the Road: Tash's Festival, Travellin' & Environmental Archives.'
Website: http://tash.gn.apc.org
Email: tash@gn.apc.org

Pete Loveday is a jobbing artist, 'self-buried in Devon', as his neighbour Tom Hodgkinson has described him. As the creator of the comic *Russell, the saga of a peaceful man*, he retains a unique place in British counter-culture, with his acute observations of traveller and festival history – and the absurdities of the law.
Telephone: 01598 710679

Contributors

Tim Malyon is a former drugs counsellor, who ran the Release festival welfare unit during the early years of the Stonehenge Festival, before becoming a photographer, writer, radio journalist and organic farm manager. He succeeded in getting through the police Beanfield blockade to photograph the 'battle' for *New Statesman* and *City Limits* magazines, and afterwards was escorted off-site by a horrified police officer who wanted people to see what had happened that day: 'I didn't become a police officer to do this', he told Tim. 'There was no breach of the peace until the police came onto this field.'

Gareth Morris co-directed *Operation Solstice* with Neil Goodwin and Russell Morris. He lives in London, and, as he describes it, 'attempts to make a living making environmental documentaries.'

Graeme Strike is a photographer who contributed to Alan Dearling's book *No Boundaries*. He lived and travelled with the Dongas tribe and was allowed to record their lifestyle as a photographic essay. Alan last heard of him living in Cornwall.

Jez Tucker is a print/publishing designer and co-founder of *Squall* magazine. He was a squatting activist during the late eighties and nineties and these days works primarily in environmental and public health, having recently helped set up a new publishing company in the substance misuse sector.
Email: jez.tucker@ntlworld.com

Andy Worthington is a freelance historian, who specialises in looking at how people in the modern world relate to ancient sacred sites and the wider landscape, particularly through paganism and political dissent. He is the author of *Stonehenge: Celebration and Subversion* (Alternative Albion, 2004), and has written for a number of publications including *The Guardian, Fortean Times, Festival Eye, SchNEWS, British Archaeology, Pagan Dawn, Pentacle, 3rd Stone* and the *Nth Position* website. He lives in south London with his wife Dot and his son Tyler.
Website: www.andyworthington.co.uk
Email: a.worthington@britishlibrary.net

Bibliography

The following are books – and pamphlets, articles and websites – consulted and/or specifically referred to in the text...

ABBOTT, Tim (1990), 'Eye Witness', *Festival Eye* 1990

AITKEN, Don and Alex Rosenberger (1991), 'Beanfield Battle Trial', *Festival Eye*, Summer '91

AYERS, Nigel, (1996), 'Where's Wally?' *Transgressions*, 2/3, Salamander Press, online at: www.earthlydelights.co.uk/netnews/wally.html

BROWN, M.D. (1995), *Do Police Officers base their assumptions of 'New Age' Travellers on stereotypical images rather than empirical evidence?*, MA thesis, University of Plymouth

BUSSMAN, Jane (1998), *Once in a Lifetime*, Virgin

CAREY, Jim (1997), 'A Criminal Culture?' *Squall*, online at: www.squall.co.uk/squall.cfm/ses/sq=2001061806/ct=2

CHIPPINDALE, Christopher (2004), *Stonehenge Complete* (3rd edition), Thames and Hudson

CLARKE, Michael (1982), *The Politics of Pop Festivals*, Junction Books

CRAIG, Sheila (ed.) (1986), 'Stonehenge '85: Souvenir Issue', Unique Publications

CRYER, Dominic (1993), 'A visit with the Dongas Tribe', online at: tash.gn.apc.org/dongas.htm

DAVIES, Nick (1985), 'Inquest on a rural riot', *The Observer*, June 9th 1985

DEARLING, Alan (2001), 'Not only but also... reminiscences on the festies, the Stones and the new Travellers, 1969-2001', unpublished MS.

DONGA Gary (1995), 'Gary's Story - From Printer to Donga', online at: tash.gn.apc.org/gary.htm

EARLE, Fiona, Alan Dearling, Helen Whittle, Roddy Glasse and Gubby (1994), *A Time to Travel: an introduction to Britain's newer Travellers*, Enabler Publications

ELSTROB, Lynne and Anne Howes (1987), *The Glastonbury Festivals*, Gothic Image Publications

EVANS, Kate (1998), *Copse: the Cartoon Book of Tree Protesting*, Orange Dog Productions

FARREN, Mick and Edward Barker (1972), *Watch Out, Kids*, Open Gate Books

FESTIVAL ZONE: The Great White Shark's colossal online resource, 'The Archive: UK Rock festivals 1960-75 & UK Free festivals 1965-1985.' Main menus at:
www.festival-zone.0catch.com/free-festivals-menu.html
users.bigpond.net.au/the-archive/
tinpan.fortunecity.com/ebony/546/index.html

FIRSOFF, George (1986), 'Robin's Greenwood Gang Yearbook 1985', privately published

FIRSOFF, George (1992), 'Why we need Stonehenge', privately published

GARRARD, Bruce (ed.) (1986), 'The Children of the Rainbow gathered in the Free State of Avalonia at the Christian Community of Greenlands Farm', Unique Publications

GARRARD, Bruce (ed.) (1986), 'The Green Collective: The best from the mailing 1985', Unique Publications

GARRARD, Bruce (ed.) (1986), 'Rainbow Village on the Road: Poems and writings from Rainbow Fields in exile February/March 1985', Unique Publications

GARRARD, Bruce and Steve Hieronymous (eds.) (1986), 'Stonehenge '86', Unique Publications

GREEN, Jonathon (1988), *Days in the Life: voices from the English Underground 1961-1971*, Heinemann

HESTER, Richard (1998), *Mediaeval Brigands? Sedentarism and Postmodernity: The Social Control of 'New Age Travellers' 1985-1995*, PhD thesis, The University of Birmingham

HESTER, Richard (1999), 'Policing New Age Travellers: Conflict and Control in the Countryside' in Gavin Dingwall & Susan Moody (eds.), *Crime and Conflict in the Countryside*, University of Wales Press

HETHERINGTON, Kevin (1999), *New Age Travellers: Vanloads of Uproarious Humanity*, Cassell

HUTTON, Lord (1999), in House of Lords, 'Opinions of the Lords of Appeal for Judgment in the Cause Director of Public Prosecutions (Respondent) v. Jones and Another (Appelants) (On Appeal from a Divisional Court of the Queen's Bench Division)', 4 March 1999, online at: homepages.tcp.co.uk/~ait/judgment.html

HUTTON, Ronald (1999), *The Triumph of the Moon: A History of Modern Pagan Witchcraft*, Oxford University Press

JARVIS, Kevin (1995), 'V.E. Day at Stonehenge', online at: tash.gn.apc.org/veday.htm

JONES, Hilary (1998), 'Dialogue with Hilary, Wes and Paul' in Barbara Bender, *Stonehenge: Making Space*, Berg

KENRICJ, Donald and Colin Clark (2000), *Moving On: The Gypsies and Travellers of Britain*, University of Hertfordshire Press

KRYSTOF (1989), 'Stonehenge Festival: Towards a New Beginning', Festival Eye 1989, online at: www.phreak.co.uk/stonehenge/psb/scfestiv.htm

LODGE, Alan, 'Tash's view – Stonehenge and the Battle of the Beanfield', online at: tash.gn.apc.org/sh_bean.htm

LOVEDAY, Pete (1989), 'Stones Again', *Festival Eye*, Summer '89

LOVEDAY, Pete (undated), *Big Trip Travel Agency, volumes 1-4*, AK Press

LOWE, Richard and William Shaw (1993), *Travellers: Voices of the New Age Nomads*, Fourth Estate

MCKAY, George (2000), *Glastonbury: A Very English Fair*, Victor Gollancz

MICHELL, John (1983), *The New View over Atlantis*, Thames and Hudson

MICHELL, John (1986), 'Stonehenge, Its History, Meaning, Festival, Unlawful Management, Police Riot '85 & Future Prospects', Radical Traditionalist Papers No.6

MONBIOT, George (1997), 'Multi-issue politics', *The Times Literary Supplement*, February 21st 1997

NCCL (National Council for Civil Liberties) (1986), 'Stonehenge: A report into the civil liberties implications of the events relating to the convoys of summer 1985 and 1986', NCCL

PENDRAGON, Arthur and Christopher James Stone (2003), *The Trials of Arthur: The Life and Times of a Modern Day King*, Element

PLOWS, Alex (2003), in 'Not only but also...some historical ramblings about the English festivals scene', compiled by Alan Dearling, online at: www.members.aol.com/adearling/enabler/nointro.htm

RIMBAUD, Penny (1981), 'The Last of the Hippies: An Hysterical Romance' in The Crass Collective, *A Series of Shock Slogans and Mindless Token Tantrums*, Exitstencil Press, online at: www.southern.com/southern/label/CRC/text/09438.html

ROSENBERGER, Alex (1986), 'Last summer: how the public was lied to', *Festival Eye*, June '86

RUSSELL, Phil (1973), 'The Windsor Free Festivals: Free press issues 1973-74', online at: tinpan.fortunecity.com/ebony/546/freep-30th-aug-73.html

SANDFORD, Jeremy and Ron Reid (1974), *Tomorrow's People*, Jerome Books

STONE, C.J. (1996), *Fierce Dancing*, Faber and Faber

STONE, C.J. (1999), *The Last of the Hippies*, Faber and Faber

SUBURBAN GUERILLAS (1991), 'Miscarriage of Justice UK' in 'The Trial of the Beanfield', Suburban Guerillas Publications 9

WILTSHIRE CONSTABULARY (1981), An overview of policing Stonehenge from the 1950s to the 1980s, reproduced as 'The Police Viewpoint', online at: www.festival-zone.0catch.com/henge-police.html

WORTHINGTON, Andy (2004), *Stonehenge: Celebration and Subversion*, Alternative Albion

... and these are the audio + visual necessities:

Operation Solstice, the 1991 documentary on the Beanfield, directed by Neil Goodwin, Gareth Morris and Russell Morris. Described by C.J. Stone as 'a film which should be seen by everyone. It should be on the National Curriculum.' Copies of the video are available from Housmans Bookshop in London or online from Culture Shop (www.cultureshop.org) or Active Distribution (www.activedistribution.org). There are hopes that a DVD of the film will be available sometime in 2005.

Roisin McAuley's 'In Living Memory' programme on the Beanfield for the BBC, originally transmitted on Radio 4 in November 2002.

Try Alan Lodge's website for videos of other valuable programmes, including the 1986 BBC panel discussion *Seven Days at Stoney Cross*.

Also relevant, if you can get hold of them, are two programmes recently broadcast on BBC4 and BBC2: *New Age Travellers*, an excellent Timeshift programme looking at traveller and free festival history, and, for more recent events, the two-part National Trust documentary on Stonehenge, which looked in detail at the politics of access to Stonehenge and the recent solstice gatherings.

Undercurrents videos 1-10, video activists alternative news videos (www.undercurrents.org)

And this lot is a list of potential further reading (but some will be quite hard to find):

ACTON, Thomas (1997), *Gypsy politics and Traveller identity*, University of Hertfordshire Press

BARNES, Richard (1983), *The Sun in the East: Norfolk and Suffolk Fairs*, R.B. Photographic

BOOTH, Steve (1996), *Into the 1990s with Green Anarchist*, Green Anarchist Books

BUCKE, Tom and Zoe James (1998), *Trespass and protest: policing under the Criminal Justice and Public Order Act 1994*, Home Office

CHIPPINDALE, Christopher, Peter Fowler et al. (1990), *Who Owns Stonehenge?*, Batsford

COLLIN, Matthew (1997), *Altered State: The Story of Ecstasy Culture and Acid House*, Serpent's Tail

DEARLING, Alan (1998), *No Boundaries: new Travellers on the road (outside of England)*, Enabler Publications

DEARLING, Alan with Graham Meltzer (2003), *Another kind of space: creating ecological dwellings and environments*, Enabler Publications

EARLE, Fiona and Ross Huelin (2002), *Tess the Traveller story books*, Educational Advice for Travellers/Travellers Aid Trust

EARLE, Fiona and Steve Witt (undated), *Working with Travellers: a practical guide for play, youth and community groups*, National Playbus Association

FRIENDS, FAMILIES AND TRAVELLERS SUPPORT GROUP (1996), *Confined, Constrained and Condemned: Civil rights and Travellers*, FFT

GARDNER, Peter (1987), *Medieval Brigands – pictures in a year of the hippie convoy*, Redcliffe Press

LOVEDAY, Pete (1991), *Russell - the saga of a peaceful man*, John Brown Publishing

LOVEDAY, Pete (1993), *Russell - the saga of a peaceful man Part 2*, John Brown Publishing

LOVEDAY, Pete (1995), *Russell's Big Strip Stupormarket*, John Brown Publishing

MCKAY, George (1996), *Senseless Acts of Beauty: Cultures of Resistance since the Sixties*, Verso

MCKAY, George (ed.) (1998), *DiY Culture: Party and Protest in Nineties Britain*, Verso

MILBOURNE, Paul (1997), *Revealing rural 'others' – representation, power and identity in the British countryside*, Cassell

MORRIS, Rachel and Luke Clements (1999), *Gaining Ground: Law Reform for Gypsies and Travellers*, University of Hertfordshire Press

SCHNEWS (2004), *SchNEWS At Ten* (and other *SchNEWS* annuals – see the website for details: www.schnews.org.uk)

SEARLE, Catherine (1997), *Gathering Force: DIY Culture – Radical action for those tired of waiting*, The Big Issue

THOMSON, Tony (1997), *Traveller*, Friends, Families and Travellers Support Group

Enabler Publications
Books to feed the mind and spirit
Specialising in publishing and distributing books about creative work with young people, environmental action and the diverse counter-cultural DiY scene.

Another kind of space: creating ecological dwellings and environments.
Alan Dearling with Graham Meltzer. £13.99.

" A very good combination of the more adventurous and the more conventional approaches to new ways of sustainable living,,,it's interesting to see the likes of low impact villages rubbing shoulders with intentional communities, scrap-rafts, eco-tourism, modern nomads and the international green community."
John Perry, Director of Policy, Chartered Institute of Housing.

"Inspirational examples from across the world."
New Internationalist.

"Packed with great ideas and rubber-necking detail about alternative living."
Friends of the Earth.

Alternative Australia: celebrating cultural diversity.
Alan Dearling with co-pilot Mook Bahloo. £13.95.

"As unstructured as the subcultures it celebrates, 'Alternative Australia' is a diverse collection of writings, first person narratives, poems, cyber scribblings, photos, drawings, by people who live on the edge of normalized society in a variety of ways. There are doof warriors, feral forest blockaders, community dwellers, shamens, musicians, fluoro faeries, pot farmers, artists. Unheard voices – Dearling gives them centre stage to express their reasons for living as they do, their rituals and beliefs.

It made me smile and question – which, in the end, is all you can ask of a book." Kate Hamilton in The Sydney Hub newspaper.

A Time to Travel? An introduction to Britain's newer Travellers.
Fiona Earle et al. £8.99.

"This is essentially the definitive book on Travellers. Let's hope it doesn't become a history book." The Levellers.

Words, pictures and illustrations by Travellers themselves. The realities of life on the road; who they are; why they want to live this way; how they deal with basic services and the law.

"A warm and vivid self-portrait in words and pictures…remember the price of freedom is vigilance." Fortean Times.

No Boundaries: new Travellers on the road outside of Britain.
Alan Dearling. £10.50.

"No Boundaries is a beacon of hope for both now and the future. You can't afford to miss it!" Friends and Families of Travellers Newsletter.

Personal accounts about travelling in France, Spain, Romania, Goa, Germany, Greece, South Africa and more. These are the real lives of new Travellers and other members of the DiY counter culture – their lows and highs, struggles, defeats and victories.

"…side stepping the boundaries that the State tries to fence us in with." Shelanagig. Paul in Spain: *"The priest will probably never see as many dreads, tattoos, combat boots, or indeed English speakers in his tiny church again!"*

Copse: the history of road protesting (in the UK). *Kate Evans. £10.50.*

From the heart of the DiY culture comes the ultimate Tree Love story. One woman,

one man, one tree, several hundred other men and women, a hundred thousand more trees, rather a lot of dogs and a planet on the brink of environmental collapse.

Cartoons, pics, writings and more from some of the most committed and inventive of the UK's road protestors.

Sadly, the post and packing costs can come to quite a lot. In the UK, we charge £1.50 for all the above titles, except *Another kind of space, Copse* and *Alternative Australia*, which, being heavier, are charged at £2.50 each for p&p. For other countries we charge the actual cost of airmail post and packing. We appreciate payment in sterling made out to *Enabler Publications*. We can't accept credit card payments – sorry. E-mail us with any queries.

Enabler Publications, 16 Bitton Avenue, Teignmouth, Devon, UK TQ14 8HD
Tel/Fax +44 (0) 1626 773145   E-mail: adearling@aol.com

Stonehenge:
Celebration and Subversion

Andy Worthington

'It's by far the best bit of modern
British social history I've seen.'
John Hodge *SchNEWS*

'This is a fine book in every way, well written,
carefully researched and with a remarkable
story to tell.' John Michell *Fortean Times*

This innovative social history looks in detail at how the summer solstice celebrations at Stonehenge have brought together different aspects of British counter-culture to make the monument a 'living temple' and an icon of alternative Britain. The history of the celebrants and counter-cultural leaders is interwoven with the viewpoints of the land-owners, custodians and archaeologists who have generally attempted to impose order on the shifting patterns of these modern-day mythologies.

The story of the Stonehenge summer solstice celebrations begins with the Druid revival of the 18th century and the earliest public gatherings of the 19th and early 20th centuries. In the social upheavals of the 1960s and early 70s, these trailblazers were superseded by the Stonehenge Free Festival. This evolved from a small gathering to an anarchic free state the size of a small city, before its brutal suppression at the Battle of the Beanfield in 1985.

In the aftermath of the Beanfield, the author examines how the political and spiritual aspirations of the free festivals evolved into both the rave scene and the road protest movement, and how the prevailing trends in the counter-culture provided a fertile breeding ground for the development of new Druid groups, the growth of paganism in general, and the adoption of other sacred sites, in particular Stonehenge's gargantuan neighbour at Avebury.

The account is brought up to date with the reopening of Stonehenge on the summer solstice in 2000, the unprecedented crowds drawn by the new access arrangements, and the latest source of conflict, centred on a bitterly-contested road improvement scheme.

ISBN 1 872883 76 1. Perfect bound, 245 x 175 mm, 281 + xviii pages, 147 b&w photos, **£14.95**

Available post free from Andy Worthington
164A Tressillian Road, Brockley, London SE4 1XY. Cheques payable to A. Worthington.
Website: www.andyworthington.co.uk

For full details of all Heart of Albion titles please see the online catalogue: **www.hoap.co.uk**